POSTCOLONIALITY
AND
INDIAN ENGLISH POETRY

POSTCOLONIALITY AND INDIAN ENGLISH POETRY

A STUDY OF THE POEMS OF NISSIM EZEKIEL, KAMALA DAS, JAYANTA MAHAPATRA AND A.K.RAMANUJAN

SUBRAT KUMAR SAMAL

PARTRIDGE

A Penguin Random House Company

To order additional copies of this book, contact
Partridge India
000 800 10062 62
orders.india@partridgepublishing.com

www.partridgepublishing.com/india

CONTENTS

ACKNOWLEDGEMENTS

The project ***POSTCOLONIALITY AND INDIAN ENGLISH POETRY*** would not have seen the light of day without the supervision of Dr. S.P. Swain, Former Principal and Head of the Department of English, Gandhi Mahavidyalaya, Rourkela and the co-supervision of Dr. Itishri Sarangi, Asst. Professor, Department of Humanities, KIIT University, Bhubaneswar. In my endeavours and findings, my Guide and Co-Guide, Prof. Swain and Prof. Sarangi, have been constant motivators and it is through their unflinching guidance and undaunted efforts that I could go forward in the process of my research and make it a reality. I am immensely grateful to them for their astute and meticulous guidance in the execution of the project. I am also grateful to KIIT University for the invaluable help they have provided in the execution of my Ph.D project and the facilities they have rendered for my research work. I am indebted to Dr. Bijay Kumar Das, Professor, Burdwan

University, West Bengal, who initiated me into the world of research. I am also grateful to Professor M.Q. Khan, Former Professor, Ravenshaw University and Vice-Chancellor, Berhampur University, Odisha, for his timely and perceptive advice in the preparation of the project.

I wish to place on record my thanks to Prof Sudarsan Nanda, Research Chair, KIIT University for his rare comments and advice from time to time which helped me to overcome all obstacles in the pursuit of my research project. I ventilate my deep sense of gratitude to Dr. GeetaSatapathy, Dean, School of Humanities, for her learned advice and constant encouragement..

I also express my deep sense of gratitude to my colleagues Prof. S.P. Kabisatapathy, Prof. Sanjay Kumar Mohapatra and my student Mr. Asish Kumar Biswal for their timely assistance rendered in typing and proof reading of the manuscript. I also thank Mr. A.K. Palit for his valuable help as regards the completion of the research project.

I gratefully remember my mother, brothers, sister and my father whose words inspired and strengthened me in my literary endeavour. I am bound in love and gratitude to my wife, son and little daughter whose silent support has made it possible for me to pursue my studies and research work.

My thanks are due to the authorities of National Library, Kolkata and EFL University, Hyderabad; Director, IACIS, Hyderabad without whose precious help, the project could not have been completed. I am also grateful to Orient Longman Limited, Oxford University Press, Sterling Publishers Pvt. Ltd., Atlantic Publishers and Distributors, Sarup and Sons Publishers, Adhyayan Publishers and Distributors, University of Georgia Press, Penguin Books,

Prakash Books Depot, Prestige Books, Kalyani Publishers, MotilalBanarsidas and McMillan whose materials (Text/ Criticism), I have profusely and liberally used in the preparation of my research project.

Subrat Kumar Samal

ABSTRACT

The project deals with 'postcolonialism' as a unique trend in world literature not only in terms of artistic creativity but also in its historical perspective. It analyses the cause, effect and remedy for all wrongs committed by the colonialists. The concept 'nativism' in the second chapter defines the basic character and concern of the postcolonial poetry. It not only makes a poet nationally conscious but also nationally accepted. The third chapter enlists the obstacles and hindrances in the realization of a poem as truly 'postcolonial'. The fourth chapter elaborates upon this matter by dealing exclusively with the problem of 'marginalization'. The project concludes with the analysis and justification of the works of modern Indian poets as true to all tenets of postcolonialism.

INTRODUCTION:

Postcolonialism, as a phenomenon, has a universal appeal. As the British Empire had its hold upon half of the globe, all the colonized people on earth have expressed their thoughts and feelings in the Postcolonial form of literature. It is not only limited to the nostalgic memories of loss but also to the objective details regarding the present scenario. Bill Ashcroft, Gareth Griffiths and Helen Tiffin use the term postcolonial "to cover all the culture affected by the imperial process from the moment of colonization to the present day" (*The Empire Writes Back* 02). Definitions of 'postcolonial' vary widely. Sometimes it is used synonymously with "a post-independence historical period in once-colonized nations" (Slemon 3).

OBJECTIVES:

The project aims at the study and analysis of poetry of the first four major poets of the postcolonial trend in the Indian context. It examines and explores the various aspects and characteristics of their poetry which can qualify them on the double standards of both being Indian and modern at the same time in a justifiable manner. The project intends to show how these poets carved out a niche for themselves and achieved a highly admirable goal in the field of modern Indian English Poetry by bringing in new trends as well as a purely Indian 'idiom' to their works. Their most significant contribution in this regard is the development of a modern 'nativist' trend in Indian English Poetry, replete with native imagery, themes and subject which impart a unique Indian flavour to their poetic art. Moreover, the poets under study make a fervent attempt to reach the 'centre' from their 'marginalized' position.

METHODOLOGY:

The project concerned is purely a literary work, done qualitatively with proper and detailed inter-textual and comparative study. All the primary and referential sources related to the poets in context have been thoroughly analysed to maintain the gravity and propriety of the work. The latest edition of MLA style sheet has been adhered to. Parenthetical references in the text of the paper (known as in-text citations) have been followed. Traditional methodology of footnotes/end notes has been completely avoided in order to maintain the appropriateness of the structure of the project. The in-text citations refer readers to a list of works at the end of each chapter known as 'Works Cited'.

REVIEW OF LITERATURE:

Realism and disillusioned vision have both remained the hallmark of Nissim Ezekiel's poetry. His holistic approach towards life is well reflected in his poems which are based upon all possible subjects ranging from urban life and culture to ancient traditions and spiritualism. In her review of the book *Form and Value in The Poetry of Nissim Ezekiel* by Anisur Rahman, Sukrita Paul maintains that a systematic awareness of the poet's cultural milieu, his social standing and involvement, his peculiar touch of the 'otherness' has made the reading of the book a worthwhile venture. What is noteworthy is that this awareness does not interfere with an objective analysis of his poetry. To her, form and content are deeply dependent on each other. Form and content leads him to discover the form of the poet's vision, his authentic self and the discovery of value lies in the discovery of the form. According to her, the central metaphors- the moral self, the pagan woman and the putrid city are studied seriously, poem after poem. The chapter on images and symbols, and another one on language and diction, to the reviewer make Ezekiel a major Indo-Anglian poet. The poet's striving to reach the ultimate forms the focus of his poetry (51).

Primarily known as the Bard of Odisha's rich cultural heritage, Jayanta Mahapatra's poetry evinces his sympathy and concern for the undeveloped India. Prema Nanda Kumar has reviewed the book *Modern Indian Poet Writing in English: Jayanta Mahapatra* by Laxminarayana Bhat in which she says Jayanta is a third-generation Christian who is marvelously responsive to Hindu myths. To her in Jayanta's poetry, one reckons a constant and varied pulls because of the received tradition and a forced alienation from one's own birth right. She says that there are tensions of growing up, of parental authority and angularity, of one's own fears and self-denials. According to her Dr. Laxminarayana's analysis of the poems is carefully executed and he rightly says that "Mahapatra's poetry may be truly regarded as his rhetoric of possibility mediated in his characteristic *lingua franca*"(68). Jayanta Mahapatra like W.H. Auden is unable to explain the mystery of life and death. His philosophy of life is basically incomprehensible in nature. Opposites, contradictions and highly paradoxical perspectives and perceptions co-exist in his poetry.

A.K.Ramanujan, the third poet concerned in the study is a truly modern poet with an added qualification of being a 'diasporic' poet. B. Parvathi has reviewed B.K.Das's *Perspectives on the Poetry of A.K.Ramanujan* in *The Critical Endeavour*, Vol-XX, January-2014. Her review reveals the various approaches by which the poems of the great poet can be analysed. According to her, the book speaks about the development and maturing of the poet's art and his poetic devices in four chapters. The fifth chapter shows how formalist, inter-textual, humanistic, reader response, myth, and postcolonial approaches can be made in reading Ramanujan's poetry. According to B.Parvathi, Das finds an unbroken continuity in the early/last poems of Ramanujan; he says that the poet wrote poetry with "both Sanskrit and English in his bones"(416).

The first female poet of the modernist trend of Indian English poetry was undoubtedly, the bold and ingenuous Kamala Das. An unflinching realist, with an undaunted obsession with the sensual and even the obscene details of physical love, she has remained at the forefront of various controversies inside as well as outside the literary circle. Sukrita Paul in her study of Kamala Das's poetry by Anisur Rahman highlights the poet's 'psychic striptease' in her poetry. Anisur Rahman's perceptive mind receives her experiences with an open mind and discovers in the poet the manifestation of an 'expressive form'. The study of Kamala Das, to the reviewer follows a rather interesting pattern and is an exploration of the poet in the tradition of 'confessional poetry'. Kamala Das, as the critic points out, is preoccupied with typically feminine concerns which obviously touch her inner self. Anisur Rahman introduces Kamala Das through a study of her poetry rather than her life story. This critical approach makes the critic more convincing and the poet more intriguing (51).

EXCLUSIONS/ LIMITATIONS:

The project excludes any reference to British English Literature. As it is primarily a study of Indian Poetry in English, its stress is on facts relevant to the chosen field only. Textual citations and supporting critical comments have been felicitously chosen, keeping in mind all the rules and regulations of project-writing. No such passage or citation has been quoted which is bereft of the necessary details such as its author, source (book, article or magazine) etc. Even, references to other poets have been avoided as far as practicable to keep the project point focused upon the poets concerned and to make the study concentrated and semantically theme-based. No translation of the original vernacular work of the poets has been used in the execution of the research work.

As the project attempts an in-depth study of the poets, namely Nissim Ezekiel, Jayanta Mahapatra, Kamala Das and A.K. Ramanujan, it traces their emergence on the scene of modern Indian Writing in English and is concerned with the socio-cultural background of these poets, as well as, the unique individual characteristics of their poetic craftsmanship. Citations have been given from some of their poetic volumes according to their relevance to the chapters concerned. In fine, the project delineates their contribution and uniqueness to modern Indian Writing in English. Thus the scope of this study limits itself within the periphery of Indian Poetry in English with reference to the four poets concerned. Further the project undertakes a study of only the theme concerned. No attempt or effort has been made as regards to the style or technique of the poets in context.

The First Chapter of the project is concerned with 'postcolonialism' as a trend of literature. It is not only an expression of talent, erudition or creativity but also a historical account of the conflict and reconciliation of different civilizations and cultures. It depicts both directly and indirectly the stigma suffered by most of the Afro-Asian countries under the exploitative and draconian rule of the colonizing European nations. It was first placed under terms like 'Commonwealth Literature' or 'Third-World Literature', but gradually the term 'Postcolonial' became its acceptable identity. Its root can be traced to the Afro-French writer Franz Fanon, whose *White Skin, Black Masks* and *The Wretched of the Earth* for the first time raised its voice against colonialism. His psycho - analytical theory was succeeded after many centuries, by another theory, Orientalism by Edward Said. Then came Bhabha's theory of 'mimicry' and 'ambivalence' with the publication of his book *The Location of Culture*. Ultimately Gayatri Spivak put forward the theory of 'marginality' in her celebrated essay "Can the Subaltern Speak?" In this manner, the postcolonial discourse grew in scope and size, with more and more new elements like migrancy, diaspora, rootlessness etc. Even the earlier form of this term with a 'hyphen' in between the words 'post' and 'colonialism', was strongly debated upon by critics like Harish Trivedi and T. Vijay Kumar. Due to the negative implication of the 'hyphen' its use was ultimately dropped.

Postcolonial Indian English poetry stands for all the English poetry written in India or by Indian writers outside India, in the post-independence era. While some of them like Ezekiel, went to the west, only to return disillusioned, others like Ramanujan remained there despite all disillusionments. Both, however, rooted to their respective places, ventured upon a deep inward quest for their cultural moorings. It is from this search, that the fruit of postcolonial Indian English poetry emerged. At first, it faced a lot of controversy for its radical unconventional nature as well as for its anti-English feelings. The supporters of the Bhasha or vernacular literatures, denied the very existence of any such thing as the Indian English poetry. The modern Indian English poets persevered all such odds and by bagging the Central SahityaAkademi awards for their works, silenced all their critics. Most of the Indian English Poetry "has been in the combined shadows of two major happenings: the Indian mythopoeic tradition and English Romanticism" (Harrex, *JIWE, 143*).

The first Indian English poet to receive this Award was Jayanta Mahapatra, who is also known as the 'Bard of Odisha'. After him, comes Nissim Ezekiel, who can even be called as the father of modern Indian English poetry. Then comes, the fierce feminist poet Kamala Das, whose bold and blatant use of sex in her poetry makes even the boldest of men tremble. Finally, the famous Indian expatriate poet, A.K. Ramanujan has also been taken into consideration. He has achieved the special feat of discovering his cultural roots and identity in an alien soil. Along with this four poets, who are the focus of the project, other poets like Dom Moraes, Adil Jussawala, Keki N. Daruwalla and R Parthasarathy, have also been discussed in this context as the other doyens of postcolonial Indian English poetry.

The Second Chapter deals with the elements of nativism in the poetry of the four postcolonial poets. Nativism is the hallmark of all postcolonial poets across the world. The Indian postcolonial poets are no exception to this. Nativism pervades every piece of postcolonial poetry in the form of native imagery, myths, folklore, socio-cultural traditions and contemporary problems. Hence, Srinivasa Iyengar states: "What makes Indo-English literature as Indian literature…is the quality of Indianness…in the choice of subjects, in the texture of thought, play of sentiment, in the organization of material in terms of 'form' and in the creative use of language" (Qtd. by Sahoo, *Tension and Moral Dilemmas in Nissim Ezekiel's Poetry* 6). While we find Nissim Ezekiel dealing with urban imagery and national problems like corruption, JayantaMahapatra derives his inspiration from the past and present of the socio-cultural traditions in India. He is also conscious about incidents like Bhopal Gas tragedy, which have a national import. His poems, though written in English, strongly reflect the 'Rasa' system of Indian poetics, showing his inalienable relation with Indian traditions. Following him is the poet Kamala Das, who for the first time, introduced the elements of aggressiveness and unconventionalism into the docile and submissive Indian women in her poetry. Resembling the ancient systems of Indian mysticism like the 'Koulas and Sahajas', she also seems to be in search of transcendental bliss with a literary recourse to sexual experiences. Yet, the epithet of being the most uniquely native Indian English poet can be given to none else than A.K. Ramanujan. His poetry is replete with his deep affinity for the Dravidian culture and ethos. The intense desire of the poet to redeem the ancient Dravidian heritage seems to burst in the lines beginning with: "… Deliver us O presence/ From proxies/ And absences…" ("Prayer to Lord Murugan" 113).

The Third Chapter deals with the problems encountered by the poets concerned to carve out a niche for themselves in Indian socio-cultural matrix. Each of them had a direct or indirect drawback regarding their identity. In fact, the crisis of identity is one of the most integral features of postcolonial literature. M.K. Naik observes: "Identity is in turn shown as a sham, as mistaken and confused, fractured and fragmented, merged and super-imposed, subjected to oblivion and dwarfed and reduced to animal level, totally lost and as barren and sterile" (46). While Nissim Ezekiel is a Jew, whose ancestors were refugees in this country, Jayanta Mahapatra belongs to an apostate family in a Hindu majority society. Kamala Das was a non-conformist to male patriarchal system of India and A.K. Ramanujan, went against traditions first by marrying a Christian woman and then settling abroad. In this context, the best example that can be cited is that of Kamala Das. She is unable to adjust herself either to the laceration of her own Nayar community or to the patriarchal structure of the Hindu community. She finds her roots and identity in the anguish of the countless Indian women and other such social groups like the untouchables, prostitutes, eunuchs and the insane, who are shunned or exploited by the mainstream Indian society. Her self-identification with the masses, is most lucidly ventilated in the following lines

> I am sinner
> I am saint. I am the beloved and the
> Betrayed….
> ("An Introduction" 22).

The Fourth Chapter concerns itself with the conflict of these poets to reach the centre from their marginalized stance. As stated in the Third Chapter, all the four major postcolonial poets find themselves in a marginalized position due to their nonconformity with one or another convention. Bruce King maintains: "These poets as a group tend to be marginal to traditional Hindu society not only by being alienated by their English language education but also more significantly by coming from such communities as the Parsis, Jews and Christians, or by being rebels from Hinduism and Islam or by living abroad" (Qtd. Das, *Aspects of Commonwealth Literature* 31-32). Yet, all of them work out their self-redemption in a most effective manner. Ezekiel adopts and admires the mythology and ancient wisdom of the Hindu Scriptures. Jayanta Mahapatra dedicates his poetry to the ancient glory and contemporary plight of Odisha. Simultaneously, he also touches upon every aspect of the socio-cultural conditions in India. Like Kamala Das, he also identifies himself with the masses of India, stifled with terror and pain:

> Watching behind the wall, I see
> It plays over people, piled upto their silences….
> ("A Rain" 11)

CONCLUSION/FINDINGS:

The Conclusion portrays a short description of how the tradition of Indian English poetry, beginning with Toru Dutt and persevering through severe criticism from both inner and outer circles, has ultimately began to blossom in the form of modern Indian English poetry. With the poets, Ezekiel, Mahapatra, Kamala Das and A.K. Ramanujan, we have perhaps, the most wholesome and indigenous form of English literature, that we can ever dream of. The chapter establishes them in the social matrix of Indian culture and tradition, and refutes all allegations of their rootlessness and marginalization. We specially find that even Ezekiel, a poet without any ethnic roots in Indian culture has successfully hybridized and acclimatized himself with the Indian cultural milieu. This feeling of self-marginalization and a profound belongingness resulting thereof, makes him say: "I want my hands/ To learn how to heal/ Myself and others" ("At 62" 273). A philanthropic urge to do something good for others evinces that his mind is now in a state of tranquility to contemplate upon the well-being of not only his framed self but also of other societal selves.

Like Ezekiel, Ramanujan also deals with scientific facts as well as cultural traditions. Due to his Dravidian origins, his poetry shows a strong inclination for the native Dravidian culture and consciousness. His unique features lie in his harmonization of mysticism and rationalism, a self-probing analysis and the mark of the classical Dravidian poetry and poetics upon his works in English.

As a poet, Kamal Das represents the aggressive resurgent spirit of the suppressed consciousness of Indian womanhood. Her poems show a unique combination of mystical contemplations as well as erotic passions. She can be thus termed as a sexual mystic, a feminist rebel and overall a true seeker of herself.

Jayanta Mahapatra's poetry is formed as much of the soil of Odisha, as his own body. Yet, instead of an inert geographical unit his consciousness stretches throughout India from one end to another. Elements of radicalism are one of the major constituents of his poetry, but he also retains many traditions like that of the 'Rasa' of Indian Sanskrit poetics. Due to the painful legacy of his grandfather's conversion, he suffers from a feeling of perpetual alienation from the Hindu tradition and masses of Odisha, in the early days of his poetic career.

WORKS CITED

PRIMARY SOURCE:

Das, Kamala. *The Old Playhouse and Other Poems.*. New Delhi: Orient Longman,1986. Print.

Ezekiel, Nissim. *Collected Poems.* New Delhi: OUP, 2005. Print.

Mahapatra, Jayanta. *A Rain of Rites.* Athens: University of Georgia Press, 1976. Print

Ramanujan, A.K. *Collected Poems.* New Delhi: OUP, 2005. Print.

REVIEWS:

Kumar, Prema Nanda. Rev. of *Modern Indian Poet Writing in English: Jayanta Mahapatra,* by Laxminarayana, Bhat P. *The Journal of Indian Writing in English,* Vol-29, Jan. 2001:68-70. Print.

Kumar, Sukrita Paul. Rev. of *Expressive Form in The Poetry of Kamala Das,* by Anisur Rahman. *The Journal of Indian Writing in English,* Vol-12, Jan. 1984:51-52. Print.

Kumar, Sukrita Paul. Rev. of *Form and Value in The Poetry of Nissim Ezekiel,* by Anisur Rahman. *The Journal of Indian Writing in English,* Vol-12, Jan. 1984:51-53. Print.

Parvathi, B. Rev. *of Perspectives on the Poetry of A.K.ramanujan,* by Bijay Kumar Das. *Critical Endeavour,* Vol-20, Jan. 2014:416-417. Print.

SECONDARY SOURCE:

Ashcroft, Bill, Gareth Griffiths and Helen Tiffin. *The Empire Writes Back,* London: Routledge, 1989. Print.

Das, Bijay Kumar. *Aspects of Commonwealth Literature.* New Delhi: Creative Books, 1995. Print.

Dwivedi, A. N. *Kamala Das and Her Poetry.* Delhi: Doaba House Book Sellers and Publishers, 1983. Print.

Harrex, S.C. "Small-Scale Reflections on Indian English Language Poetry", *JIWE,* Vol 8, Jan-Jul 1980, No. 1. Print.

McLeod, John. *Beginning Postcolonialism.* New Delhi: Viva Books, 2013. Print.

Naik, M.K. *Studies in Indian English Literature.* New Delhi:Sterling Publishers, 1987. Print.

Sahoo, Raghunath. *Tension and Moral Dilemmas in Nissim Ezekiel's Poetry.* New Delhi: Sarup and Sons Publishers, 2012. Print.

Slemon, Stephen. "The Scramble for Post-colonialism", in Tiffin and Lawson (Eds.) *Describing Empire:Post-colonialism and Textuality,* London: Routledge, 1994. Print.

CHAPTER 1

POSTCOLONIALITY AND INDIAN ENGLISH POETRY

An attempt has been made in this chapter to define 'Post-colonialism' and make a diachronic study of the Indian English Poetry within that theoretical framework. The term 'Post-colonial' has three distinct levels of meanings. It is a historical marker which distinguishes between the two time periods – Pre-independence and Post-independence. Secondly, it is a Post-Structuralist approach with reference to literary texts. Thirdly, it is a renaming of the 'Commonwealth Literature'.

For the proper understanding of the nature and significance of 'Post-colonialism' one should first be very much aware about the history and impact of colonialism. It is highly necessary in this regard as colonialism and post-colonialism are two aspects of the same phenomenon. Like the bud and the flower, they are integral and identical to each other. The roots of colonialisation lie in the search for the sea route to India, the fabled land of gold and spices. Though, Columbus was not successful in finding India, his discovery of America, added new over-sea territory to Spain's domain. The easy conquest of an entire continent with immense stores of wealth to plunder fired the lust for establishing over-sea empires. Almost all European nations, with Portugal and Britain at the front, joined this rush. Soon, large tracts of Asia and Africa began to be conquered for the dual sake of exploitation as well as for preparing markets for European goods. Though, Europeans claimed to bring the light of redemption and enlightenment to the native people, the lust for exploitation was too strong to be hidden under any noble garb. Colonial rule affected not only the commercial and political life but also the cultural and intellectual life of the natives, mostly in a negative manner. The most malevolent impact of the colonial rule however was the inferiority complex engendered in the native population regarding their culture and nationality. The conscious intellectuals among the native masses soon realized it. They raised their voice against the root of all their misery - The Colonial rule. Ultimately, after more than a century of struggle, all of the colonized nations (of Asia and Africa etc.) regained their independence within the first half of the twentieth century.

The tide of fortune which turned against the colonial masters with the end of their rule, made them desperate for the goodwill and friendship of their once-colonized subjects. An attempt to keep them in good humour was the formation of the group of Commonwealth Nations, which consisted both the United Kingdom and all its once subjugated nations. One of the attempts to group together all these nations under a single banner was to brand their literary output in English by the collective term 'Commonwealth Lliterature'. This term stood exclusively for all literatures written in English in the former British colonies during the second half of the twentieth century, which fell outside the Anglo-American tradition. The term raised great controversy because of its political connotation. Critics like George Woodcock from Canada sneered at it as an attempt "to build academic principalities" (Qtd. by Das, *Critical Essays on Post-colonial Literature* 2). Further, the continuous influx and out flux of the members of the group blurred the criteria of the term. So, a necessity arose for a more valid and appropriate term to contain the extensive mass of literatures in English written in countries other than the United Kingdom and the United States. It was under such circumstances that the new term 'Post-colonial' came to occupy the centre stage of the literary activities in English in the once-colonized nations.

The term 'Post-colonialism' started gaining ground from the Bandung Conference of 1955 and the Tricontinental Conference at Havana in the year 1966. The Tricontinental Conference was much significant for the beginning of a journal with the same name (i.e. Tricontinental). It featured the writings of prominent 'postcolonial' theorists and activists like Franz Fanon, Che Guevera and Jean Paul Sartre. Its popularity increased with the publication of *The Empire writes Back* (1989) by Bill Ashcroft, Gareth Griffiths and Helen Tiffin and *The Encyclopedia of Post-Colonial Literatures in English* by Benson, Eugene and Connolly. Yet, considering in a historical manner, it is from the French psychologist Franz Fanon that the colonial discourse makes its beginning. He was the first person to observe and criticize the harmful effects of the French colonialism. Belonging to African origins, he himself faced racial discrimination both during his academic as well as professional years. The contemporary French philosophers and poets such as Jean Paul Sartre and Aim`e C`esaire inspired him with zeal to oppose this injustice. His two publications, *Black Skin, White Masks* and *The Wretched of the Earth*, express his heart felt resentment against the oppressive and derogatory effects of colonialism over the colonized. In his book *Black Skin, White Masks*, he speaks of his own experience of being publicly discriminated on the basis of his colour: "On that day, completely dislocated, unable to be abroad with the other, the white man, who unmercifully imprisoned me, I took myself far off from my own presence, far indeed, and made myself an object..." (Qtd. by McLeod 20). Here, Fanon applying his typical psycho-analytical method presents before us the experience felt by him as the result of racial discrimination. He shows how he is made to see or consider himself as an object, instead of a living human being. The whole book similarly depicts the way in which inferiority complex is imbibed in the minds of the subjugated native population regarding their nationality, culture and colour etc.

The second figure after Fanon, important in regard to the field of oriental discourse is Edward W. Said. Said has explored the various facets and impacts of the process of colonisation on the Eastern countries. He puts the once-colonized countries under the collective term- the Orient. Based upon the study of the Orient, he has written his book *Orientalism* (1978) to explain the colonial phenomenon. Unlike Fanon, he emphasises more upon the colonizers than the colonized. He derives much of his inspiration from the Marxist theories of power, the political philosophy of the Italian intellectual Antonio Gramsci and France's Michel Foucault. In his book, he gives his observations about the justification of the subjugation of the natives by their colonial masters. He reveals that the people of the West rarely ever did try to understand the people of the East or their culture, traditions etc. Even their communication with the natives was also severely restricted by their racial prejudice. Therefore, most of the observations made by them present the natives in a negative colour as of being morally bankrupt and sexually degenerate. All such views rest simply on the basis of the assumptions made by the former. It is upon these flimsy grounds, that the colonists gave free play to their political and economic lust under the holy garb of spreading the light of civilization and redemption. So, in Said's view, the counter process of colonialisation would not involve only the transfer of power from the hands of the ruler to the hands of the ruled. Rather it should be a complete transformation of the false views of the colonizers framed against the colonized. Like Fanon, he also expresses his dissent upon the objectification of the Orient. According to him under the colonial view, the Orient becomes an object: "… Suitable for study in the academy, for display in the museum, for reconstruction in the colonial office, for theoretical illustration in anthropological, biological, linguistic, racial and historical theses about mankind and the universe, for instances of economic and sociological theories of development, revolution, cultural personality, national religious character" (Said 8).

The third figure of interest in this area is Homi K. Bhabha. He added new dimensions to the Post-colonial approach by including the elements of 'ambivalence' and 'mimicry' to it. In his book *The Location of Culture*, Bhabha refers to these elements through his second essay, "Of Mimicry and Man: The Ambivalence of Colonial Discourse". This essay presents before us the 'ambivalent' or the 'split' personality of the colonized or at least as imagined or projected by the colonizers. To the colonizers, the natives by nature are savage, wild, untamable and given to lust and anarchy. Though the rulers claim that under their rule, they become civilized, domesticated and harmless, yet on the other hand they believe that a native can never leave his original traits. Bhabha himself refers to these repeated claims of the colonizers as: "… the same old stories of the Negros' animality, the coolie's inscrutability or the stupidity of the Irish must be told (compulsively) again and afresh and are differently gratifying and terrifying each time" (Qtd. by McLeod 54). In his aforesaid essay "Of Mimicry and Man", Bhabha shows the development of the ambivalence of the native into 'mimicry.' In his own words, it is one of the most elusive and an effective strategy of colonial power and knowledge (Of Mimicry and Man 85) and as such is a direct threat to the colonial masters. The colonizer trains and teaches the native into his own way, to make him a 'Mimic' man. But that does not make the native either powerless to resist or enslaved to his master's ways. Rather they acquire the power to disrupt the myths fabricated by the colonized against them, through their nativist 'ambivalence.' The native finally challenges the colonist interpretations and redefines them in his own manner. So, 'Mimicry' as Bhabha puts it up: "… is thus, the sign of a double articulation; a complex strategy of reform, regulation and discipline, which 'appropriates' the other as it visualizes power" (Of Mimicry and Man 87).

Till now, all the theorists, whose views and ideas we observed and studied are males. Though, Edward Said speaks of the colonialist view of effeminizing the Orient or perceiving the Orient as basically of an effeminate nature, he does not speak anything significant about the effect of colonialism upon women. Bhabha's 'theory of mimicry' remains neutral due to no specific mention of any gender. The absence of female voice or female representation raised many voices against this shortcoming of the colonial-discourses. The critic Carole Boyce Davies even raised the question: "Where are the women in the theorizing of post- coloniality?" (80) There was yet another aspect of this problem as is reflected upon by Helen Carby in her essay "White Woman Listen ! Black Feminism and the Boundaries of Sisterhood" (Qtd. By Mc Leod 181). In this essay, she recognizes the fact that whatever feminism is present in the postcolonial discourse is predominantly of the 'first–world' nature. All the female critics are western not only by nationality but also by their sensibility. This renders them rather unsympathetic to the problems and views about the colonial rule as experienced and expressed by the women of Afro- Asian countries. What actually created the alienation between the female masses of the east and the west was a strong politically motivated movement in the west under the veil of universal female emancipation and empowerment. Just as the noble watchwords of French revolution 'equality, fraternity and justice', became mere words under the French ambition of imperial expansion, similarly the women of the west had no or least concern about the women of the eastern colonies. In their view it was rather a benevolent boon for the women of the colonies to be protected and instructed by the noble British administration. This is exactly the reason which led the colonial critic Robert J.C.Young to assert: "historically, it is true that feminism was a western political movement that began in the eighteenth century"(*Postcolonialism: A very …* 98). It was on such a scenario that Gayatri Chakravarti Spivak made her appearance with her unique 'Subaltern' approach towards the theory of post- colonialism. Her choice of this term is influenced by the Italian thinker Antonio Gramsci, who used it for referring to a position of subordination in terms of class, gender, race and culture. In her essay "Can the Subaltern speak?" Spivak reveals the way in which 'Subaltern' type of woman came in to existence on the ideological level. Yet, she is either absent, silent or even if tries to speak, is not listened to. It is this silence or absence of women in the postcolonial context, which is the main concern of her essay. She argues that between the ideological conflicts of patriarchy and imperialism as well as subject constitution and object formation, the figure of woman becomes marginalized in the middle of the spheres concerning tradition and modernization.

Her use of the term 'Subaltern' covers in its criteria, not only women, but also the blacks and all those who consist of the colonized and the working class. The term, in literary usage, is suggestive of the repressive dominance of the western thought. It is also used as an allegory for the displacement of the gendered and colonised subject through the imposition of the narratives of inter-nationalism and nationalism. She is against the rather disinterested data-collection or highlighting about the 'Third-World' women as is done by the usual 'First-world' critics. She herself confesses how she used to think in her early years of youth about her empowered position to speak and write about the colonised women due to her western education. She now claims that to be a fallacy. The extent of complicacy in this context can be measured from her views regarding this topic. According to her, the wide area of 'Subaltern' encompasses all the sections or classes that are suppressed, depressed or repressed. Yet, the issue of gender-based identity remains a stark truth as all the representations of subaltern expressions of revolt or opposition are based with the supremacy of the male gender. The problem, thus created is explained by Spivak in the following words: "As objects of colonialist historiography and as a subject of insurgency, the ideological construction of gender keeps the male dominant. If, in the context of colonial production, the subaltern has no history and cannot speak, the subaltern as female is even more deeply in shadow" (Spivak 82-83).

Thus, the question raised by Spivak puts us in doubt regarding the female representation in the colonial discourses. She herself expresses this opinion that the search for an indigenous, sovereign and concrete female consciousness for subjective analysis by intellectuals can yield no results. The reason is the inability of the subaltern female to communicate with the listeners at the first place. Even when they speak, their words are interpreted according to some fixed standards and no exception is allowed. Therefore, the inability of the subaltern, especially as a woman, to speak is mainly due to the lack of proper interpretation.

Apart from all these theories and views about the nature, scope and necessity of the post- colonial discourses, a very interesting aspect involves the term itself. The 'hyphen' that separates the 'post' from the 'colonial' is looked upon as a highly controversial feature of the entire post-colonial theory. There are numerous contentious and mutually contradictory interpretations of this mere punctuation mark, which to the critics appears as a deliberate conspiracy of western prejudice. The famous critic, Harish Trivedi, has clearly stated the objective of the post-colonial discourses in the following words: "Unlike with feminism or post-structuralism or even

Marxism, the discourse of post-colonialism is ostensibly not about the west where it has originated but about the colonized other" (*Interrogating Postcolonialism: Theory Text and Context* 120). In the same essay, he has tried to highlight the different implications of the prefix 'Post' to the term 'post-colonial.' By a comparative study of the English term 'Post-colonial' with its Hindi or Sanskrit equivalent 'Uttar- upaniveshavad', he has come up with the above implications that emerge from the use of the prefix post:

i) After, or latter (as against former), so that, in the present context, if what obtained formerly was colonialism, what came or obtained latterly would be *Uttar-colonialism*.

ii) Later but not separate from (as in the title *uttararamacharitam*, the later life of Rama). In this sense, it would be later stage of colonialism, i.e. complicit post- colonialism.

iii) Higher, more advanced, more so. In this sense, it would be an advanced stage of colonialism, i.e., neo colonialism.

iv) Answer or refutation (as in *Purva-Paksha* and *Uttar-Paksha*) (ibid, 126).

In this sense, it would be what is opposed to, or what resists, counterpoises or counteracts, any of the above forms of (post/neo-) colonialisms. By these above implicated meanings, the critic tries to establish that how an Indian interprets the very term 'post- colonialism' according to his Indian sensibility.

The issue of the hyphen has been dealt in a more serious manner by the post- colonial critic, T.Vijaya Kumar. He has tried to elucidate three integral aspects of the term 'post-colonialism'. He has tried to explain the 'hyphen' in the following manner: "Firstly, by splitting the word into two, the hyphen effectively prevents/defers the integration of the colonial past into the post-colonial present. The lack of integration can be seen in 'Post- colonial' history, culture, and literature (…) when we refer to a literature as 'post-colonial', we do not only over- emphasize its continuing concern with colonial experience, but also hinder its integration into the tapestry of literatures written in the local languages"(196). In the same context, he also alleges that how the 'hyphen' not only sends, the 'post' to a rather backstage position but also places 'colonialism' at a central position. Thus it marginalizes the 'post' and obscures the individual identity of the colonialised. It results therefore, in a stagnant situation where no change is possible in the 'post-colonial' condition. The 'hyphen' also categorizes the 'post-colonial' discourse and as such prevents the marginalized voice of the colonized to occupy the central position of the colonist. So, we finally observe that the 'hyphen' is not only unnecessary for application but is rather negative in its implication. For all such reasons, the use of hyphen in the book has been omitted so as to become more expressive of the Indianness of the postcolonial discourse.

To this point, the text has undergone the study of multiple theories and thoughts on postcolonialism. A very common feature that can be noticed in all of them is a very reserved and limited view of all the matters that come within the criteria of postcolonialism. In this regard, Bijay Kumar Das, comments: "Semantically Postcolonialism means something that has concern only with the national culture after the departure of the imperial power. But in actual practice, it has to be understood only in reference to colonialism. Like colonialism, post-colonialism is a state of consciousnesses, a crucial stage in the continuum of our cultural process and self awareness. Colonialism involves two types of imperialism- political and cultural. Therefore, myth and history, language and landscape, self and the other are all very important ingredients of post-colonialism" (*Critical Essays on Post-colonial Literature* 7). The same views are reflected in the words of yet another critic of repute, Srinivas Aravamudan, when he says: "To consider that we are beyond colonialism in any way is to misrecognize-dangerously- the world's current realities" (16). Here a question may naturally arise about the role of language, as in this context the English language, in the entire process of colonialisation. The simple answer to this complex question is that language being the most potential mode of human communication, no social, political or intellectual human phenomenon can take place without it. In the view of the Kenyan novelist Ngugi Wa Thiong'O as quoted by John McLeod: "Language carries culture, and culture carries, particularly through orature and literature, the entire body of values by which we come to perceive ourselves and our place in the world. How people perceive themselves affects how they look at their culture, at their politics and at the social production of wealth, at their entire relationship to nature and to other human beings. Language is thus inseparable from us as a community of human beings with a specific form and character, a specific history, a specific relationship to the world" (18-19).

Though there are different allegations about the term 'Postcolonial', its meaning and justified implication, the truth is that the postcolonial writers don't really write back to their former master. The real purpose behind their literary endeavour is to declare their independence from the colonial master and to establish their mastership over the ruler's language. Thus, intellectually independent of any domination, they have used it to express their own indigenous creativity. The result is that English literature has lost its coveted place to other literatures or the localized 'englishes.' Every once-colonized nation uses its own version of the Queen's or Standard English, as it was once called. This is the reason for the linguistic varieties, we find in the global literary sphere like the Australian, the American and the Carribbean English. However, it is also true that 'resistance and subversion' form a very integral part of this type of literature. Therefore, all the elements of culture such as national identity, landscapes, rituals and national culture and tradition, combiningly constitute the national character of the postcolonial poetry. The current trend in the postcolonial poetry is to assert one's national identity and to glorify his or her country in all the aspects. Thus, we can say that in stead of praising the colonial master in his language, as was the fashion in the colonial period, the postcolonial writer hits them back by glorifying his own nation, culture and race instead.

Writing in English started in India during the colonial times itself. There is a good deal of prose literature written by Indian intellectuals from the time of Raja Ram Mohan Ray himself. The number of poets, and that also of some repute, are however quite scanty in number. India's entry into the field of English poetry started with Toru Dutt. Her poems though have passed more than a century; still inspire awe and admiration due to their highly evocative nature and a strong Indian sensibility. Apart from her Michael Madhusudan Dutt, Sarojini Naidu and Rabindra Nath Tagore are some of the colonial stalwarts in Indian English poetry. Many spiritual figures such as Swami Vivekananda and Sri Aurobindo also have produced some good poems, marked by skill and innovation. V.K.Gokak has classified the pre-independence poets into two broad categories- "The neo-symbolists" and "The neo-modernist" (Qtd. by Das *Critical Essays on Postcolonial Literature* 18). The neo-symbolists were the mystic poets while the neo-modernists were the humanist poets. C.D Narasimhaiah even accredits Sri Aurobindo of not only being an eloquent poet but also of being a critic of poetry, with a very fine power of observation and analysis. He is also accredited for creating an 'idiom' in English, which fulfilled much of the demands made by the Indian intellectual. The sensuousness and highly aesthetic poetry of Keats's style was successfully produced on the Indian soil and on its themes by Sarojini Naidu. Last but not least, the bagging of the Nobel Prize for literature by Rabindra Nath Tagore, for his exclusive masterpiece *Geetanjali* proved to the world that finally the Indians have mastered and assimilated the very essence of their master's language. However, with independence, there was a great upheaval of the existent situations. With an overall transformation of the socio-political scenario, there were new demands on the social, political, economical and even on the intellectual sphere of the country. A more humanistic, realistic and modern approach to the national life and its problems became inevitable. It was in such conditions that the 'Postcolonial' form of Indian English poetry came forward to fulfill the aforesaid demands.

Whatever the critics may say, the fact remains that Indian English poetry, which could compete with the Anglo-American modern poetry, came to be written only in sixties. The modern poets of India took the Anglo-American modern poets and poetry as their ideals. This was a very negative and unfortunate beginning as many of them actually started imitating not only their outlook but also their style and subject. The politeness and high grade refinement of the English poets and the confessional style of the American poets, though adopted by the Indian poets, remained obscure for the common people without proper Indianization. Slowly, this trend died out. But, Indian English poetry went on its own way by itself. It slowly achieved the qualities of robustness, variety, responsivity and enjoyability. In fact; it has developed itself into a quite unique and, independent and resourceful kind, relying totally upon indigenous sources of inspiration. This postcolonial Indian English Poetry, though to a great extent is a protest movement against its past, is still another form of continuation. The elements of modernity in the modern Indian English poetry can be easily identified by the following characteristics:

i.   A past-oriented vision, which is associated with a sense of loss and hopelessness - a sort of cultural pessimism.
ii. A future-oriented vision, associated with a desire to remake the world.
iii. A present oriented attitude, which is ahistorical, amoral, neutral, stoic, ironic, ambivalent and absurdist.

There are also two modes of expression in the modernist trend in Indian poetry:

i.   One may turn an introvert and join a 'voyage within'.
ii. One may develop an ironic observation of reality and becoming an extrovert, join a 'voyage without'.

Sometimes one may think what is the thing which imparts that sense of Indianness to these literatures written in English by Indian intellectuals. The answer is that the sense of nationality comes not from the theme but the 'idiom' in which a particular piece of literature is written. It is this idiom which gives the mark of originality to the various postcolonial literatures, though all of them are written in English. This idiom is achieved by earnest efforts of recreating characters and situations of one's native language in English. This idiom, along with the application of certain other literary techniques, imparts the nationality to a certain literature and thus they come to be known as American, Australian or Indian etc. Indian English poetry of the 1960's and after is highly distinct and authentic in nature. There is a great genuineness in it as it is the outcome of deep and honest feelings and an address to the whole community. Everything which is a part of the vast culture and tradition of India forms a part of it. Thus myth, culture, religion, rituals, superstitions, folk beliefs and everyday situations from the normal Indian family life, all find a place in it and contribute to its beauty and charm. Not only these but even very current problems, typical to India or the present modern world are also taken as themes for the creation of modern poetry. Various personal issues like loss of identity, loss of faith in God, religion, failures, alienation and isolation form the themes of the major portion of modern Indian English Poetry.

The emergence of the 'Postcolonial' trend in India marked a completely new epoch in the history of not only Indian but also in that of World English literature. It is not that other countries have not suffered under the yoke of colonial rule or have not expressed their feelings in Standard English. But, due to some specific reasons, India has always occupied the centre-stage of Postcolonial discourses. The western critic Robert Young has rightly remarked in this context: "In comparison to the extensive work done on India, meanwhile, Africa remains comparatively neglected…. the greater attention accorded to India still seems to perpetuate the differing evaluations that the British accorded to the various parts of their empire. It was always India that received the greatest economic, cultural and historical attention from the British. In the same way, today India quite clearly retains that position of pride of place, the jewel in the crown of colonial-discourse analysis"(*Colonial Desire: Hybridity*... 165-66). India's advent into the arena of postcolonialism is marked by the publication of Salman Rushdie's novel *Midnight's Children* in 1981. Like most of the pre-independence novels, it presented India in its most exotic variety. Yet, its uniqueness can be found in the fact that in this book, India has come alive in a 'flesh and blood' existence. It reveals to the westerners, that what 'true' India is like beneath all the multiple layers of assumptions, fabricated myths and fantasies of the western mind. In his review on *Midnight's Children* for the "Times Literary Supplement," Valentine Cunningham praising the wide scale representation of India suggests: "A novel pretending to India as a subject can't avoid the question of how novels in general may claim truthfully to cope with the daunting vastness, the multiple cities of things and persons." (Qtd. by Smale 12)

The Post-independence literary activities in India were marked with all the basic traits of postcolonial trend. Various aspects like the issue of split existence resulting due to the effect of colonization, rootlessness, search for self identity, issues of migrancy, ambivalent attitude of the colonized subject, hybridity, sense of alienation, nativism, irony and the relation between the centre and the periphery have been discussed as being integral to the postcolonial temperament. Various theories have been formed upon all the aforesaid elements of postcolonialism. While the Psycho-analytical method of Franz Fanon deals with the problem of split existence, Homi K. Bhabha speaks about the ambivalent aspect of the post colonial discourse. Similarly many other theorists, critics and intellectuals have dealt with these matters and have given their views after much consideration. Another very interesting feature of the postcolonial trend is the problem of 'Diaspora'. It refers originally to the dispersion of the Jews during and after the Babylonian exile and their mass migration to lands of foreign language and culture. In the wake of independence, many Indian intellectuals like Salman Rushide, A.K. Ramanujan and V.S.Naipaul left the Indian shores for greener, intellectual pastures.

Besides the erstwhile factors 'marginality' plays a significant and crucial role in moulding and re-shaping the core of Indian Poetry in English. Shantinath K.Desai as quoted by B. K. Das; in his article "Indian Writing in English: The Predicament of Marginality" makes a keen observation of the effect of marginality upon the Indian English Writers and how they behave under its effect. He writes:

"The Indian writer in English", particularly in the Post-Independence period which is characterized by nativistic assertion, has to make a choice to go to England or America or, like Nissim Ezekiel, to stay where he is (Das, *Aspects of Commonwealth Literature* 30).

He should have added: "My remote place too is where I am"(Ezekiel 181). "Marginality affects the Indian writer in

English to where he should stay. He chooses to do one of the following: either he goes to England or America and is an exile there or stays here in India and is an exile here" (Desai 33). In another place of the same article he further observes:

> The post-Independence Indian writers in English who have their particular commitment to India, present interesting variations of the predicament they are in (a) Some, like Ezekiel, cultivate a cool and detached view of things, accepting the predicament of living in an environment in which they feel alien. They write slick, competent poetry, dessicated and extremely reductive. They adopt a kind of ironic, existentialist, a historical stance, and after the first or second book of poems, which are generally interesting because of the early 'living' emotional tensions generated by the necessity of coming to terms with themselves and their environment, they vanish into the safe bourgeois corridors of academics or advertisement firms. If they persist in writing - and some do, for one reason or another they get the Sahitya Akademi Awards for their thin volumes of poetry. (ibid, 35)

The concept of marginality however doesn't end with a single note. There are many different and highly inter-connected aspects of it. Not only this, they are highly self-contradictory in nature, as almost none of the critics have presented a clear view of their judgement. One example can be quoted from Bruce King as quoted by B.K.Das in *Aspects of Commonwealth Literature:*

These poets as a group tend to be marginal to traditional Hindu society not only by being alienated by their language, education but also more significantly by coming from such communities as the Parsis, Jews and Christians, or by being rebels from Hinduism and Islam or by living abroad (Das 30-31).

However, in the same book, he contradicts himself when he writes that Indian English poetry has become a self-sustaining tradition with recognizable models. The poets have purely indigenous forms, styles, subjects and voices and are forming a national tradition recognized throughout the world. He finally contradicts his previous outlook by the comment "Can we say then that Indian English poetry is marginal?" (ibid, 4)

Some other critics also in the same fashion condemn and cheer Indian English modern poets and poetry in the same breath. Even a poet himself, R. Parthasarathy while calling Indian English poetry with relation to Indian poetry as a whole 'marginal' also accepts that "it is a legitimate expression of universal experience," (*Ten Twentieth Century Indian Poets* 11), and is highly significant in its own position. S.K.Desai also follows the suit and says that the Indian writing in English "is always part of Indian literature-though marginal." Saying so, he in a way is turning a blind eye to the fact that no literature in any Indian language except perhaps Hindi, commands as much readership nationwide as does English literature. Further Desai continues with the question of the 'locale' of the modern Indian English literature. "Where should Indian writer in English stay?" asks Desai and suggests: "he chooses to do one of the following: either he goes to England or America and be an exile there or stay here in India and be an exile here". (ibid, 33). Desai seems to forget the All-India status given to an Indian English writer. Like Sanskrit in ancient India, English today is the language of the intellectuals throughout the country from east to west and north to south. Indian English literature now constitutes an integral part of the college syllabi and most of the M.Phil and Ph.D dissertations are now written on Indian English Literature. Keeping all these facts in mind, no reasonable man would say that an Indian English writer is an 'exile' here.

No introduction of any art and its history is complete without a reference to the artists, who invent and help in its process of evolution. Likewise it would be very odd to close a chapter of discussion about modern Indian English poetry, without explaining the role of various prominent poets who contributed in its genesis and evoulution.The history of post-colonial or modern Indian English poetry starts from the publication of Nissim Ezekiel's first collection of poems titled *A Time to Change*, which was published in London, in 1952. This event heralded a new age of Indian English poetry, of a totally new kind. Like Eliot, who gave shape to the modernist form of English poetry in the western world, it was Ezekiel in India, who was responsible for deciding 'a local habitation and a name' for the post-independence Indian English Poetry. It was with him that a new style of writing and a new mode of thinking were initiated into the realm of Indian English poetry. It was from him, that the later Indian English poets like R.Parthasarathy and Dom Moraes drew inspiration for creating their own poems. The critic Adil Jussawala rightly points out that: "Ezekiel is perhaps the first Indian poet consistently to show Indian readers that craftsmanship is as important to a poem as its subject matter" (Qtd. by Das 19).

Nissim Ezekiel belonging to the Bene-Israel Jewish community, which settled in India many generations ago, lives in Mumbai. His poetry as such is relevant to contemporary situations. It has a secular outlook and a cosmopolitan attitude. It was he who started the use of free verse instead of the closed forms like the heroic couplet, though he can write regular stanzas in metrical verse also. Like W.B Yeats, he also revises all his creations to the extent where he feels completely satisfied of its perfection. In his own view, a poem and poetry are two different things, whose differences he draws out in the following lines of his poem "Poetry,"

> A poem is an episode, completed
> In an hour or two, but poetry
> Is something more. It is the way
> The how, the what, the flow
> From which a poem comes,
> In which the savage and the singular
> The gentle, familiar,
> Are all dissolved, the residue
> Is what you read, as a poem, the rest
> Flows and is poetry (13).

Ezekiel is also credited for liberating the modern Indian English poetry from both, Anglo-American influence and also that of the imitative and romantic trend of the pre-independence poets of India. His poetry, according to J.Birje Patil: "… Constitutes a revolt against the incipient romanticism and vapid narcissism which had long made it impossible for Indian poetry in English to be a criticism of life" (*Interior Cadences: The Poetry of Nissim Ezekiel: The Literary Criterion 12:2-3*).

It was he who started using 'irony' as a powerful instrument to describe the corruption in our contemporary society. It is by this instrument that he is able to grasp the perfect attitude towards Indian situation. In a number of poems, he has shown his commitment to social causes and made ironical comments on the subjects or persons concerned. Some examples of such poems are: "Very Indian poems in Indian English," "Guru," "Entertainment," "Ganga," "The Couple," "The Truth about the Floods," "Jewish Wedding in Bombay," etc.

After independence and more particularly during the 1950s and 60s, when a respectable national identity has been achieved, Indian Poetry in English, under the guardianship of Nissim Ezekiel began to make its newness felt. Poetry became inward-looking rather introspective and introvert in nature, much more realistic; the poetic utterances became authentic, the poetic voice original and human. Rather than celebrating the past golden days of the nation, the poets began to scan and critically examine the rhythms of the nation. There was a shift from the rhetoric of the nation to the rhetoric of the self.

Ezekiel's poetry shows his sharp wit, apt observation of life and events which transcend the limitations of time and space. His poems gave a direction, shaped an idiom and gave a sense of purpose to Indian English poetry. There is a great variety in his poems- realism, love, philosophy, prayer, advice, and specific use of Indian English idiom. Paradox, irony and antithesis play freely in his volumes of poems such as *Latter-Day Psalms*. One of the main characteristics unique to him is that like Eliot, sometimes he seems to believe God but at the same time ridicules all the outer forms of religion. In the poem "Healers," becoming prophetic, he advises: "Know your mantra, meditate, release your kundalini, get your/ shakti awakening and float with the spirit to your destination" (*Collected Poems* 232).

In yet another poem he talks of highly unconventional subjects like poverty, sex and related contents which have many a time outraged the orthodox traditionalists. However, they don't make it pornographic, instead they give a spiritual version of true love and sex.It is to be noticed that Ezekiel doesn't advocate free sex; he only praises the consummation that takes place during sexual intercourse between two lovers. Ezekiel ironically criticizes the present pseudo-spiritual saints in his poem "Guru". In fact, his poetic world is warm, palpable and dynamic with lively personages. His poems are the expressions of his own self. They are self-assertive in nature.

After Ezekiel, the second important Indian English poet whose name comes to the reader's mind is Kamala Das. She is perhaps the first woman poet of India to write modern poetry which can very well be compared with Ezekiel. She was the fourth Indian English poet to win the Sahitya Akademi award for her book *Collected poems Vol-I* in 1985. Born in Kerala, brought up in Calcutta, and living in Metros like Delhi and Mumbai, she is firmly rooted in the Indian soil and has a very sound knowledge of its customs, tradition and culture. All these give the stamp of reality to her writings, making her fully aware of the direction and purpose of her writing. Her poems are usually rich with images and warm with emotions. Her images also have a very wide range, from natural landscapes to highly explicit sexual images. All her poems are full of ideas and abstractions, images of man and woman on several planes, the complex of emotions centering round human activities such as love, sex, companionship and problems relating to her own art. In her most acclaimed poem "An Introduction," she universalizes her desires: "I am every/ Woman who seek love…" (*The Old Play House…* 27)

Though she has written various poems about the different spheres of life like childhood, youth and others, her deeply feminine sensibility finds its fullest expression in her poems dealing with love. The matriarchal tradition of her Keralite family deeply influences her outlook and understanding of love and sex. She is truly a poet of love as seen from the perspective of a woman. According to her, the real achievement of a woman's life is not to worship her husband but to attain consummation in love.

Her poetry is, basically lyrical in form and can be divided into three main categories like positive poems, negative poems and poems relating to her family, childhood and ancestral legacy. The poems where she expresses satisfaction in love are known as positive poems whereas the poems where she resents against unrequited love are known as negative poems. Much like Ezekiel, she also creates a new Indian English idiom in her love poems. A large number of new and unconventional words like 'menstrual blood', 'the musky sweat between the breasts', 'the Jerky way he urinates', 'lesbian', 'frigid', 'queer', 'schizophrenia', 'eczema', 'ischemia' etc are found in abundance in her poetry. This can be taken as Kamala Das' contribution to Indian English idiom. Her Indian sensibility is highly lucid and the use of the mythical divine love of Sri Radha-Krishna affirms this fact. Krishna, who for thousands of years has been a symbol of divine love and a source of great inspiration for Indian poets, finds a very exalted place in the usually unconventional and even irreligious poetry of Kamala

Das. She imagistically portrays the minds of Mira, the great devotee; and Radha, the beloved of Krishna; creates some poems like "Ghana Shyam," and "Radha," which are full of divine passion and love. In yet another poem, "Krishna," the protagonist expresses her love in the following words:

> Your body is my prison, Krishna,
> I cannot see beyond it, Your
> Darkness blinds me.
> Your love words shut out the wide world's din (75).

Her language is quite effective in articulating her feelings, and the linguistic pattern she uses are flexible enough to facilitate communication of her intuitions. It is not surprising that speech, language, words, meanings etc. form the core part of her poetry. Her poetry is lyrical, conversational and the fact is that though she is an outright feminist but still is very much rooted with her own tradition and culture; instead of following the Anglo-American especially the confessional American poets, though in many poems she speaks in a tone very much like them. The famous critic cum poet Eunice De Souza pays her a tribute in the following words: "writers owe a special debt to Kamala Das. She mapped out the terrain for post-colonial women in social and linguistic terms. Whatever her vernacular oddities, she has spared us the colonial cringe. She has also spared us what in some circles nativist and expatriate, is still considered mandatory: the politically correct 'anguish' of writing in English. And in her best poems she speaks for women, certainly, but also for any one who has known pain, inadequacy, despair" (8).

One of the most important poets without whom the history of modern Indian English poetry would remain incomplete is, A.K.Ramanujan. He was one of the pioneering poets of the modern trend in Indian English poetry. Born in Mysore on 16 March, 1929, he belonged to a highly orthodox Tamil Brahmin family. This helped him to imbibe the rich mythology, folklore and cultural knowledge of both the Tamil as well as Kannada traditions. He left India in 1958 for his academic research in the Indiana university U.S.A. It was from here that he obtained his Doctor's Degree in Linguistics for generative grammar of Kannada in 1963. As a person having the knowledge of multiple subjects, there can be few who can match his intellectual variety and width. Basically a man of literature, he shows remarkable acquaintance with philosophy, psychology, sociology and the cross cultural heritage of India. Also, while referring to various facets of Indian history in terms of society, religion or culture; he never loses track of the contemporary realities. His poetry gives a double view of both the mythical past and the current present. On one side, a reader finds the mystic and the devotional aspects of Hinduism in his poetry, on the other one may come across the most controversial topics related to Freudian psychology, namely, sex and taboos. He has himself acknowledged the fact that while English and other scientific disciplines contributed in the formation of the body of his poetry, the soul has been formed from his early life in India and the knowledge about its customs, traditions, literature, culture, philosophy, religion and mythology. Furthermore they have so well assimilated or intertwined with each other that, now even the poet himself is unable to distinguish between them.

While some praise him in lofty terms, others find various faults in his abilities. In the context of Ramanujan's poetry S.K.Desai comments: "One way of facing the situation is to cultivate extreme sophistication of language and be in line with the modernist, ironic, ahistorical kind of writing and for 'identity' and for effect use the Indian memories to illustrate your attitude"(34).

Ramanujan's poetry, as one can understand from the above mentioned statement serves as an example for an Indian English poet to draw his strength and inspiration from his own roots, i.e. his culture and tradition. Like any common Indian householder, he has great attachment with his family and his poems reflect his nostalgia concerning his family. But unlike others who after migrating to other country become a part of it and forget their own land, culture and tradition; he instead has become more attached to it. In fact, he is very much at home in a foreign land. His poems are mini albums of Indian rural pictures. His Hindu consciousness serves as a central point of thinking. By its help, he still remains attached to his tradition though he lives in a different country. The title poem of the "Second Sight," states this unambiguously:

> You are a Hindoo, aren't you?
> You must have second sight
> (*Collected Poems* 191).

However, unlike his poetic ancestors he doesn't follow the tradition in a blind manner. His poem "The River," is a good example of his unconventional attitude. In his poem, instead of praising the river during flood like the ancient poets did, he picturises the tragic loss faced by the villagers living near the river, the loss of cattle and the loss of life in flood. His poetry is a fine blending of the oriental vision and the occidental mind in the harmonious way.

After these three luminaries in the sky of Indian English poetry, the star which draws our immediate attention is Jayanta Mahapatra. He was the first ever Indian English poet to win Sahitya Akademi award for his book of verse, *Relationship* in 1981. He is a highly dynamic poet who till now has produced sixteen volumes of poetry. This has earned him the fame of the poet producing the largest number of poems in English in India. He has been successful to a great extent in acclimatizing English language to an indigenous tradition. His poetic masterpiece *Relationship* combines the three elements of history, myth and vision. It draws its subject-matter from the land of 'forbidding myth' of the twelve hundred artisans working with full dedication under the fear of their emperor, to construct the grand temple of the state and the chivalry of the Kalinga warriors, who fought to their last breath resisting Ashoka's imperialistic designs and whose blood turned the river Daya red, are dealt with a highly artistic and evocative manner. After telling all these myths, he laments the loss of desire in the present sons of the soil and the successors of that great race of warriors and traders, to regain their glory and fame. He is mentally pre-occupied with the soil of Odisha, which is adorned by great places. He is in quest of his self in such a land of bewildering contradictions! In his poems, it appears as if Mahapatra becomes one with his soil, a chief characteristic of leading Postcolonial Poets.

In his second endeavour, *Bare Face* (2000), Mahapatra brings before everyone his concern for national identity. The poem is a vast storehouse of scenes from a typical Indian village, with all its daily routine work and rural scenes of natural beauty. In this poem, he had tried to establish the significance of villages in the context of the present times. In another poem called "In a Time of Winter Rain," the poet tries to interconnect the landscape with the people and tells us how the evocative memory of the past recreates the present. He tries to make a picture of the typical Indian atmosphere by giving a vivid description of Indian sky, landscape, birds and even abandoned temples. The poet in his poem "Abandoned Temple," gives an authentic picture of the conditions of such a temple in the following words:

> A wandering boy hurls a rock through the ruined entrance.
> Shadows in retreat fly: the serpent-girls, elephant-gods, fiery birds. Mosquitoes slap the Siva-linga in ignorant stillness a long shiver running down the shrine. (Himal, August 999)

Like all the postcolonial writers, he also tries to describe the indigenous culture and thereby assert his nationality that is both lovable and enduring. Though sometimes touching other unconventional subjects like sex etc., his main aim seems to confirm the glory of his nation and national culture. In many of his poems, he eloquently praises Gandhi. Further; he ventilates his despair as to how people have forgotten their principles. He raises his voice mostly for the pathetic conditions of women in India. Various poems written by him, clearly ventilates his feelings of outrage against the continuous crimes against women such as rapes, acid-attacks, sexual exploitation, the burning of brides for dowry and female infanticide etc. It is the combination of these widely ranged and mutually different aspects in his poetry, which makes it uniquely wholesome in nature. The eminent critic, M.K.Naik, as quoted by Rabindra K. Swain; has rightly observed about him that: "His style has an admirable colloquial ease, punctuated by thrusts of striking images. His muted brooding occasionally results in extremes of either excessively cryptic statement or verbal redundancy and in weaker moments he is seen echoing other poets"(68). Thus as a creator of new national myths, Jayanta Mahapatra deserves to be called a true postcolonial poet.

Apart from these four major poets, who shaped the form and style of the modern Indian English poetry, there are many other poets of fame and repute, who have made significant contributions to the volume, beauty and variety of Indian English poetry in their own way. Poets like Keki.N.Daruwalla, R.Parthasarathy, G.S Sharat Chandra, O.P Bhatnagar and many others have done great service to Indian English poetry by writing very good poems in purely Indian style and on Indian themes. It would be a great injustice to them if we would end this chapter without a slight introduction and description of their works and achievements. Shiv.K.Kumar is one of the prominent Indian English poets, who imparted a new dimension and shape to modern Indian English poetry. In fact, one of his greatest contributions is that he has developed a totally unique and indigenous Indian symbolism and freed Indian English poetry from the use of the western symbols. His approach to the things and events around him is modern and rationalist, though he doesn't outrightly criticise every old custom and belief. In his poems, he has bitterly criticised the performance of rituals in an irrational and mechanical way. He has written many poems on superstition, and useless rituals like, "Crematorium in Adikmet, Hyderabad," "At the Ghats of Banaras," "Pilgrimage," "Kali," and "An Encounter with Death," which bring before us the dark side of the religion we follow so fervently. His portrayal of the cremation ground in Adikmet is very realistic and lively to each single word:

> Incessant din of beggars
> And chants…
> Perched on the wall a vulture cogitates
> Upon human avidity-flesh offered
> To flames, bones and ashes
> To the Ganges. No leaving
> For the living…
> The priest chants louder for a generous tip (47).

In many of his poems, he has written about the western viewpoint of observation of our rituals and beliefs. In America, people would not believe in the miracles of the Ganges or holiness of the cows. His later poems show his spiritual confusion and anguish concerning the manifold sufferings of life. In a way he has become more conscious of the spiritual way of life like Ezekiel. Kumar also deals with a wide range of subjects, both of national and transnational interest, poverty, superstition, injustice, hypocrisy, double-standards, failure in married life and betrayal in life in the contemporary society-all come within the criteria of his poetry. In his poetry, the whole length and breadth of India becomes the local-a priest at Varanasi, a crematorium at Hyderabad, the pavement sleepers in Bombay, a temple in Calcutta, women at the village wells any where in the country and the death of the Australian missionary, Graham Staines with his two little sons-all become his source of inspiration and evoke powerful emotions in him. His poems are in general vibrant and enjoyable with the east and west coming together. According to Bijay Kumar Das: "Images of 'India' are handled with a consummate skill and keenness of intellect in Kumar's poetry. Unlike other postcolonial Indian English poets, Kumar writes a number of poems on the West and sees it from the Indian viewpoint. His poetry fits into the definition of postcolonial literature, which states that the postcolonial writer writes back (the empire writes back)"(*Shiv K. Kumar As A Postcolonial…* 45).

Keki.N.Daruwalla, after Mahapatra and Ezekiel, is the third Indian English Poet to win the Sahitya Akademi award. He began writing poetry in the seventies and has written eight volumes of highly admirable poetry. He gives great stress on Indian landscape and his poems are famous for the description of the natural scenic beauty of India. Daruwalla, in his introduction to *Two Decades of Indian Poetry 1960-80*, writes: "My poems are rooted in landscape which anchors the poem. The landscape is not merely there to set the scene but to lead to an illumination. It should be the eye of the spiral. I try that poetry, relate to the landscape, both on the physical and on the plane of the spirit. For me riot-stricken town is landscape" (21).

Except natural beauty and landscape, social concern is also a favorite theme of the poet. His two famous poems like "The Keeper of the Dead," and "Pestilence in Nineteenth Century, Calcutta," are glowing examples of his sympathy for the poor and middle-class Indians suffering due to unhealthy conditions and lack of medical facilities in the country. Like most of the modern poets, he is greatly averse to the hypocritical Hindu rituals. In his poems upon the holy city of Benares, we find a strong feeling of repulsion as quoted by Sunanda Sinha, in the following lines:

> Behind the heat- raise rising from the fires,
> Objects shimmer, dance, leviate,
> You face reality on a different plane
> Where death vibrates behind a veil of fire
> There is no lament. No one journey here
> To end up beating his breast. This much the mourners learn
> From the river as they form a ring of shadows
> Within whose ambit flesh and substance burn.
> (Boat Ride Along the Ganga 186-187)

R.Parthasarthy is one more poet of fame, whose name is synonymous with the modern Indian English poetry. Like A.K.Ramanujan, he is a great admirer of traditions, myths and beliefs of his country. His poems like "Ganesh," and many others, show his great mastery and craftsmanship of Indian mythology. In "Ganesh," he gives a description of the Ganesh myth of how the God was beheaded by his father, Lord Shiva and then became the elephant-headed god, worshipped first in all occasions for the purpose of removing all obstacles.

Here, we should not jump to the assumption that he is a blind believer of age-old traditions or religious myths. There is an implicit question in all his poems which leaves the attentive reader pondering for the answer. For example, he raises the question about the fate of the elephant, whose head was cut to restore that of Ganesh:

And no one ever bothered to find out
What happened to the elephant
Whose head, you wonder, will roll next ?
(Qtd. by Das, *Postmodern Indian English...* 35)

His later poems show a transition from the normal melancholy and gloom to contentment and acceptance. Yet, it is mainly the melancholy and frustration which receives the attention of the critic. In this regard the critic William Walsh comments: "Disappointment is the principal theme, whether with the edgy complications of love, with the insoluble problems of poetic composition or as with England in face of the actuality of what he expected. He accepts disappointment with an irritable but unprotesting glumness, a slightly morose recognition of the way things are" (Qtd. by B.K.Das, 1983: 84)

G.S Sharat Chandra is an expatriate Indian English poet who like Ramanujan is a great master of irony and also a skilled delineator of human ties and tangles. His poems such as "Heirloom," in which he fumbles before the question of belongingness and is unable to develop a proper sense of belongingness either to the country he is living in or the country, where he took birth. He seems to be in search of this answer in his poem "In the Third Country". There he contemplates over the ritualistic funerals in India involving lot of emotionalism as well as spiritualism. When he compares it with his new home, he finds a rather dry and unaffectionate approach towards death. The lines which describe the after death situations in a foreign country are expressive of the disillusionment of the poet:

In the country you went for
Your ex-wife arrives
By the next available flight
The children as usual
Are at the summer camp
For want of religious clarity
You are hearsed the public cemetery(...)
Your friends in town bewail you in a bar
Someone reads a poem or two
Someone mentions you on the telephone
(Qtd. by Das *Postmodern Indian English...* 36)

Thus one can see literally the pain of rootlessness and confused identity explicitly expressed in his poem. In the words of Naik and Narayan: "Sharat Chandra is still preoccupied with the memory motif, but is, at the same time, moving in the new-direction a mere objective kind of verse, with a marked dramatic element"(137).

O.P.Bhatnagar, came to be known as a poet with the publication of his volume of poetry *Though Poems* in 1976. He is highly efficient in the use of irony and humour.His subjects are mainly topical and he lays emphasis on 'nation and nativism'. Like Daruwalla, he is greatly devoted to the cause of his country. His great unhappiness concerning the brain-drain is very well expressed in his poem "Look Homeward Angles," in which he begs to the intellectuals going to foreign countries, to show some concern for their motherland. He is dead against the trend of 'brain-drain' and relentlessly opposes all those who support it in any way. He criticizes the intellectuals as selfish beings who fail to look beyond glamour and good. Ultimately he lashes out at the entire country for the vices of lethargy and selfishness which lies at the root of all brain – drain as quoted by Kanwar Dinesh Singh:

> What resilience holds us our condition!
> What inertia keeps us back from action!
> Even a bee stings, an ant pinches:
> Alas! A tortoise can but save his neck.
> (Make Wind Visible 65).

Thus, Kanwar Dinesh Singh is completely justified in the following observations, which he makes about the poet and his choice of subject: "The poet in O.P. Bhatnagar has been imbued with a sheer sense of awareness of the contemporary social realities and human predicaments. He especially concerns himself with the woes of the common man who is reluctant to transgress moral taboos. (ibid, 63). His conversational tone and free verse and swift streaming lines make his poems highly interesting and engaging to readers.

Dom Moraes is one of the most prolific post colonial Indian English Poets, known for the sharpness and clarity of his views. As the sixth Indian English Poet to bag the Central Sahitya Akademi award, he holds a unique position in the field of modern Indian English poetry. His poems mainly deal with his interest in history and anthropology as well as his nostalgia about the past. It was the archaeological bent of his mind that led to the creation of his poetic masterpiece *Serendip*. In his autobiographical poems, he has written down the fears, obsessions and desires of his life. He has admitted to the imperfectness of his life without hesitation. Yet, he has no regrets over it and seems to be quite at ease over this matter. In his poem "A Man Dreaming," he has spoken of the ultimate ripening of his spiritual sense. The maturity of this composition and depth of these lines leave little scope for surprise when one comes to know that the poet was still an undergraduate at Oxford, when he received the coveted Central Sahitya Akademi award for his work *Serendip* in 1994. P. Lal's comment in this context would therefore be highly appropriate to quote: "There is no doubt at all that Moraes is one of literature's most extra-ordinarily precocious people" (1972:139).

Among those Indian postcolonial poets who followed the socio-realistic poetic tradition of Ezekiel, Adil Jussawala's name has a unique significance. Like Ezekiel, he also was born in Bombay and received his higher education in England. Like the former, he too returned to India after being disillusioned about the western world. His literary output is quite scanty because of his unambitious and rather contemplative nature. Being a blatant practitioner of realism, most of his poems reflect the present 'crises of faith' due to the prevalent hypocrisy, impropriety and vulgarity in the modern times. In his first volume *Lands End,* we find a profuse use of Christian symbolism and references to Christian mysticism. Like Wordsworth, he becomes romantic more in the lap of nature, than the surroundings of artificial or sensuous beauty. Yes, there are also references to his childhood experiences of the Second World War as quoted by Sunanda Sinha:

> Violence is culture found on playgrounds
> Cities fall to let their children breathe.
> (A Bomb-Site, Land's End 296)

He adopts a 'Fanonite-Marxist' approach in the pursuit of his true identity. The themes of rootlessness, self-implied exile and the loss of identity stain most of his poetry with the colour of gloom and melancholy. The feel of alienation has been aptly brought out by V.A Shahane: "Imitative of Eliot's poetic technique, Jassawalla's poetry exposes loneliness and alienation of human beings as a contemporary reality, Marxist-economist's view of poverty-stricken people, limitation of colonial heritage, grim cultural climate, and personality crises etc"(Qtd. by Nigamananda Das, *The Poetry of Jayanta*...11).

With all these poets, many others like A.K.Mehrotra, Gieve Patel, Eunice de Souza, Arun Kolkatkar, Bibhu Padhi and Shanta Acharya are among the numerous poets whose creations have helped in the beautification and glorification of the vast storehouse of Indian English poetry. All poets from Ezekiel to the most current poet writing in English have their own significance in the history of modern Indian English poetry. With each new poet, the trend takes a step further and the Indian English 'idiom' becomes more and more rich and vast. All of them have helped in their own way to provide that sense of Indianness to the modernist trend of Indian English poetry and have made it reach to the point of glory where it is now.

As stated earlier, the Post-independence Indian English poetry is marked with all the basic characteristics of postcolonialism. One can find that the native identity and consciousness pervades the poetry of all the postcolonial Indian English poets. There is the use of various popular myths related to the epics and the Puranas in the poems of A.K.Ramanujan, Jayanta Mahapatra and Kamala Das. In the poems of A.K.Ramanujan, one can even find references to the local folklore of South India. Through various descriptions of religious and festive traditions, the poets assert the individual identity of their own culture. Their whole body of poetry seems to be on incessant search for their tradition and roots. Their nativist emphasis is very much reflected from their mentioning of intricate details about not only the cultural practices but also the most authentic portrayal of Indian landscapes. In the poems of all the postcolonial poets including Ezekiel, Kamala Das and Jayanta Mahapatra, the rural as well as the urban scenario of India comes alive before the eyes of the readers. One can even state, that to a certain extent, the reader can feel the very pulse of Indian culture, geography and philosophy in their poems.

A very unique feature regarding the tone of the postcolonial poetry is its stark realism and outspokenness. Unlike the colonial poets who either praised their colonial masters or glorified their own nation and its cultural heritage with an unparalleled zeal, the post – independence poets were rather objective in their approach and realistic in their outlook. While Kamala Das depicted the plight of the women in the traditional Indian society, Ezekiel spoke about wider problems like corruption, callousness on the part of the government officials and the communal prejudice prevalent in India. The poet Jayanta Mahapatra speaks about all the social and political vices prevalent in India but he is more vocal about the crimes and atrocities committed against women. Similarly, A.K.Ramanujan is also highly critical against the hypocrisy and stereotype attitude of the Indian society. All of them have, in the most unreserved manner, tried to depict the contemporary realities. This realistic depiction sometime makes the tone of their poetry ironical. It also provokes a sort of existential attitude towards life. The post-modern influence upon it is quite easily discernible with features like 'Feminism' and 'Diaspora' forming a major element in much of the postcolonial poems. Though originally a movement of western origin, the feminist ideology has become quite Indianized due to the Indian postcolonial poets. They considered it from an Indian perspective and has thus hybridized it, so as to become a mouthpiece for the women masses of this country. The cultural confusion which occurred as an aftermath of the colonial rules end, resulted in a lot of displacement of people as both groups and as individuals. While some of the reasons were borne out of socio-political causes, others were the result of the intellectual dissatisfaction caused by the unpatronising conditions at the home-land. Many postcolonial poets migrated to foreign countries for the intellectual satisfaction they were seeking. Though only a few of them achieved what they desired, yet even the realization, they had there, helped by giving a new zeal to their poetry. In the process, they have been successful in creating a purely 'Indian idiom' which is quite comfortable with the original Indian words as well as their synonyms in English. The most prominent contributors in this field are Jayanta Mahapatra and Kamala Das. Both of them have imbibed a lot of Indian vocabulary into the frame of their poetry and have set it in the most appropriate manner.

Though the number of social, cultural, personal or universal issues are too vast to be covered by one individual poet, yet each of the postcolonial poets has tried his best to meet the contemporary demand in at least a few of the subjects. Everyone of them, with his/her unique approach, literary style and power of expressiveness, has brought before us glimpses of many such facts about contemporary India, of whom we generally remain unaware. It is also true that with the changing times, everything including the moral perceptions, socio-cultural views and the very fibre of family life in India has undergone great changes. This has led to the defining and redefining of the various issues arising out of personal, social or national matters. The vision of India as an idealistic and altruistic 'heaven of freedom' as envisioned by the great visionary poet, Rabindra Nath Tagore, is yet to be realized. The great heights of perfection, plentitude, power, prosperity and prestige, as spoken by the saintly fathers of Indian nationalism- Swami Vivekananda and Sri Aurobindo, remains to be achieved. Still, as told by Benedict Anderson, in context to his literary approach of incisive analysis, such visionary details of the nation in art and literature is what we call as "Imagining the nation" (Qtd. by McLeod 94). It is this symbolic representation of the nation, which is the source of inspiration for all the nationalist feelings. As nationalist literature is basically a product of the postcolonial trend, it is their decolonizing and self-assertive nature which counts their real value. As per the words of the critic Elleke Boehmer: "Every new instance of independence, therefore- and some might say each new stage in the process of winning independence- required that the nation be reconstructed in the collective imagination; or that identity be symbolized anew" (185). So, ultimately we find that the overall goal of the postcolonial Indian English poets was to retrieve or redeem their self-identity, which had been blurred due to the archetypal colonial representations. For this purpose, these poets adopted the two-fold means of maintaining the individuality of their writings as well as keeping the tradition of national literary themes alive. The critic Elleke Boehmer, in this context, observes that:

"Indian, African, and Caribbean nationalist writers focused on re-constituting from the position of their historical, racial, or metaphysical difference a cultural identity which had been damaged by the colonial experience. The need was for roots, origins, founding myths and ancestors, national fore-mothers and – fathers; in short, for a restorative history" (185-186). So, we can conclude that all the postcolonial Indian English poets, thus, were the seekers of the 'native' soul of India and 'native' culture and tradition of which it is constituted.

WORKS CITED

Aravamudan, Srinivas. *Tropicopolitans: Colonialism and Agency,1688-1804.* London: Duke U P, 1992. Print.

Ashcroft, Bill, Gareth Griffiths and Helen Tiffin. *The Empire Writes Back: Theory and Practice in Postcolonial Literatures.* London: Routledge, 1989. Print.

Bhabha, Homi K. "Of Mimicry and Man: Ambivalence in Colonial Discourse." *The Location of Culture.* London: Routledge, 1994. Print.

Boehmer, Elleke. *Colonial and Postcolonial Literature.* New York: OUP,1995. Print.

Das, Bijay Kumar. *Aspects of Commonwealth Literature.* New Delhi: Creative Books, 1995. Print.

____. *Critical Essays on Poetry.* New Delhi: Kalyani Publishers, 1993. Print.

____. *Critical Essays on Postcolonial Literature.* New Delhi: Atlantic,2007.Print.

____. *Post Modern Indian English Literature.* New Delhi: Atlantic, 2006. Print.

____. *Shiv K. Kumar as a Postcolonial Poet.* New Delhi: Atlantic Publisher, 2001.Print.

____.*Trends in Postcolonial Poetry: Critical Essays on Post-colonial Literature.* New Delhi: Atlantic publishers, 2007. Print.

Das, Kamala. *Collected Poems.* New Delhi: Orient Longman, 1984. Print.

Das, Nigamananda. *The Poetry of Jayanta Mahapatra: Imagery and Vision.* New Delhi: Adhyayan Publishers, 2006. Print.

Daruwalla, Keki N.(ed.) *Two Decades of Indian Poetry.* Ghaziabad: Vikas Publishing House,1980.Print.

Davies, Carole Boyce. *Black Woman, Writing and Identity: Migrations of the Subject.* London: Routledge, 1994. Print.

Desai, Shantinath K., "Indian Writing in English: The Predicament of Marginality" *IJES,* Vol. XXVI, New Delhi:Sahitya Akademi,1987. Print.

De Souza, Eunice. *Nine Indian women poets:- An Anthology.* New Delhi: OUP, 1989. Print.

Ezekiel, Nissim. *Collected Poems.* New Delhi: OUP, 2005. Print.

Khan, M.Q. and Bijay Kumar Das. *Studies in Postcolonial Literature.* New Delhi: Atlantic, 2007. Print.

Kumar T.Vijay, "Post-colonial or Post-colonial? Re-locating the hyphen," *Post-colonialism. Theory, Text and Context.* Ed.Harish Trivedi and Meenakshi Mukharjee. Shimla: Indian Institute of Advanced Study, 1996. Print.

McLeod, John. *Beginning Postcolonialism.* New Delhi: Viva Books, 2013. Print.

Naik, M.K. and Shyamala A. Narayanan (ed.). *Indian English Literature 1980-2000: A Critical Survey.* Delhi: Pencraft International,2001.Print.

Patil, J Birje. "Interior Cadences: The Poetry of Nissim Ezekiel" *The Literary Criterion.* Vol-12,2-3, 1976.Print.

Ramanujan, A.K. *Collected Poems.* New Delhi: OUP, 2005. Print.

Said, Edward. *Orientalism.* London: Routledge, 1978. Print.

Singh, Kanwar Dinesh. *New Explorations in Indian English Poetry.* New Delhi: Sarup and Sons,2004. Print.

Sinha, Sunanda. "Annotating the Reality of the Indian Context: A Study of the Poetry of Nissim Ezekiel, Keki N Daruwalla, Adil Jussawala and Gieve Patel." *Indian Poetry in English: Roots and Blossoms.* Ed. S.K.Paul and Amarnath Prasad. New Delhi:Sarup and Sons, 2007. Print.

Smale, David. Ed. *Salman Rushdie: Midnight's Children/ The Satanic Verses.* New York: Palgrave Macmillan, 2001. Print

Spivak, Gayatri Chakravorty. "Can the Subaltern Speak?". *Marxism and the Interpretation of Culture.* Ed. Gary Nelson and Lawrence Grossberg. London: Macmillan, 1998.Print.

Swain, Rabindra K. *The Poetry of Jayanta Mahapatra, A Critical Study.* New Delhi: Chamman Offset Press, 2000. Print.

Trivedi, Harish. "India and Postcolonial Discourse". *Interrogating Postcolonialism: Theory Text and Context.* Shimla: Indian Institute of Advanced Study, 1996. Print.

Young, Robert J.C. *Postcolonialism: A Very Short Introduction.* New York: OUP,2003. Print.

Young, Robert. *Colonial Desire: Hybridity in Theory, Culture, and Race.* London: Routledge, 1995. Print.

CHAPTER 2

INDIGENOUS TRAITS (NATIVISM) IN THE FOUR REPRESENTATIVE POETS OF THE POSTCOLONIAL TREND

The most essential difference which distinguishes the postcolonial from the colonial form of literature is its emphasis on the 'native subject' rather than on the 'foreign master'. The postcolonial discourse probes into the 'native' concept of culture, literature and ethics and tries to re-establish the self-esteem of the subjugated and the colonized. On account of this 'Nativism' or the ideology defining the concept of 'Nativity', is one of the most popular subjects of discussion in the contemporary literary circles. Literally, this term seems to be simply speaking about the elements 'native' to a person, community or country like language, customs, beliefs and culture etc.But in reality, this is a loaded term which defies exact classification and meaning. According to G.N.Devy, one of the most prominent critics on nativism in India, the term 'native' derives its root from the word 'naïve' found in ancient European languages. This word was used, usually to describe a person who was deeply attached with his locality (commonly the village he lived in) and his soil, who by nature was land-locked, i.e. who didn't travel much, and who served his community by producing items of practical use for it. Thus he or she can be viewed as a soil bound, innocent and harmless person committed to the service of his or her community or nation. In the medieval age, the Spanish literature created an anti-figure of the aforesaid 'native character'. This new character called 'Picaro' was completely different from that of the 'naïve' character. It preferred reckless traveling, was adventurous by nature and had no particular emotional binding with its land or community. Its attitude was also that of a selfish and aggressive nature (8). The German literary critics of the eighteenth century used these two opposing models to classify literature into two broad groups. In their view, the unconventional literature created by the emotional tides of the heart was of 'naïve' character. It certainly affected the emotions of the readers but created no lasting impression. This type of literature was also known as Romantic literature in more popular usage. Contrary to it, the 'Picaro' variety of literature was highly sophisticated and was appreciated by the elite class. It was deemed to be of a lasting quality. This group came to be acknowledged as the 'classical' by the German critics. However all the intellectual endeavour of the critiques of the naïve wasn't enough to push it to the dark corner of marginality. Though, the 'Picaro' or 'Picareo' became the role model for the colonizing nations of Europe, the 'naïve' found its voice and representation in the various cultures opposed to the colonial ideology. Yet, it was only in the nineteenth century that this term 'naïve' or 'native' took the form of a full-fledged ideology called 'Nativism'. It was the result of an intellectual and cultural movement in the U.S.A, which aimed to safeguard the rights of the native Americans. In the same manner, the movement in Italy for upholding the native cultural traits resulted in the emergence of nationalism. Further in the first part of twentieth century, a similar movement started in Ireland. This movement referred to, by W.B.Yeats in his literary works, known as the Irish Literary Renaissance. It attempted to revive the imaginary fictional image of Ireland with the help of its myths and legends. This 'revivalist' nativism, which acknowledged race, nation and myth as the three principles of self-recognition and selfhood, was gradually accepted by the various nations of Africa and Asia, as a weapon to fight the hegemonic Western Cultural effects imposed upon them during the colonial rule.

In India, 'Nativism' in recent years has become a favorite topic of discussion in the literary circles. But it doesn't mean that the original term or the ideology is new to India. Even before the advent of the English, there are instances of nativist feeling in some of our ancient and medieval intellectuals. With the passage of time and due to the influence of various cultural, social and political factors, this concept, as in various other nations, has undergone great change in India also. Prior to the arrival of the English, nativistic attitude showed itself in the sayings and literary creations of various poets and saints, belonging to different regions of India. Especially those were the Bhakti saints like Dhyaneshwar, Tukaram, Namdeva, Meerabai, Tulasidas, Guru Nanak and Kabir, who laid the foundation of the modern vernacular languages and their literatures. They not only preached and wrote in the language of the local people but also strongly advocated its use instead of classical languages like Sanskrit or Persian. Even the great Marathi Saint, Dhyaneshwar is also known to have proclaimed "we will demonstrate how sweet our deshi-Marathi language" (Paranjape 236). This concept of 'deshi' which stood for native in Indian context was a counter and to some extent an anti concept to the concept of Margi or the classical Sanskrit tradition. However the 'deshi' was not as much a symbol of contempt as the English term 'native'. The Europeans used this term for all the subjugated races of Asia and Africa, whom they thought to be inferior in all ways and also destined to be ruled by them forever. The racist feelings in the English show themselves in the meaning of the term given in the not very old, 1971 Edition of the Oxford English Dictionary, as quoted by Nemade:

> The original or usual habitant of a country,
> As distinguished from strangers and foreigners,
> Now especially belonging to a non-European and
> Imperfectly civilized or savage race: a colored
> Person, a black (Paranjape 237).

Not only this, the prejudice of the English can be ascertained by the very fact that such ethnic groups of England, which can justifiably be called 'native', when fight against oppression, aren't branded 'native'. They are rather dismissed by being labeled as Welsh Separatism, Scottish Nationalism, Gaellic Revivalism and other such but never as a 'native' movement. In India also there were various evils in the past ages, like untouchability and the various bindings of the caste system. But, still there were two factors working in the Indian system, which accorded a place to anyone who came to India. They were-(i) Jati or the caste system and ii) Desh or domicilation. Once a person gets himself set within a particular caste and a region, he becomes a native of India. This is the way by which the various foreign races which came to India, settled and in course of time became a part of Indian social fabric. This nativisation process however didn't hamper with their original native character and wherever a particular group of people settled, they comfortably carried on with them their own language, religion, dressing and food habits, traditions and so on.

The task of translating these three terms was taken up by yet another critic of fame, Makarand Paranjape. In his *Nativism-Essays in criticism*, he translates the three terms as nativeness, nativism and nativity respectively. All the three terms though related to the same topic, stand for its different aspects. So, while 'nativeness' is natural and 'nativism' is aggressive, 'nativity' combines both the aspects within it. According to Nemade, while true universalism or cosmopolitanism is based upon appreciating the native culture of an individual society, the present concept of universalism is against it. Though he is not in support of reserved nativism, yet he feels that the aspects of nativism should not be given up under foreign influence. In his view, there is no real Indian English poetry as Indians are not the native speakers of English. Logically, this statement cannot be considered as true because India has produced a very extensive series of literary output in English right from the colonial period to the modern times. Though in all these literary pieces, the mode of expression is English, yet there can be no doubt raised about all of them being Indian in spirit and matter. In the words of C.D Narasimhaiah: "What one has in mind is a shared tradition, a community of interests, and a set of values that a people live by, all of which give a sense of identity to individual and nations"(Qtd. by Raghunath Sahoo, *Tension and Moral Dilemmas in Nissim Ezekiel's Poetry* 6). The same view is echoed in the words of Srinivasa Iyengar, who asserts more upon the nature of the spirit rather than the choice of the medium or body: "what makes Indo-Anglian literature as Indian Literature…. is the quality of Indianness… in the choice of subjects, in the texture of thought, play of sentiment, in the organization of material in terms of 'form' and in the creative use of language (ibid, 6).

The aggressive aspects of nativism has been examined and tried to be sorted out by various intellectuals. The Marathi critic Vasant Palshikar, warns us about its militant nature in the following words: "A nativistic movement has mixed motives and not all of them are constructive or positive. A nativistic movement can easily go chauvinistic: the aim is to exclude, to restrict, to whip up an anti-feeling, which ordinarily is part of the power game" (Paranjape 169). Taking nativism in a new and a rather broader sense, he rejects the traditional notions about nativism bound by geographical or political boundaries. In his words, a non-native can be described as "someone who is rootless, some one who is no longer 'at home' in any one place, amongst any people and culture" (Paranjape 172).

The question yet remains how to ascertain the criteria to determine a particular literary work as nativistic. For this, one has to take the help of nationalism and decolonization. Many Indian writers and poets have done praiseworthy work in the direction of liberating English from the colonial influence and bringing it to a more indigenized, rather 'native' form for the benefit of all the Indians. Nemade also in the same perspective, considers the freedom movement under Gandhi's leadership as a good example of a nativistic movement. Palshikar though seems to support it, holds the view that such movements: "are often meant to create a power base for the traditional elite class which had been displaced earlier by some one or the 'other' outsider" (173). Shantinath Desai remarks "Nativism is, like Negritude, an attitude of assertion, the assertion being that one's peculiar national and cultural identity" He further adds: "Nativism is not primarily an attitude of Swadeshi but an attitude of Swaraj" (173). As a literary genre it gives preference to "the indigenous over the outlandish: whether it is genre, style, form, or content"(Paranjape 175). Finally, in Makarand Paranjape's view, though the contribution of nativism is notable, it is unable to cope up with the present demand for a more flexible, broad-based, and eclectic tradition of contemporary criticism. The present requires such a liberal and absorbing tradition which would bring up an understanding between the various opposite concepts and ideas about nativism and internationalism, which would refer not only to our ancient literary traditions of Sanskrit and Tamil but also to the medieval regional literary trends. Side by side, it should also continue to interact with the western literary and interpretive theories, both classical and modern. In this regard, we can on no account neglect or do away with the English language, which is not only the best but also the most well known instrument for the purpose of exploring western knowledge. It is also the only medium of self-expression on the global level due to its universal acceptability. Even in the context of India, it has become a bridge for communication across all the barriers of race, language, regionalism and culture. The postcolonial critic Elleke Boehmer is thus quite accurate in his comment: "So, the best option for writers is to participate in the process of indigenization already taking place: to make a virtue of historical necessity by manipulating English to suit their own creative needs" (*Colonial and Post-colonial Literature* 210). The task is not too difficult also as English has done away with most of its inflections a long ago. Due to its un-inflected nature, it has a very strong adaptability for absorbing words from almost any language of the world. It has a very astonishing tendency to become naturalized in any terrain of this planet by assimilating the native phonemes, vocabulary and translated versions of local proverbs etc. The critic Elleke Boehmer therefore evaluates its worth in the most unbiased words: "It has been grafted on to different cultures, adjusted to local conditions, mutated and mongrelized. It has also promoted feelings of solidarity among nationalist middle classes. In large multicultural nations such as India or Nigeria, English is paradoxically the only language which allows communication and cultural exchange between elites in different regions" (ibid, 210).

All this, would combiningly give rise to a tradition which would not only safeguard the native and national interests and values but also enable us to have a foothold in the international literary sphere. With a strong background of our native culture enhanced with national pride, we would be immune to the sense of loss of identity or roots, with which many intellectuals following western ideology are suffering. Thus with a new sense of belongingness, national pride and enthusiasm, we would be able to cope up with the highly complicated literary trends formulated in the west and also to formalize our own critical and interpretive literary trends.

Nissim Ezekiel, like T.S.Eliot, can be taken as the originator or founder of the modernist trend of Indian English poetry. It was his style of writing and choice of subjects, which gave a 'local habitation and a name' to Modern Indian English poetry. Like any other ideal postcolonial poet, he also has a great affinity with the country he lives in and all other features of it like its landscapes, culture, tradition, philosophy and even its present conditions. He originally belongs to the Bene-Israel Jewish community which had taken refuge in India many centuries ago and thus in reality lacks any possible roots in the Indian culture and traditions. Still, he has made this country, its culture and philosophy his own and the high degree of Indianness he has imbibed in himself, shows itself with great clarity, in his poems. Though, like a typical modern poet his outlook and style are highly rational, modern, cosmopolitan and revolutionary in nature, still the natural beauty of India, the wisdom of its ancient scriptures, the living conditions in its big cities like Bombay and the various problems like degrading morality etc, which it is facing now, are referred to frequently in his poetry. The trend set by him is different from that of the colonial poets whose poems were highly romantic or mystical in nature. His poems are highly realistic, simple, and down to earth and have a nature of revealing many facts about which we normally remain unconcerned even after coming across it in our daily life. His poems in general highlight the various problems which India is struggling with in the present times. Subjects like poverty, fall in moral standards, poor sanitary conditions, political disturbances and other such of the same type appeals to his imagination and he makes poetry out of such tasteless subjects also.

In his poems like "The Railway Clerk," and "Ganga," he has talked about the difficult life led by most of the Indians due to poverty and inflation. In the first poem, he portrays the sufferings of an average government official:

> My wife is always asking for more money.
> Money, Money, where to get money ?
> My job is such, no one is giving bribe,
> While other clerks are in fortunate position,
> And no promotion even because I am not graduate
> (*Collected Poems* 184).

The poet also satirizes the Indian sense of morality which prides itself on patronizing or sustaining the poor people, who work as servants in our houses. Though we look upon them with contempt and suspicion, still we know that they are quite essential for our comfort. This notion is well expressed by the poet in the closing lines of this poem:

> … but we are used to it.
> These people never learn (202).

The above stated lines clearly portray the hypocrisy and double-standards of the average Indian morality.

All common elements of nature like heat, dust, sun and floods, and common people like professors, officials, clerks, shop-keepers, politicians, beggars, destitutes and hypocritical God men, all find a worthy place in his poetry. In his poems, like "Passion Poems," "At the Hotel," and "Morning Walk," the changes in emotional and spiritual values and the decay in relationship and love go side by side with the description of scenes from Indian daily life in cities and villages. His wide range of images is purely Indian in their essence. It seems as if India is the fountainhead of his imagery. His poetic language is of the English which common Indians speak and his style is highly conversational. His whole body of poetry seems to consist of only Indian elements and even the English words and sentences used by him have their own sense of Indianness.

Ezekiel has written some highly admirable poems like "Very Indian poems in Indian English," "Healers," "Hangover," "Touching," "Family," and many others. His poem like "Night of the Scorpion," gives a very realistic picture of the ignorant, superstitious and backward yet simple and pure-hearted people of Indian villages. When the poet's mother gets stung, many people gather to console and comfort her. They try to treat her in all superstitious and irrational ways, from known medicines and herbs to chants, rituals and incantations. Here the poet has also presented before us, the paradoxical picture of the educated Indians. As a rationalist his father tried various pseudo-scientific methods instead of applying for some magical cure. Yet, ultimately due to the strong influence of his surrounding milieu and the pressure of desperation, he gives away to all sorts of absurd and unscientific measures of treatment:

> My father, sceptic, rationalist,
> Trying every curse and blessing,
> Powder, mixture,herb and hybrid.
> He even poured a little paraffin
> Upon the bitten toe and put a match to it (131).

This shows that how in India; the people have a strong weakness for any easy and absurd mean for achieving their objective.

Finally when the pain and poison become ineffective the mother only thanks god, by saying: "Thank God the scorpion picked on me.../and spared my children." (Night of the Scorpion 130). This line throws light on the highly loving and selfless nature of Indian mothers. Other poems like "Tribute to the Upanishads," and "Hymns in Darkness," show the influence of the ancient Indian metaphysical knowledge of the Upanishads on his mind and intellect. However, his centre of attraction is always the city in which he was born and grew up (i. e. Bombay).Though he tried to go away from it; he was unable to do so due to a deep sense of belonging attached with it, despite all its negative aspects. His poems like "The Unfinished Man," and "The Exact Name," show the different kinds of outlook, with which the poet observes the city during different stages of his life. He looks at the city with an avid interest and a highly assimilative liberalism. All the multiple aspects of the city of Bombay are a part and parcel of his consciousness and he remains actively fascinated with all its colours - whether dark or bright. In one of his early poems titled "Morning Walk," he observes the city with much disgust as is expressed in the following lines:

> Barbaric city sick with slums
> Deprived of seasons, blessed with rains,
> Its hawkers, beggars, iron-lunged
> Procession led by frantic drums,
> A million purgatorial lanes,

And childlike masses, many tongued,
Whose wages are in words and crumbs
(*The Collected Poems 119*).

Here, with the admirable use of a purely Indian idiom, he has highlighted the gloomy and dark aspects of the city, normally held to be the citadel of Indian glamour. For him, it is rather like a 'Purgatory,' devoid of fresh air, good weather and natural surroundings. In spite of all this, he seems to be attached with his 'locale,' not only in a physical but also in a psychological and spiritual manner also. With the gradual passage of time, he seems to come to terms with the city and have adapted himself to it, while adopting the city and its lifestyle. In fact, unlike many other fellow poets, he refuses to leave even Bombay, what to say of leaving India. His attachment for the city and his determination to stay here is demonstrated in his poems "Island," and "Background, Casually," in the following lines:

I cannot leave the island
I was born here and belong (182).

In another poem he affirms this by saying:

I have made my commitments now
This is one: to stay where I am,
As others choose to give themselves
In some remote or backward place
My backward place is where I am (179).

A poet, to identify him with a particular nation, should respond to its natural beauty, culture and tradition. In his exhortation to the youth of India regarding the development of a truly Indian spirit, D.Ramakrishna says: "All growth independent of one's environment has an alienating effect. It's like living in the woods dreaming all the time of the mountains or the other way around" (3). Ezekiel's success in this field can be estimated from the compliment of C.D.Narasimhaiah in the following words: ".....to the extent he has availed himself of the composite culture of India to which he belongs, he must be said to be an important poet not merely in the Indian context, but in a consideration of those that are writing poetry anywhere in English" (Qtd. by Raghunath Sahoo 25). As a poet, Ezekiel concerns himself not only with the physical or geographical and the social surroundings, but also the political and intellectual scenario of the country. In his poem "The Truth about the Floods," he has described the apathetic and the lethargic attitude of both the volunteers and the government officials towards the victims of natural disasters like floods etc. While the students have their own motives behind distributing a meager amount of relief, the government officials were nonetheless passive in this regard. Their callousness in shifting their blame upon nature has been presented by the poet in a very interesting manner:

> The district authorities
> at Balasore
> Admitted they had failed,
> But they claimed they could not have done better.
> Nature, they said,
> Had conspired against them.
> 'Write the truth' they said
> 'in your report' (188).

Here we also see the lively descriptions of the rural areas suffering from flood, common to India. Also the use of Indian idioms like 'Paddy fields with knee-deep water' and 'shelter on tree-tops' gives a real native touch to the poem. One can almost feel the native touch of Indian temperament in the irresponsible attitude of the 'district authorities at Balasore'. In his poem "The Professor," he has presented the pitiable condition of intellectuals after retirement. With virtually no company either from family or friends and with nothing to invest their time, they feel greatly abandoned. The plight and helplessness of the old people at the present times is very-well depicted in the following lines:

> If you are coming again this side by chance,
> Visit please my humble residence also.
> I am living just on opposite houses backside
> (239).

As a true adherent of social realism and practical approach towards life, no aspect of corruption escapes his notice or his pen. While he criticises the government officers for their lethargic attitude, the corruption of the common people, whether of the urban or rural areas; also comes under his criticism. In his poem "Rural Suite," he vehemently criticises the exploitive nature of the affluent farmers, who during the after-harvest period, singing devotional songs go door to door and collect much gifts of rice, fruits, nuts and chillies. The poet condemns such shameless practices in his lines:

> It's a shameless exploitation
> Of the people's ignorance.

It's not even as if they need the food
Most of them are wealthy farmers
From the neighbouring villages
With a taste for hoarding gold
(*Collected Poems* 197)

Similarly in his "Poverty poem," he makes fun of the notions of the foreigners, who visit India. In the poem concerned, he is amused by the views of a female foreigner upon the friendliness of Indian people. Though he is able to surmise that, she herself is in doubt of her statement, he lets her remain in that false conviction, as it would make her feel comfortable in India:

Perhaps she thinks it best
Not to argue. I think so too.
(*Collected Poems* 231)

Here we find that the poet has a strong sense of practicality due to which, he avoids revealing the dark truth about India. This is one of the most integral features of his poetry. The poet accepts all the aspects of his country as a part and parcel of it. He neither complains nor shows pride over anything. Like a mute witness, he watches everything in a most detached and objective manner. For him everything, good and bad, moral and corrupt, pure and vile, all are the parts of the Indian consciousness and sensibility.

Religion has always been one of the most basic necessities for any nation. India is no exception to this need. Every average Indian in one or other way practises religion and tries to establish contact with the Almighty. While few persons do it out of pure devotion, most of the people in general do it out of one or other desire. The desires may vary from getting a wish fulfilled, a pending work done and having problems solved to becoming free from a guilt consciousness due to some mistake or immoral act committed knowingly. Unfortunately enough, it is this sentimental weakness of the Indians for religious succour that has been used to cheat and exploit them throughout the ages. Even today, after the spread of modern science and education, people still seek divine grace or intervention as the first remedy to all their problems. With the increase in the complexity of the modern age, the stress and strife in the life of an average Indian has also increased. This has also increased the chances of cheats and charlatans to exploit the gullibility and devotion of the general public. In the poem "Guru," we find a very disheartening description of the so-called spiritual masters, who claim to be our redeemers. Though claiming to be the men of God, they do not possess any godly quality of piety, compassion, self-control and love for others. This rudely shatters the faith of a devotee:

> Witnessing the spectacle
> We no longer smile.
> If saints are like this,
> What hope is there then for us? (192).

The poet also speaks of the various ways in which such people try to attract more and more disciples. He points to their high sounding claims in a most sarcastic manner:

> Sex is prohibited or allowed.
> Meat and drink are prohibited

Or allowed. Give up
Every thing or nothing
And be saved. The master
Knows the secret (281).

Yet another poem "Family," belonging to the volume *Songs for Nandu Bhende*, speaks about the spiritual sickness of the people in the modern times. The people feel uprooted from their spiritual and religious traditions. Therefore, they seek spiritual solace from every possible source. The poet as the speaker speaks again and again of this pseudo-sickness from which the average Indian feels himself to be suffering with. As everyone tries to get peace or bliss in his or her own manner, the family gets divided on theological level:

Let father go to Rajneesh Ashram
Let mother go to Gita classes.
What we need is mediation
Need to find our roots, Sir
All of us are sick, sir (243).

Thus, we find that the poetry of Nissim Ezekiel is native not only in form and taste but also in spirit. While most of the poems of his early volumes express his sense of alienation from the socio-cultural traditions of India, his later volumes show a steady search for roots in the Indian socio-cultural background. It is in the *Hymns in Darkness* (1976) that he finally affirms a sense of true belongingness to this country.

It is his attachment to his country, which makes him use the 'Indian idiom' profusely. All his poems of repute like "Background, Casually," Healers," "Guru," "Rural Suite," "A

Morning Walk," "In India," and "Night of the Scorpion," have enriched the Indian idiom by using not only words from Indian languages but also for using English words or phrases expressive of the native Indian sensibility. In his poem "The Truth about the Floods," his descriptions are true to the fact in every possible sense. Similarly "Ganga," "Professor," "The Patriot," and "The Railway Clerk," give us the most realistic pictures of our contemporary society. The city of Bombay, which is the centre of all his poetic consciousness, comes again and again in his poetic volumes with all the graphic details of its squalor, strife and sufferings. His poem 'In India,' details all the representations of fatigue, poverty and wretchedness, one can ever find in any of the major cities of India:

> Always, in the sun's eye,
> Here among the beggars,
> Hawkers, Pavement sleepers,
> Hutment dwellers, slums,
> Dead souls of men and gods,
> Burnt-out- mothers, frightened
> Virgins, wasted child
> And tortured animal (131).

The above stated style of description is a marked characteristic of all post-colonial poets, who believe in adoring and representing their country as it is in reality. Unlike, the colonial poets like Henry Vivian Derozio or Sarojini Naidu, they do not believe in deifying or glorifying in the face of the rampant poverty, corruption and other problems it is suffering from. This is one of the prominent reasons for his frequent use of irony and satirical tone underlying most of his poems.

His style and temperament has been well summed up by the critic A.N.Dwivedi, who states: "The austerity of his art, the economical accuracy of his language, the condensation of his style, the impressiveness of his imagery, the sharpness of his wit and irony, the contemporaneity of his subject matter, all these immediately render him a 'modern' poet of great relevance and significance" (65).

The poet who, made Indian English poetry get the honour it deserved by bagging the Central Sahitya Academy award for the first time is no other than Jayanta Mahapatra.Born in Orissa, he has not only elevated Indian English poetry to a global status but has also enlivened the ancient heritage and glory of Odisha. His masterpiece, *Relationship* for which he got the Sahitya Academy award in 1981, is infact a virtual representation of Odisha. Odisha, with all its natural beauty scattered in its landscapes and rural country sides as well as its architectural wonders in the form of Konark, Puri, Bhubaneswar; its ancient glory, rich tradition, highly colourful culture and its present deplorable condition, has been picturized in a highly vivid manner. The book is in fact, not an ordinary collection of poetic observations, presented in the form of an arrangement of words but a well-constructed poetic edifice built upon the theme of Odisha and the 'forbidding myth' associated with it. This is the reason for which he dedicated the Sahitya Akademi Award to his motherland with the following words: "To Odisha, to this land in which my roots lie and lies my past and in which lies my beginning and my end, where the wind knees over the grief of the river Daya and where the waves of Bay of Bengal fail to reach out today to the twilight soul of Konark. I acknowledge my debt and my relationship" (Dodiya 176). Yet, Odisha has not bound the sensibility and consciousness of the poet within its physical boundaries. He is ever-conscious of all problems of his country whether of political, social or economic nature. He renders his heart bare in his poems and one can feel the surge of pain rising in his heart at the present scenario of crime against women, rampant corruption, decreasing patriotism and social injustice against the downtrodden castes of India. Actually, he can be claimed as a true 'native' poet on the very ground that he does not overlook even the most unappealing and repulsive aspects of his 'native' land. In this context, he seems to justify the statement of the critic Judith Wright in a most befitting manner: "Before one's country can become an accepted background against which the poet's and novelist's imagination can move unhindered, it must be observed, understood, described as it were, absorbed. The writer must be at peace with his landscape before he can confidently turn to its human figures" (Qtd. by Bijay Kumar Das *The Poetry of Jayanta Mahapatra...* 7).

The first part of the volume *Relationship* highlights the historical importance of the Mahanadi, the most important river of the state, the temple of Konark and the ancient harbours like Chilika and Chandipur.There is a deep sense of nostalgia and pain intermingled in the course of the poem. The poet laments upon the present plight of Odisha.Once upon a time, Odisha was famous for its prosperous and far-stretched maritime trade. But now we have only vague traces of it embedded in the traditional observation and celebrations. The poet bemoans the loss of such a glorious heritage:

> Time
> And the boat,
> and the initiation into the mystery of the place,

the soiling ships of those maritime ancestors,
who have vanished in the black day without a
trace (*Relationship* 39).

He also remembers his brave ancestors who fought bravely to their last breath with the great Mauryan Emperor, Ashoka. The battle which was fought near the river Daya was so terrible that the water of the river is said to have turned red with the blood of the dead soldiers. The high scale destruction of that war enlightened Ashoka about the true nature of military conquests and he became a deeply religious man, a follower of the path of peace, preached by Lord Buddha.

However, now, the people have not only lost the power to retain but also have become undesirous of regaining those instincts of bravery, courage and chivalry. So, the poet laments:

How would I pull you out
Of the centuries of fallen stone?
How would I hold the Linga in the eye
Until the world is made all over again?
(*Relationship* 28).

The poet is highly appreciative of the natural beauty of Odisha and feels as if he is one with it. He keenly observes the annual migration of birds from far North Siberia to the warm waters of the Chilika Lake on Odisha's Southern shores. This wonderful natural process in a highly surprising manner only helps in increasing the agony of the poet because the birds and animals inferior to humans have retained their habits from ages but he and his people of Orissa have been segregated from the heroic traditions of their ancestors. This fact makes the poet analyze the 'golden deer' myth of the land which deluded Rama and Sita,for knowing the true meaning of life. He further goes on to the ancient myth of the Sun God and the Konark temple associated with it. The temple famous for its architecture is surrounded by various mythical stories and historical facts. The story of its construction is also not less romantic and thrilling. The description of twelve hundred artisans working day and night, under the fear of royal punishment, to give a shape of reality to the dream of the King Narasimha Deva is highly touching and moving to the heart of the readers. However, the re-telling of all the myths and lores of the land by the poet is not a purposeless nostalgic reaction but a purposeful and earnest effort on his part to put up a comparison of all the myths with the present miserable conditions so that, the people inspired by the greatness of the ancestors may strive for regaining it once again. In the tenth section of the poem, the poet recounts the tale of Lord Buddha and the advent of Buddhisim on the soil of Orissa. Along with these, the poet also brings back into our memory, accounts:

> Of broken empires and of vanquished dynasties
> And of ahimsa's whimpers (*Relationship* 34-35).

The poet thus standing among the mental ruins of a glorious past and haunted by the voices of closed ones from it, writes poems which "smells of the rancid fat of the past" (*Relationship* 35). In the view of the poet, for the better understanding, appreciation and durability of the present, it should be thoroughly analyzed in the light of the past.

His other poems such as "Dawn at Puri," "A Country Festival," and "The Captive Air at Chandipur-on-sea," are highly evocative with number of images, native to Odisha, the land of the poet. His *Bare face* in its opening stanza present before us a scene common to all the Indian villages. A village woman arriving at a pond to bath, her letting the hair loose before bathing and the mild rain wetting the bamboo groves near the place, all evoke a perfect native scenario in our minds. In another poem called "In a Time of winter Rain," the poet tries to bring out the relation of nature with man along with the recreation of the present by the evocative memory of the past. His aim is elucidated by the following verse:

> We learn to smile in a time of winter rain.
> Under a wet sky it's no meager comfort
> To feel the radiance of noon in our palms
> The almond-eyed boats clutching time in their fists
> In the Mahanadi River, the right shoulders
> Of peaceful lotuses floating motionless
> (*Bare Face* 18).

Not only the elements of nature like the sky, landscape, waters and birds of India but even the dilapidated or abandoned temples also inspire the poet and find mention in his poetry. In a poem titled "Abandoned Temple," he gives a very lively description of such a temple:

> A wandering boy hurls a rock through
> The ruined entrance. Shadows in retreat fly:
> The serpent-girls, elephant-gods, fiery birds
> Mosquitoes slap the Siva-Linga in ignorant stillness
> A long shiver running down the shrine.
> (Himal August 999)

As a poet, Jayanta Mahapatra started his career with the publication of his first volume of poetry *Close the sky Ten by Ten* in 1971. In this volume he has tried to transform the wide body of his experiences into poetic words. It is the attempt of the poet as a novice in the field of poetry to make his mark. In this volume, the nature of his poetry is highly experimental. There is no practical balance between the language and the emotions. Somewhere, the emotions fail to cope up with the strength of the words and at other places, it is the language which is unable to keep up its pace with the flow of emotions. The themes with which the poems of this volume deal are earth, life and language. All the forty-nine poems in this volume are expressive of feelings like loneliness, love, absence, ancestral fear, the awkward despair, momentary impressions, his early childhood experiences, his relationship with his family, his sexuality, his alienated state in context to the Hindu tradition and society. The poem "Myth," in this volume is a strong evidence of his feeling of alienation from the Hindu society. Though he is fascinated to the traditions, rituals and places associated with Hinduism, he still remains apprehensive of any possible question from a priest, who may suddenly ask him… "Are you a Hindu?" (*Selected Poems* 15). This volume is followed by two other volumes- *Swayamvara and other Poems* and *A Fathers Hours*. Both these volumes, acting like sequels to the first volume, expressed the poet's views and feelings over the subjects stated earlier, in a much refined and balanced manner.

It is the next four volumes, which shaped the poetic genius of the poet to its present magnificence. The volumes- *A Rain of Rites*, *Waiting*, *The False Start* and *Relationship*, record the gradual condensation and crystallization of his poetic consciousness. These volumes mainly deal with a search for identity with the mainstream Hindu tradition and culture; and a gradual effort to root oneself in his own native environment by being conscious to all its possible aspects. In these volumes, we also find a growing consciousness about the contemporary problems of the Indian society, like the plight of women, poverty etc. The very first poem of the volume *A Rain of Rites*, "Dawn," describes the pathetic condition of Indian woman, who live only by the dictates of the male dominated society.

> …an Indian woman, piled up to her silences
> Waiting for what the world will only let her do (1).

His *Waiting* and *The False Start* are also works of an acute human sensibility, which is strongly expressed by the poet's literary reactions to the socio-cultural scenario of his native country. The poems "The Indian Way," and "Taste for Tomorrow," in *Waiting* show the intensity of the poet's attachment with his national tradition and culture. The best example of this would be his fourth volume of poetry *Relationship*, which can also be considered as his Magnum Opus. This entire volume abounds in images from his native land, its society, culture, religion, its history and its contemporary problems.

The third phase of the poetic career of Jayanta Mahapatra showed great maturity of style, vision, theme, technique and imagery. It is in this phase that he steps outside the circle of disillusioned Romanticism into the vast field of post-modernism. From here on, all post-modern elements like existential anguish, rationalist outlook towards life and an uninhibited portrayal of the grotesque or the grim elements of the modern society and contemporary scenario started occupying his poems. The first poetic volume of this phase, *Life Signs* is a chronicle of the tragic experiences of the poet, of both personal as well as impersonal nature. One of its most famous poems is "Grandfather," which is a re-telling of the tragic conditions during the great famine of Odisha, which forced his grandfather, Chintamani Mahapatra, to embrace Christianity. Others like "The Lost Children of America," "Violence," and "A Country," show the poet's sensibility towards the communal, social and political problems, which are at the roots of all the suffering, misery and disturbance in this poem. The next volume *Dispossessed Nests* centers around various tragic incidents which have marred the consciousness of the nation. The Bhopal Gas Tragedy and the Khalistan movement in Punjab were some of the most tragic episodes in the Indian History. In the eighth poem of this volume, he has narrated the frightful episode of the hijacking of Flight 405 by Pro-Khalistani terrorists:

> ... Even days after
> The nightmare it's hard to believe
> The Kapurs shouting long live Khalistan
> Alongwith the terrorists in unison,
> Like well trained protestors...........
> (Dispossed Nests: The 1984 Poems 21)

The last volume of this phase is *Burden of Waves and Fruit* which shows a growing inward search for the answers searched by him through the years of his poetic evolution. The mood of the poet here becomes more philosophical and contemplative. It even tends towards a mysticism of its own type. For example in a poem of this volume, the poet himself declares his confusion to understand his own poetic zeal:

> Can one tell
> Why various writers
> Have emptied themselves to the cruel caricature
> Which memory dangles
> As bait before them ?
> (*Selected Poems* 76).

In spite of this increase in internal search, the poet does not leave the ground of reality upon which he is firmly established. Other poems of the same volume like "A Summer Afternoon," "Events," and "Burden of Waves and Fruit," justify that even while soaring in the skies of internal space, his eyes are bound to the earth, darkened with all types of vices, corruption and injustice.

The interval between the third and the last phase of Mahaptra's poetry is marked by the volume *Selected Poems*. This volume presents the very essence of all the volumes of Mahapatra, published by then. The phase which continues thereafter consists again of three volumes *Bureden of Waves and Fruit* (1988), *Temple* (1989) and *A Whiteness of Bone* (1992). The first volume is a multilayered depiction of Odisha's landscape in different seasons with deep spiritual significance. The rural life, sensibility for death, abuse of women and children and a mystic introvertness are a few of the major themes of this volume. It is also famous for its 'rain' imagery which is depicted in many of its poems like "Rains in Odisha," "Another Day in the Rain," "A Rain Poem," "This is The Season of The Old Rain," and "Again The Rain Falls,". In the next volume

Temple, he both glorifies and satirizes the feminine concept in Hinduism. The body of a woman is as sacred as a temple with the halls of Dancing, Offerings and Sanctum Sanctorum corresponding to her youth, marital life and motherhood. Yet, this temple is regularly desecrated by various acts like rape, sexual abuse, prostitution etc. The poet by placing the myths about the Shakti cult and the present state of women as reported in newspapers, side by side, exposes the hollowness and hypocrisy of the Hindu society. The last volume is a compendium of poems selected from various periodicals and anthologies. It presents the internal disturbance of the poet's mind over the prevailing conditions of the state and the society. Referring frequently to death, despair and tragedies, his tone becomes quite replete with existential anguish. By talking over and over about grim topics like rapes, murders, assassinations, and mass tragedies; he seems to be expressing his views about the world being a rather unfit and miserable place to live in. The titles of the major poems of this volume like 'Unreal Country," "Shadows," and "Bone of Time" are symbolic of the despair and disillusionment that pervades the entire gamut of this volume. In one poem 'The Waiting," we became aware of the constant fear of the poet regarding any mishap that may happen:

> I can easily tell the sound
> Of someone being hit with an iron pipe,
> The sound of a body falling
> Or being burnt after doused in petrol,
> And the sound of someone seducing my woman-
> These are like the sun and air
> On my face now (*A Whiteness of Bone* 35).

The last phase of the poet's creativity comprises of three volumes again, *Shadow Space* (1992), *Bare face* (2001) and *Random Descent* (2005). The first volume refers to the space or the gap between the two polarities of Westernism and Indianism, Christianism and Hinduism, scientific and artistic temperament, and above all the colonial and post-colonial approach towards contemporary things. His poetry thus depicts both the contrast and confluence of all these opposite factors. The next volume *Bare Face* is again a typical monument of hopeless, desperate and gloomy expression of the poet's melancholic heart. Its most lengthy poem "Requiem," while tracing the origins of the great Indian tradition from the Vedic ages to the present, laments its death and the resulting misery with which we are suffering. In the same poem, referring to hypocritical attitude of Indians towards Mahatma Gandhi's great ideals of ethics and humanity, the poet comments:

> What you have left behind are
> Faded pictures on bare office walls. A day
> Every year as a national holiday.
> Growing, seething leper colonies.
> (*Bare Face* 29)

The last volume *Random Descent*, justifies its title by the random thoughts of the poet. The contemplative mind, the sympathetic heart and the pro-existentialist view of life have rarely undergone any major changes. The imagery of fear, violence, grief, poverty, wretchedness and exploitation are abundant throughout the volume. All the three parts bearing the names-Old Violins of Legends, Another Ruined Country, 2002 and Shores of Darkness and Light ; are symbolic of the poet's nostalgia, existential anguish and spiritual dilemma. There is also reference to contemporary problems in poems like "The Stones," "Scream," "Scenario," and "A Walk of Wild Feet,". The critic Pradip Kumar Patra is completely justified in his statement that: "In *Random Descent* each and every poem is a portrait not of the physical world but of the mental world. Most significant is the delineation of Odisha, its culture, its lost glory and the contours of Odia life. Hence, here is a poet who has not only grasped Odisha, but also assimilated it in his entire being"(89-90).

As a poet, Jayanta Mahapatra qualifies all the norms for being a true or ideal native poet. A befitting evidence in this context would be an evaluation of his poetry in the tradition of Indian Poetics. Indian Poetics is one of the oldest systems of poetry and music in the world. Its most unique feature is the theory of "Rasa" or aesthetic pleasure. Its earliest propounder Bharata Muni, had prescribed originally eight Rasas in his treatise "Natya-Shastra". However, later on a ninth Rasa, "Shanta" or the "tranquil" was added to it. From then onwards, it is these nine-fold Rasas which have been accepted and used by all the Indian poets following the code of Sanskrit Poetics. The eminent authority upon Sanskrit poetics, Abhinavaguptacharya, in his treatise Abhinavabharati, upon the principles and theories of Sanskrit poetics; quotes the following verse from the Natya-Sastra –

Shringara-Hasya- Karuna-Roudra- Veera-Bhayanakaah
Vibhatsa-Adbhuta-Shantascha nava natye rasah smritaah (vi.16)

Shringara-(Amour), Hasya-(Comic/satire), Karuna-(Pathetic), Roudra-(Terrifying), Veera-(Heoric),

Bhanayaka-(Ferocious), Vibhatsa-(Grotesque), Adbhuta-(Surprise) and Shanta-(Serene), are the nine fold rasas of Natya.

So, "Rasa", to be interpreted in the simplest manner, is the aesthetic pleasure that one derives from an artistic expression or representation of the nine-fold fundamental states of human mind. Though, many of the later exponents of "Rasa" theory have tried to reduce or increase the number of Rasas, yet it has remained constant till now.

Due to its Post-modernist inclination, the major part of Jayanta Mohapatra's poetry, takes and portrays the grim aspects of life and society. However, as a true poet with a genuine Indian sensibility, the element of beauty and love, or Shringara Rasa doesn't escape his pen. Whether consciously or unconsciously, his own attachment to natural beauty, the cultural panorama of his native state 'Odisha' and his own experiences regarding love and passion; drag the element of beauty or love within the usually grim realm of his poetry. In his volume of poetry, *Waiting*, he has depicted the states of 'Abhisaram' i.e pre or extra marital relationships between lovers, and 'Viraham' i.e. the intense craving of lover for his/her beloved, in the most evocative yet compact lines. The feeling of timelessness due to the ecstasy of such experiences is marvelously worked out in the following lines:

> We could return again and again
> To the movement
> That is neither forward nor backward,
> And let the sun and moon take over,
> Trailing their substances and shadows.
> (The Indian way; *Selected Poems* 24)

Apart from poems upon personal themes, the aesthetic consciousness of the poet is also perceptible in poems depicting his love for the beauty of his own culture and native land. He mesmerizes the reader with the lucid and symphonic lines of the fourth poem of his volume, *Relationship*. The explicitness and sublime nature of Shringara Rasa, in this context proves his genuinely Indian sensibility:

> And now, you
> My ancient love of a hundred names,
> Of rains and endless skies and morning mists,
> Of wind-beaten evenings of owl-calls and of
> Rice harvests in December,
> My love of gold nose-rings and laughing earrings,
> Of towering ruins of stone panting in the dark,
> Of loyal lions guarding the diamond navels of shrines,
> Of amber breasts and secret armpits,
> Of cries and the soft steel of thighs,
> and of the old emptiness of my own destiny.
> (*Collected Poems* 43).

"Hasya", the second Rasa, actually pertains to the element of the comic or the humorous. However, in the post-modern context, it is more representative of 'Vyangya' or Satire, which is held as a lower from of this usually delightful Rasa. 'Vyangya' as a mode of humiliating the wrong-doers or the wicked publicly, was a very popular literary device in the traditions of India. Even at present times also, it has become an efficient measure of showing contempt to one's enemy, without inflicting any physical violence in the least possible manner. As a poet, Jayanta Mahapatra's poems target no individuals.

Rather, they take to task the Government's callousness and inefficiency as well as some of the exploitative and parasitic sections of the Indian society. For example, in this poem from the volume *Relationship*, the poet satirizes the condition of the records and files kept in a state office:

> ... like state cupboards which are going black
> with the smells of the rancid fact of the past
> (*Relationship* 35).

In these lines, he has indirectly revealed the extreme carelessness and irresponsibility, which haunts the government offices in India. In such places due to the continuous accumulation of dust without any ventilation, the place itself starts smelling in a typical manner. This smell is not only symbolic of the uncleanliness of the place, but also that of neglect and apathetic attitude of the government towards the people.

In yet another poem "Total Solar Eclipse: Puri, February 16, 1980," the poet makes satirical comments upon the Brahmin Community, who have exploited the superstitious nature of the credulous masses of India for centuries. He compares them to crocodiles hiding in deep water, which here is symbolic of the temples or religious institutions:

> And cautiously the crocodile
> Pushes its long snout from the deep water
> Like the fearsome Brahmin priest in the temple
> (*Collected Poems* 54).

The third Rasa "Bibhatsa" or the grotesque is perhaps one of the most pervading and prominent element of Mahapatra's poetry. Quite a large number of his poems are unique examples of this Rasa in the modern context and style. "Bibhatsa" aims at horrifying the audience to the point of repulsion, so, as to force out their dormant moral sensibility in denouncement of corruption or immorality. In his *Life Signs*, he describes the brutal rape of a poor under-aged girl, first by a priest's son and then by four policemen:

> In the Hanuman Temple last night
> The priest's pomaded jean-clad son
> Raped the squint-eyed fourteen-year fisher girl
> On the cracked stone platform behind the shrine
> And this morning
> Her father found her at the police station
> Assaulted over and over again by four policemen
> Dripping of darkness and of scarlet death
> (The Lost Children of America, *Collected Poems* 63).

Here, our sensibility is forced to exert itself to the extremes to assume the ghastly nature of this incident. The rape of an innocent girl, in a place like temple and that also of the god of celibacy, shocks us out of our wits. That this act was committed by a priest's son, whose community represents the very ideals of holiness, character and virtue, repulses us greatly. But even after this the repetition of the crime again, this time by policemen, the guardians of law at a police station, the primary seat of law, leaves us with a most bitter taste in our heart and mind.

We find more instances of this Rasa in other volumes like *Dispossessed Nests* etc. In *Dispossessed Nests*, the poem no-19 and 32 are a few of the examples of the explicit use of this Rasa. While the first poem depicts the inhumanity to which our sensibility has degraded regarding women, the other poem horrifies the readers by revealing the truth about children in big cities, being vulnerable to the dangers of sexual abuse and prostitution:

> Never say that their years are flayed from them.
> Never say that those flowers are for their hair.
> Never talk of pity, or beauty, laughter or honour
> Remember their breasts are meat, the dram city's
> share.
> (*Dispossessed Nests* 54)

"Karuna" or Pathos is one of the strongest themes of his poetry. As a Rasa, it is generally categorized in the category of the Sattvica or pure and noble Rasas. Therefore, the presence of such a Rasa in the poems, determines the nobility and purity of the poet's heart and character. When one goes through the intensity of this Rasa found in Jayanta Mahapaptra's poetry, one can not help but admire his humane and noble spirit. In the volume *A Rain of Rites*, he gives a most heart-rending description of the lot of widows, who reside in the holy city of Puri, in the strictest discipline of austerity and self-neglect, only in hope for salvation:

> Her last wish to be cremated here
> Twisting uncertainty like light
> On the shifting sands (14).

Another poem of the same volume "Hunger," depicts the plight of the poor people of coastal Odisha, who in order to sustain themselves are sometimes driven to the most desperate measures. The poem tells us how sometimes hunger drives a person to the most shameful acts like selling her own daughter's body for prostitution. 'Hunger,' as a theme, has always been one of the most frequently used, by the poet. After all it was hunger only, which was the root of all the rootlessness, socio-cultural alienation and religious dilemma faced by the poet. Due to starvation, his great grandfather had embraced Christianity during the great famine of Odisha. This had forever alienated him and his descendants from the socio-religious mainstream of Odisha. The poet in his volume *Life Signs* presents the trauma that forever remained with him after the conversion:

> The separate life let you survive, while perhaps
> the one you left wept in the blur of your heart.
> (Grandfather 67).

As a post-modern poet, Jayanta Mahapatra rarely glorifies idealistic heroism or chivalry, yet there are occasional streaks of Heroism or "Veera" Rasa in his poetry. Like any other Indian, he is also unable to remain uninfluenced by the feelings of nationalistic pride upon the traditions of heroism of his native land. In his volume *Burden of Waves and Fruit,* he refers to the heroic and patriotic spirit of Shivaji, which helped not only in liberating Maharashtra but also left a legacy of everlasting pride for India:

When the great plains beside the Sahayadri
flamed to flower
With the blood of the day and rested satisfied.
(At Shivaji's Fort at Panhalla: Looking across the
Western Ghats 18)

In yet another volume, *A Whiteness of Bone*, he speaks of the bravery of Tipu Sultan, who fought till his last breath to save the freedom and honour of his kingdom:

History closes
Behind us its tale of disinherited princes,
The clear music of freedom, a magic circle
Of wild stripes that once flashed steel
In the bright sun of Seringapatam.
(At the Summer Palace of Tipu Sultan, Seringa
Patam, 11).

"Bhayanaka" Rasa or the feeling of fear is also a very important element of Indian poetics. As a human being, one is always prone to one or other kind of fear. The poet also has fears of his own share. His fear however, is of an impersonal nature, as it is more concerned with the safety of women, children and the depressed classes. It is the inhuman exploitation and torture, to which they are subjected, that makes the poet afraid for their well-being and future. The feeling of fear resulting from the violence and corruption, pervading his native land are beautifully expressed in the poem "Steps in the Dark,":

Darkness that comes slowly in,

Voices and feet marking time, (…)
Or emerging through strange water,
Ready and naked and of death
(*Selected Poems* 29).

Another poem "Writer in the City," gives a very frightening description of the wretched and pathetic condition of the poor in a city, during the harsh winter:

… Misting the answers we are afraid to ask,
Still healing those flows of life itself we do not know.
(*Random Descent* 15).

"Roudra" Rasa is an intensified form of the Bhayanaka, in which fear becomes greatly overwhelming in nature. It is somewhat similar to 'Bibhatsa' in characteristic with the exception of any feelings of repulsion resulting out of it. In his 'Dhauli," he has given a very terrifying description of the battle field, post Kalinga war:

Afterwards
When the wars of Kalinga were over,
The fallow fields of Dhauli
Hid the blood-split butchered bodies.
(*Collected Poem* 22).

Another glimpse of this Rasa can be observed in the poem "Night Coming in," where each line causes a shiver in the spine of the reader:

…Here
There is no end to the voiceless screaming
Of the heart, beside the sacred hangman
Who stands upright, cutting history bone-deep.
(*Random Descent* 62)

The "Roudra" rasa is succeeded by the element of wonder and surprise, which is known as the "Adbhuta" Rasa. This Rasa in extremity is also symbolic of perplexity, confusion and indecisiveness. The poem "Idyll," in the volume *A Rain of Rites* is quite symbolic of this Rasa:

… On the stained stone a small puddle trembles
In the ghost-light of the moon.
Is it the earth that catches its breath?
Or is one there?
Only a shredded prayer-flag keeps twisting in
the wind.
(*Collected Poems* 9).

The same feeling is expressed in a more lucid manner in the poem "Shadow," where he searches the meaning of this life-long virtual companion of all creatures:

May be this shadow of mine
Was born before I was.
Now I am never alone
Because it's always there.
(*Random Descent* 28)

The last and the final Rasa represents the final realization or enlightenment of a truly wise person. This Rasa known as "Shanta" symbolizes peace, tranquility and sublimity of the mind. This normally informs of the philosophical or spiritual maturity and depth of the poet's mind. In "Somewhere my Man," the poet has indirectly referred to the quality of flatness of the soul, by which it can co-relate itself with any place, person or thing:

> A man does not mean any thing.
> But the place
> Sitting on the riverbank throwing pebbles
> Into the muddy current,
> A man becomes the place.
> Even that simple enough thing
> (*Collected Poems* 10).

In another poem "Scenario," the poet speaks rather in a state of self realization, which proves that he finally achieves the peace of his heart:

> Today I know I contend
> With the frail moral of a little boy
> Whose eyes brighten up at any illusion before him.
> And whether I come closer to my image
> Or step for back from it
> I realize I am never anything but myself
> (*Random Descent* 68)

Many other such descriptions of his land and culture by the poet create as if a living image of the places in the mind of the readers. As 'nativism' or the tendency to give emphasis upon one's own nation, and its culture or tradition, plays a great role in shaping the imaginative and creative faculties of Jayanta Mahapatra, for which he can be without any hesitation, called as a true nativist poet par excellence.

Kamala Das was the first woman and the fourth Indian English poet who was honoured by the Central Sahitya Akademi for her service to Indian English poetry. Though born in rural Kerala country side, she has spent most of her life in the most urban metros of India and has been heavily influenced by their life-style and culture. Also the cosmopolitanism of these metros has given her a broader outlook, through which she can perceive everything from various angles. Her imaginative faculty is very much captivating to the mind of the readers due to its rich mimicry. The use of far-fetched imagery also makes its effect more durable on the mind. Her poetry is a highly varied combination of various complex elements such as the different types and stages of relationship of men and women, the myriad human emotions identical with its very existence like love, sex, companionship and universification of personal problems she faced herself. She has a deep sensibility towards her surroundings in her native land. She derives her early poetic inspiration from her experiences of childhood and adolescence in her ancestral Nalapat house. Her highly autobiographical poem "Blood," is adorned with rich verbal imagery from the native traditions. There the grandmother narrates to all her grandchildren, including the poet herself about her intense racial pride over her sanguine purity, her early marriage, the luxuries of her short nuptial life, her widowhood and the gradual decay of her ancestral house. Throughout the poem, she refers to various native images like "the snake-gods in the shrine with lichen on their hoods", "her daily visit to the Shiva shrine riding on an elephant", her "Jewel box", "the brocade from the north", "the perfumes and the oils," and "the sandal for her breasts." Her grandmother's deep attachment with the house makes the poet identify it with her old grandmother herself. This is why she even imagines the virtual death of the house itself with the death of the grandmother. Other poems like "Nani," "A Hot Noon in Malabar," "An Introduction," and "The House Builders," have derived their matter from her experiences at her native place in Kerala. In her post-marriage life, spent mostly in the metros like Calcutta, Bombay, Delhi and Trivandrum, she speaks about the urban imagery like the morning scene in Strand Street, the Victoria Gardens, garbage collectors, South Indian cafes and cosmopolitan clubs found in such cities. Thus, in her poetry, one can find both rural as well as urban images in plenty. Yet, there is no doubt that it is the urban environment and the life spent in it, which has shaped the major portion of her poetry.

Through her poems, we come face to face with the dust, the heat, the suffocating crowds, the miserable condition of the poor and the various problems faced even by the urban women in India. The reality is that she has experienced the darkest side of city life, generally covered by the glamour of the cities. The vices, the horrors and other negative aspects of it, has made her own outlook unidyllic and tinged with a certain amount of negativity. However the city has become an integral part of her existence and she is unable to do away with the impressions and memories associated with it. Instead of trying for such likely to be failure effort, she tries to strike a sort of synthesis between the changing reality of her private passions and the apparently unchanging reality of the shining sun on the Indian horizon. She is also a unique urban poet as, unlike Ezekiel she is neither ironical, nor she is philosophical like the colonial poets. Also, though not a very great admirer of the Indian landscapes like Keki.N. Daruwalla or Jayanta Mahapatra, she is not totally alienated from it and a few references to it can be found in many of her famous poems.

Kamala Das essentially is a poet of love. Love, according to her, in its ultimate form is divine in nature and merges the lover with the beloved. But; it does not mean that the physical or sexual manifestation of love is wrong or sinful. In fact, in her view, it helps in the perfection of divine love to attain the bliss to which one should surrender his or her whole existence to the beloved. In this context she seems to be influenced by the theory of the four-fold achievements in the Hindu philosophy i.e. Dharma (merit), Artha (wealth), Kama (pleasure) and Moksha (salvation). As per this theory, for achieving salvation or divine bliss, one should not only fully discharge all his duties, but should also become fully content and satisfied by enjoying all the worldly pleasures in the prescribed manner. This was said to in turn, create a feeling of vairagya or unattachment towards worldly happiness which gradually leads a person towards the attainment of supreme and eternal bliss or salvation. This concept was later more boosted by the Tantric and Sahajiya schools of philosophy, which encouraged liberal sex on the ground that it helped in the realization of supreme self through the union of the two-fold divine elements-call them Shiva-Shakti, Purusha –Prakriti or Radha-Krishna, which are present in every human being. In West Bengal, one can even find today, a mystic sect called 'Bauls', who perceive the physical union between men and women, as the greatest mean to realize the supreme and divine self. Refusing to identify themselves with any particular religion, caste or creed, their ideals, beliefs, philosophy and spiritual practices are reminiscent of the ancient 'Kaula' sect of the Indian Tantric section. All these sects either spiritualize or personify as deities, all the eight-fold forms of sexual passion. These forms, as stated in the Bramhavaivarta Puran are as follows-

> Smaranam Keertanam Keli Prekshanam
> Guhyabhasanam
> Samkalpam Adhyavasayascha Kriyanishpattih
> Reva cha
> (Vedavyasa 249).

--- 'Smaranam' (remembering or craving for the beloved), 'Keertanam' (talking about the beloved or the moments spent with him / her), Keli (to indulge in amorous foreplay or mischief), 'Prekshanam' (looking stealthily or continuously at the beloved), 'Guhyabhasanam' (to talk in coded language with the beloved), 'Samkalpam' (to intend or decide to have sex), 'Adhyavasaya' (to strive for the fulfillment of sexual desire) and 'Kriyanishpatti'(the ultimate consummation of sexual act), are the eight forms of sex (or sexual passion).

As, all these conditions or states can be realized only in a physical body, the body is of paramount importance in all these sects. There, one can find a much more fervent adoration of the body, than is done by the practitioners of the Advaita and Yoga systems of Indian philosophy. All these point towards the unique body consciousness and explicitness of sexual phenomenon, which is so common to the poetry of Kamala Das. One can in fact, get the reflection of all the

91

eight fold steps of sexual procedure in some of her prominent poems upon love and lust like "A Relationship," "Radha," "The Looking Glass," "The Music Party," "Winter," "The Joss-Sticks at Cadell Road," and "Substitute,". However, of all the steps or forms of these eight, she gives prime importance and maximum emphasis to the last (i.e. the sexual consummation of love).

Kamala Das seems to have taken this theme from the Sahajiya Vaishnava cult in which the masters taught their disciples to have sex with their partners, imagining the divine union of Radha and Krishna, by the medium of their earthly bodies. This fact becomes more justified on the ground that in many of her love poems she has frequently used the myth of the divine love-play of Radha and Krishna or the yearning for love of Mira, the greatest female devotee of Krishna. 'Krishna,' who in the Indian Hindu mythology stands for an eternal divine lover and the epitome of love itself, has for centuries inspired Indian poets through his plays of love, he used to play with Radha and the Gopis. In one of her poems, titled "Radha", Kamala Das has tried to create the first experience of love by Radha in the following words:

> Everything in me
> Is melting,
> Even the hardness at the core.
> O Krishna,I am melting,melting,Melting (15).

In another poem "Ghanshyam," she prays to Lord Krishna with a heart overflowing with devotion and joy. In it she compares the dark-hued lord with a koel, who has made its nest in her heart and for whom the poet weaves beautiful garments out of her words. There he exclaimed as "the cell of the eternal sun", "the blood of the eternal fire" and "the hue of the summer air", all the three expressions giving a feeling of his warm passionate nature. Finally he is presented as a fisherman in whose nets, cast in the waters of the mind, all thoughts of the poet race like enchanted fish. In the poem "Krishna," she finally presents the state of complete surrender, in which a true lover forgets and gets detached from all except the beloved. In her words:

> Your body is my prison, Krishna
> I cannot see beyond it,
> Your darkness blinds me,
> Your love words shut out the wise world's din
> (*Collected Poems* 75).

Thus in her love poems, she reciprocates the idea of divine bliss achieved through physical union and the ultimate assimilation of the "self" with the divine. However the use of Radha-Krishna myth should not be taken as absolute desire, only for the supreme lord. Though her envisioning of Krishna in all the men had mystic appeal to it, as she herself declares: "I looked for the beauteous Krishna in every man. Every Hindu girl is in reality wedded to Lord Krishna" (Mohanty 7). Yet, there was a rather perverse motive underlying in it which may to some extent be called sadistic also. In her words: "I was looking for an ideal lover. I was looking for one who went to Mathura and forgot to return to his Radha. Perhaps I was seeking the cruelty that lies in the depths of a man's heart. Otherwise, why did I not get my peace in the arms of my husband" (ibid, 42).

Love; however is not the only subject of her poetry. In her poetry, the unexpressed and unfilled desires of the Indian women in general have also found place. The fact that the poet herself never got true love from any man, empowers her poems with the feeling of a direct experience. In her most popular poem "An Introduction," she gives a universal form to her longings:

> I am every
> Women who seeks love...
> (An Introduction 27)

Like Jayanta Mahapatra,who desires to be rejoined with the glorious tradition of his ancestors who were both heroic and prosperous, Kamala Das also, due to the influence of Marumak Kathayam or matriarchal system prevalent among the Nayars in Kerala,is unrestricted and uninhibited in her sexual behaviour. As a true postcolonial as well as a feminist poet, the voice of revolt against any kind of colonialism is quite active in her poetry. Ever conscious of her own subjugation and abuse by her husband, she is ever ready to protest and fight for the cause of the downtrodden and the wretched of the earth. During her stay in Colombo, she was herself a witness to the anti-Tamil propaganda going on in SriLanka. In her poems like "The sea at Galle Face Green," "Smoke in Colombo," "Shopper at Cornells, Colombo," "A Certain Defect in the Blood" and "Fear," etc; she has tried to bring alive the atmosphere of fear and violence she experienced there. The pain and sarcasm, which is reflected in these lines from her poem "A Certain Defect in the Blood," highlights the views of the poet upon racial prejudice: "It was a defect/

in our blood that made us the land's inferiors/ A certain muddiness in the usual red, / Revealing our non-Aryan descent" (*Collected Poems* 17).

Her deep pride upon her Dravidian descent is expressed in the poem "Wood Ash," where she speaks about the subjugation of the Dravidians by the Aryan invasion. This feeling of belonging to a subjugated race makes her sympathise with the marginalized, the suppressed or the colonized, which can collectively be called as the 'Subalterns'. All the backward or the lower sections of the society, the working class and the women are generally included in this category. As such, the poet feels concerned for all of them and raises her voice on behalf of them. She herself derides the concept of racial pride in her poem "Blood," where she satirises her grandmother's belief that they had the oldest and purest blood in their veins. The death of her maid servant 'Nani' during her childhood, left an indelible impression on her mind. Like many women of socially or economically backward classes, Nani also fell a prey to the lust of some upper caste person. When she became pregnant and was perhaps refused any protection, she had no other option but to hang herself. In her poem "Nani," the poet describes her heart-felt feelings about her tragic death and the apathetic attitude of her family regarding the whole incident. Another poem of the same strain is "The House Builders," which shows the extent of exploitation faced by the poor people belonging to the lower castes by the upper or feudal castes. The very words of the poem are a burning testimony to caste-based exploitation that has tarnished Indian culture for ages:

> Today, they laugh at laws that punished no
> rich, only the poor

Were ravished, strangled, drowned, buried at
mid-night
behind Snakeshrines
Cheated of this land, their huts and hearts…(47).

Likewise, her heart goes on for any section of the society that is exploited, subjugated or is subjected to injustice. Her witnessing the wild dance of the eunuchs in Calcutta, inspired her to write the famous poem "The Dance of The Eunuchs". This poem in a manner identical to Eliot's 'The Wasteland,' describes the grotesque and pathetic barrenness of the world of these social outcastes. Similarly, her poems like "Lines Addressed to a Devadasi," and "Lunatic Asylum," reverberate with her concern and sympathy for the prostitutes and the lunatics also. Of late, her active humanistic tendencies also made her a strong protestor against the practice of child prostitution in India.

As a post-modern poet, the poetry of Kamala Das is marked with all the basic traits of post-modernism like, existentialism, confessionalism, humanism and overall an aggressive strain of feminism. Like most of the post-modern poets, she feels a strong emptiness or vacuum in her life, which she is unable to fill by any means. The hardness, heartlessness and tastelessness of this world has compelled her to say:

To be frank,
I have failed.
I feel my age and my
Uselessness
(Composition 9).

The most natural outcome of such existentialist feelings is a strong note of confessionalism in the literary output. In her poem "Suicide," she herself declares the underlying unhappiness of her life:

> But,
> I must pose
> I must pretend,
> I must act the role
> Of happy woman,
> Happy life (The Suicide 34)

In this context, Kamala Das becomes quite identical with the famous female poet of confessional trend, Sylvia Plath. Both of them had a strong dissatisfaction towards life and disgust for male domination over women. The poetry of both is marked with strong feelings of anxiety, alienation, meaninglessness, futility, and fragmentation, a strong sense of isolation and loss of identity. Overall, there is also the same suicidal tendency in both. In her autobiography, Kamala Das writes: "Often I have toyed with the idea of drowning myself to be rid of my loneliness which is not unique in any way but is natural to all" (Kamala Das, *My Story* 227). Yet above all, she can be distinguished purely as a true feminist poet. Referring to the vast range of feminine depictions in her poem, M. K. Naik, says: "Several faces of Eve are exhibited here-women as sweetheart, flirt, wife, woman of the world, mother, middle aged matron-and above all as an untiring seeker of the psychological processes of behind both femininity and masculinity" (Qtd. by Aroonima Sinha 93).

With all these poetry with different types of native elements, her contribution to the nativist literature in English and her position as a native poet, can't be said otherwise but highly significant. Her claim as a postcolonial poet is more than justified by her deep Indian sensibility and her contribution to the development of the Indian idioms in context to modern Indian English poetry. Again, she can also be credited to re-shape the very idea of feminism according to the native culture and consciousness of the Indian soil. Yet, her most unique service in the field of postcolonial Indian English poetry is to raise a revolt against the "Sexual-colonization". As the critic Iqbal Kaur puts her views: "Kamala Das did display tremendous courage in revolting against the sexual colonialism and providing hope and confidence to young women that they can refuse and reject the victim positions, that they can frustrate the sexist culture's effort to exploit, passivise and marginalize women" (Qtd. by K.V.Surendran 133).

As a poet, A.K. Ramanujan has played a pivotal role in the formation of both the Indian sensibility and idiom in postcolonial Indian English poetry. Born and brought up in a South Indian Brahmin family of Karnataka, he grew up in an environment, which comprised of both orthodox Hinduism and western rationalism. It was his strong affinity with the culture, language and religion of his native land, that made him more 'Indian' than most of his fellow – poets. At a very early age, he was introduced to the rich literary traditions of both the Tamil and the Kannada languages. The research which he did on Dravidian Linguistics in the later years, helped further in the sharpening of his insight into the depths of Indian culture and spiritualism. His reminiscences of India and the experiences associated with it, made him more and more attached with his native land and culture. Ultimately, a time came when, even though living in abroad, his entire personality became so permeated with an Indian spirit, that one could even feel the presence of India while talking to him. In the words of U.R Anantha Murthy, the famous Kannada novelist: "I met him often in Chicago. Each time it struck me that the space around him was either a small town in Tamilnad or a village in Karnataka"(Qtd. by Sabitha T.P. 199).

Starting from the native traditions followed at his own home, he studied the loftiest and the most refined philosophies of his country including that of Jainism and Buddhism. His migration to the west brought him more close to his country, culture, religion and traditions. His consciousness became a confluence of the eastern traditions of philosophy and spiritualism with that of western rationalism and scientific thought process. There is a marked influence of the Buddhist inquisitive approach on many of his poems. Even, Jainism also does not escape from his view as can be seen in his poem "Pleasure." It reflects upon the strange methods of self – punishment, which the Jain monks inflict upon themselves. One can find a number of poems with scientific temperament in his volumes, which denounce or satirize the blind superstitions followed by Indians. On the other hand, there are an equal number of poems, where one could find the Indian strain of emotional devotionalism typical to Hinduism or an inward search which is common to Buddhism. Even local legends and folklore is also efficiently employed by him to convey the desired feelings in the most effective manner. Still, he is also conscious of the cultural or racial fanaticism, which in the modern times is at the root of various evils like the rise of Nazism under the garb of 'Aryan Puritanism'. He himself points it out in his poem "A Report". Through the poem, he sends a message that though Hitler has died, the tendencies like xenophobia and chauvinism are still very much alive in the hearts of humanity. Therefore, for the sake of world peace and security, one should have strong restraint over any excesses even in the case of patriotism also.

Even at the very heart of the West, he remained committed to the culture and tradition of his native land. Even when he completed his Ph.D in Indiana University, U.S.A, in the field of Linguistics, he chose as his topic the generative grammar of Kannada. As both Tamil and Kannada, along with English were spoken at his home during his childhood, he had a strong affinity with these languages and the literature written in them. Even after the completion of his Ph.D, he joined as an Assistant Professor at the University of Chicago in the Department of South Asian Languages and Civilizations. One cannot but be impressed by the sheer genius and mark of individuality which is reflected in the translations of ancient and medieval works in Kannada and Tamil by the poet. While he adopts the "Akam" and "Puram" style of Tamil "Sangam" poetry; he also uses the themes of the Kannada "Vacana" poetry written by the Shaivite poets of Karnataka. While "Akam" stands for the personal intoned love poetry, the "Puram" stands for such poems which are meant for public audiences in general. His poem "Two Styles in Love," can be considered as a poem belonging to the first category, while "The River," is an example of the second category. But along with the elements of Tamil poetics, there are also instances in his poetry of the various elements of Sanskrit Poetics. The most frequently used techniques of Sanskrit poetics by Ramanujan are "Sadharanikarana" or the process of giving an universal appeal to the personal emotions and "Vakrokti" which means the indirect suggestiveness inherent in a poetry. The poems like "Saturdays," "For a Wife And Her Trees," and "Second Sight," show the use of the poetic technique of 'Vakrokti.' For example, the first poem of the "Love Poems," suggests the cold or apathetic attitude of a husband toward his wife:

> His eyes are moss – green
> His blood is cold
> His heart is a piece
> Of lead
> (*Collected Poems* 219).

With the techniques of both the poetics, the poet's creativity also combines the various socio- cultural and graphic elements from both the Aryan and the Dravidian backgrounds. One can find references to the history, society, culture and folklore of both the North and the South in his poems like "On memory," "Snakes," "Some Indian Uses of History On a Rainy Day," and "Astronomer,". In his poem "Small – Scale Reflections on a Great House," there is reference to the postage coming back due to the wrong or inappropriate addresses written upon them:

> With many re- direction to wrong
> Addresses and red ink marks
> earned in Tiruvella and Sialkot.
> (*Collected Poems* 97)

These lines point to the nation–wide acquaintance, the family of the poet maintained even in the early years of his life in India. Even in those days his family communicated with people from both the northern parts and that of the extreme south.

Yet another feature of Ramanajun's poetry is the conflict between the religious or spiritual aspects of India with that of the rationalism of the West. In the poems like "Snakes," "Astrononer," and "A Minor Sacrifice," we find a strife in the consciousness of the poet, regarding the various superstitions that has been traditionally followed at his home and the scientific temperament which he developed during the later years of his life. Even in a seemingly simple poem like "Old Indian Belief," the poet laughs upon the unscientific concepts of the Indians about the creatures commonly found around them like snakes and ants. Even the poem "Saturdays," is also a satire upon the belief in India which considers Saturday as the most malevolent and evil day. In an ironical manner, the poet concludes the poem with the following lines:

> . . . his daily dying body
> The one good omen
> In a calendar of ominous Saturdays
> (*Collected Poems* 152).

He holds a unique position in the traditions of the postcolonial Indian English poetry, for being a 'Diaspora' poet. Deriving its origin from the Greek term 'dia'-meaning 'to scatter' or 'to disperse', this term refers to the separation of an individual or a group from the land of their native roots and culture. In the latter half of the twentieth century, many Indians left India for economic or intellectual pursuits in foreign lands. A.K Ramanujan also left India in the year 1959. Though he left the physical India with all its geographical or topographical manifestations, far behind; India as a consciousness always pervaded his mind, soul and sensibility. With each of the frequent visits paid to the native land, his native sensibility became more and more pronounced and magnified. In this regard, the critic Anand Mulloo comments: "Socially, as a displaced people, the diaspora carry an idealized and fractured memory and also a new consciousness of their homeland, its cultural, social, economic heritage which they want to implant wherever they go into the reconstituted little India, China Town, etc" (130). He dedicated his life to the tremendous task of bringing the pure ethnic Dravidian culture, language and literature upon the world stage. Throughout his life and poetic career, it was the Dravidian influence which reflected in his attitude as well as literary creativity. However, whether consciously or unconsciously, the Aryan elements and the influence of the Sanskrit poetics used by him in many of his literary works, is clearly discernible.

A prominent reason for his absence of nostalgia is that he is deeply rooted in his tradition. Not only he writes about his village, his childhood fears and anxieties but also translates the poems written by Tamil and Kannada Saint Poets, in English to be read even by foreigners. His studies in Anthropology bring him back to the Kannada oral folk tales heard during childhood. Even the experiences he had in Chicago are observed through an Indian view point. But there are some differences between him and other Indian nativist poets. While other nativist poets frequently glorify their nation, traditions and culture and in a way, try to revive its past greatness, Ramanujan keeps an almost detached attitude and refers to his native elements, in either a purely narrative or in a sarcastic manner. Though attached with his traditions, he never conforms to it in his poems. In his famous poem "A River," moving away from the traditional eulogizing of the subject, he instead refers to its negative aspects in a descriptive manner. His "Hindoo" poems are also written in the same manner. Presenting a stereotype model of the orientalist Hindoo, he criticizes the various defects like lethargic attitude, heartlessness and others which have crept into the present Hindoo society. All the three poems of the series:

1) "THE HINDOO: he reads his GITA and is calm at all events,"
2) "THE HINDOO: he doesn't hurt a fly or a spider either,"
3) "THE HINDOO: the only risk,"

show their ironical attitude both by their titles and the italicized "*THE HINDOO*" words. In yet another poem "Second Sight," he has made fun of the concept of the second (inner) sight famous in the Hindu philosophy. In the poem titled "Guru," he has aimed his sarcasm upon the modern pseudo-spiritual Godmen of India, who are just blindly following long dead traditions and are unaware of the real meaning and practical implication of the instructions of the scriptures they mechanically mug-up like a parrot. Howsoever, the use of native myths and fables is also a common characteristic of a major part of his poetry. In fact there are three poems, exclusively titled as "Mythologies-1, 2 and 3," respectively. In the first poem he referring to the myth of Krishna as a baby sucking out the life of Putana, who had come to kill him, prays to the lord to suck out all the venom or negativity from him (the poet), so that he may undergo a complete transformation as Putana did after dying at the hands of the lord. In the second poem, he gives the example of Hiranyakashipu, the demon king as the symbol of all those people who think themselves as unrivalled in cleverness, by analyzing only one side of a thing or matter. The demon king as a boon had asked:

> Not to be slain by demon, god, or by
> Beast, not by day or by night,
> By no manufactured weapon, not out
> Of doors nor inside, not in the sky
> Nor on earth (226).

However, all these precautions prove worthless before Nara Simha (the lion-man incarnation of Lord Vishnu) who kills him at the threshold of his own palace during twilight hours, by holding him in his lap and tearing his abdomen by his sharp claws. The poet thus addressing the lord as an assimilator of all odds prays to purify his faith and give him the power to perceive even the invisible along with the visible aspects of all things. In the last poem of the series, he narrates the story of a famous South-Indian female saint, Akka, whose divine love won over Lord Shiva. The lady on her first night as a married woman warned her husband against touching her during her meditation. However the husband, unable to suppress his carnal desire touched her, upon which she fled away from him, to find that the great Lord himself was waiting for her in the backyard. In another poem "Fear no Fall," he gives the example of the famous Tamil saint, Arunagiri who was once head-deep into the pit of debauchery and other ill habits. Later he turned into a great saint-poet through the grace of Lord Murugan. Through this story, the poet gives hope that however deep a fall may be, there is always redemption from it.

There are also other varieties of poems written by him of a vast range. His two poems "No Fifth Man," and "No Amnesiac King," also take their matter from Indian fables and myth. The first poem recounts the story of the five Brahmanas who learning the art of resurrecting the dead, test it on a dead tigress. The fifth and ignorant one, however before the dead tigress becomes alive, climbs a tree to save him and the rest are eaten up by the tigress. The second one refers, though indirectly, to the myth of Sakuntala and Dushyanta. Some poems are in forms of simple narratives like "Pleasure," in which he describes the daredevilish way of self control, practiced by a naked Jaina monk, disturbed by the passion of sex. The practice of self- mortification has always remained central to the "Digambara" or sky- clad sect of Jain monks. Jainism as a religion, flourished greatly in the ancient and medieval South India, mainly in the states of Tamilnadu and Karnataka. Even today also, Karnataka remains a strong hold of the most orthodox Jains of the "Digambara" sect. As a true native poet, he has an all encompassive view of the socio-cultural, religious and philosophical panorama of his native land. He minutely observes the austere spiritual practices of the Jains in regard to self- discipline, control of the senses and inner purification. The method which the monk concerned employs in overcoming the sudden surge of lust within him, is terrifying to the extreme. Western rationality and sensibility can hardly fathom the spiritual ethos behind this semi- suicidal endeavour of the monk, who seems to enjoy some inexplicable bliss even in the pain resulting from the ant- bites:

> . . . A naked Jaina monk
> …crying
> his old formulaic cry
> at every twinge,
> Pleasure, pleasure,
> Great pleasure!
> (*Collected Poems* 140)

It is only a person with a most holistic Indian sensibility, who can understand the spiritual bliss that the monk believes to be deriving by punishing his evil or impure desires.

In "Smalltown, South India," in which he gives the description of a typical South-Indian city with all the elements, native to it. Of all the poems written by the poet, "Prayers to Lord Murugan," is perhaps his Magnum Opus. Written in a style imitative of the Tamil mystic Nakkirar's "Tirumurugatruppadi," it is a hymn to Murugan, one of the most primitive divinities, central to the Dravidian culture. The saint composed it as a desperate appeal to the heroic six-faced lord who is a repository of both infinite knowledge and power. Similarly, Ramanujan maintains not only the "arrupatai" form of Nakkirar's hymn, but also the same tone of anxiety and desperation as the former. The "arrupatai" or the Tamil heroic verse, exhorts a warrior to rise and destroy all opponents before him, saving those who are sheltered by him. In this context, the poet taking Murugan as the representative deity of Dravidian culture, art and religion; appeals to him to dispel all the illusive concepts about Indian native culture, caused by the influence of both the processes of Aryan Sanskritization and Western Colonization. Here the poet seems to be championing for the separate and individual identity of Dravidian culture, not in an abstract spiritual manner but rather in a form appealing to all the five senses:

> ... Lord of the sixth sense,
> Give us back
> Our five senses
> ... Deliver us O presence
> From proxies
> And absences
> From Sanskrit and the mythologies
> Of night and the several
> Round table mornings
> Of London.........
> (Prayer to Lord Murugan 113).

The strong Pro- Dravidian theme of the poem can hardly be ignored. In his conversation with Rama Jha, A.K.Ramanujan affirms that ". . . . . . my poem Murugan, for instance, could not have been written if I did not know the classical Tamil forms and even some of the images there"(7). The modern aspects of this poem can be observed in the unique employment of irony. The poet concludes the prayer by addressing the Lord as "Lord of answers" and beseeching him to cure humanity of all prayers. This may seem quite awkward but outwardly, but is in fact, a perfect testimony of the poet's sound rationality. Instead of remaining dependent upon God perpetually, he demands for such self- sufficiency as would make him complete and content in all possible ways. In fact, we can call this poem as an expression of the poet's inward search for his true cultural and spiritual identity.

As evident in all the poems referred to till this extent, there is an exuberance of native Indian idiom throughout the body of his literary creativity. All his poems, whether referring to his family experiences or his own contemplation upon the spiritual, literary and social trends of his native milieu, are rich with a keen power of observation and a liberal understanding of the various local customs or traditions. In the poem like "Astronomer," "Death and the Good citizen," "A Minor Sacrifice," "Snakes," "The Rickshaw Wallah," "Lines to a Granny," "Small town, South India," and "Conventions of Despair," one can find a lavish exhibition of both native imagery and the most authentic Indian sensibility. For example, in the poem "Death and the Good Citizen," he refers to the traditional method of cremation used by the most orthodox Hindus:

> . . . they' ll cremate
> Me in Sanskrit and sandalwood,
> Have me sterilized
> To a scatter of ash (*Collected Poems* 136).

It was this strong affinity with the Indian culture and Indian consciousness, which made the poet completely disillusioned about the West. Though he never physically left the west, yet his mind, soul and life became dedicated to India and its native culture as can be found in Dravidian language and literature. The poet declares his conviction blatantly in the following lines:

> But, sorry, I cannot unlearn
> Convention of despair

They have their pride
I must seek and will find
My particular hell only in my Hindu mind.
(*Collected Poems* 34)

Here, we find the poet's own confession affirming his devotion and adherence to the soil, culture and ethos of India. This is the foremost factor which joins a poet to his own native traditions and sensibility inspite of whatever language he uses as a mode of expression or whichever place in the world he lives in. The critic Darshana Trivedi in this context comments: "The authentic voice of the Poet his true "language" does not solely depend upon the tongue in which he chooses to express himself, the landscapes, the personal, the appropriate moods, all become a language within language. Like a native speaker, he makes infinite use of infinite means to say with familiar words what has never said before; he can say exactly what he wants to do without even being aware of the ground rules of his grammar"(Rukhaiyar 133). Whatever may be the differences; A.K Ramanujan would always be remembered for his role in the creation and development of native Indian English poetry.

Thus, all these poets achieved unique heights of glory, breaking through the conventions set by the colonial poets before them. Imbibing a new life, vigour and identity to the postcolonial Indian English poetry, they made it a unique and individual literary brand, to be recognized and accepted globally. Some of their major contributions to the development of modern Indian English poetry are, the creation of a unique and truly indigenous 'idiom' in the field of Indian English poetry and the introduction of postmodern elements into its body, like feminism, alienation, rootlessness, existential anguish, spiritual dilemma, rationalism, realism and aggressive unconventionalism etc. Even the poets, who migrated to other countries, have to their credit, of introducing the element of 'Diaspora', in modern Indian English poetry. Most of these poets, who left for other countries found themselves at a 'subalternized' or 'marginalized' position on the foreign soil. The only solution to this problem was 'hybridizing' oneself to the new soil, while maintaining the basic or essential characteristics of one's 'native' identity. So, while they had to work out their problem of belongingness to both their native and their 'new – found home' lands; they also had to forge out new identities which would be potent enough to meet the demands from both the sides. This strife not only strengthened but also refined the quality of the overall mass of Indian English poetry and won for it world- wide acclaim and recognition.

WORKS CITED

Baral, Saranga Dhar. *The Verse and Vision of A.K.Ramanujan.* New Delhi: Sarup and Sons, 2008. Print.

Boehmer, Elleke. *Colonial and Postcolonial Literature.* New York: OUP,1995. Print.

Das, Bijay Kumar. *Critical Essay on Poetry.* New Delhi: Kalyani Publishers, 1993. Print.

...*The Poetry of Jayanta Mahapatra.* New Delhi: Atlantic Publishers,1992. Print.

Das, Kamala. *The Old Playhouse and Other Poems.* Bombay: Orient Longman Limited, 1973. Print.

Das, Nigamananda. *The Poetry of Jayanta Mahapatra: Imagery and Vision.* New Delhi: Adhyayana Publishers, 2006. Print.

Devi, G.N. "Desivad: Keynote Address." *Nativism Essays in Criticism.* New Delhi: Sahitya Academy, 1997. Print

Dwivedi, A. N. *KamalaDas And Her Poetry.* Delhi: Doaba House Book Sellers andPublishers,1983. Print.

Dwivedi,A.N. "Modernity in Nissim Ezekiel's Poetry." *JIWE. Vol -14.* Jul-1986. No-2. Print. (65).

Dodiya, Jaydipsinh K. *Indian English Poetry: Critical Perspectives.* New Delhi: Sarup and Sons, 2009. Print.

Ezekiel,Nissim. *Collected Poems.* New Delhi: Oxford University Press, 1989. Print.

Jha, Rama. "A Conversation with A.K.Ramanujan". *The Humanities Review.3,* No-1. Jan-Jun,1981. Print.(7).

Mahapatra, Jayanta. *Dispossessed Nests.* Jaipur: Nirala Publications, 1986. Print.

... *Random Descent.* Bhubanashwar: Third Eye Communications, 2005. Print.

... *Selected Poems.* New Delhi: Oxford University Press, 1987. Print.

Mahapatra, Kamala Prasad. *Nature Culture Metonymy: Quest For Lost Horizons in Jayanta Mahapatra's Poetry.* New Delhi: Adhyayana Publishers, 2013. Print.

Mohanty, Niranjan. "Krishna Motif in the Poetry of Kamala Das." *Critical Essays on Indian Writing in English.* Ed. Jaydipsinh Dodiya. New Delhi: Sarup and sons, 2006. Print.

Mulloo, Anand. *Voices of Indian Diaspora.* Delhi: Motilal Benarsidas, 2007. Print.

Patra, Pradip Kumar. "Random Descent": The Still, Sad Music of Humanity in the Poems of Jayanta Mahapatra. Ed. *The Indian Imagination of Jayanta Mahapatra.* New Delhi: Sarup and Sons, 2006. Print.

Pranjape, Makarand. *Nativism: Essays in Criticism.* New Delhi: Sahitya Academy, 1997. Print.

Paul, S.K. and Amar Nath Prasad. Eds. *Indian Poetry In English: Roots and Blossoms.* New Delhi: Sarup and Sons, 2007. Print.

Perry, John Oliver. "Questioning Nativism: A Movement, Approach Or Attitude?" *Journal of Literature and Aesthetics* 8 (2000): 7-14. Print.

Ramakrishna, D. "Ezekiel's Credo". *JIWE.* Vol-14. Jul-1986. No-2. Print.

Ramanujan, A.K. *Collected Poems.* New Delhi: Oxford University Press, 1995. Print.

Radha, K. "Kamala Das". *Kerela Writers in English.* Vol- 8. Madras: Macmillan India Press, 1986. Print.

Rawat, Aniruddh. *Episteme of Desire: The Poetry of A.K. Ramanujan.* New Delhi: Adhyana Publishers, 2012. Print.

Ragharan, V. *The Number of Rasas*. Madras: The Adhyan Liberary And Research Centre,1975. Print. (13).

Rukhaiyar, U.S. and Amar Nath Prasad. *Studies in Indian Poetry in English*. New Delhi: Sarup and Sons, 2002. Print.

Vedvayasa.(Ed.) Chemanlal Goswami and Hanuman Prasad Poddar- *Brahma-Vaivarta Purana*. Gorakhpur: Gita Press, (Sambat 2055). Print. (249)

Sahoo, Raghunath. *Tension and Moral Dilemmas in Nissim Ezekiel's Poetry*. New Delhi: Sarup and Sons Publishers, 2012. Print.

Sinha, Aroonima. "The Quest For Female Identity In The Poems Of Kamala Das." *Indian Poetry in English: Roots and Blossoms*. (Ed.) S. K. Paul and Amar Nath Prasad. New Delhi: Sarup and Sons, 2007. Print.

Sivananda, Swami. *Lord Shanmukha and His Worship*. Shivanandanagar: The Divine Life Society, 1996. Print. (63).

Surendran, K.V. "Suffering and Humiliation in Kamala Das's Poetry". *Indian English Poetry: Critical Perspectives*. (Ed.) Jaydip Sinh K. Dodiya. New Delhi: Sarup and Sons, 2009. Print.

T.P.Sabitha. "Home in Exile: 'Hybridity' in A.K.Ramanujan and Nissim Ezekiel." *Indian Literature: Sahitya Akademi Bimonthly Journal*. Ed. Gopichand Narang et al. 236. Nov-Dec,2006. Print.

CHAPTER 3

THE PROBLEMATICS OF BELONGING: FORGING NEW IDENTITIES

English poetry in India has completed more than two centuries of its birth. It has now a firm tradition, history and a set of indigenous characteristics of its own to claim. A long chain of illustrious poets beginning from Toru Dutt to Nissim Ezekiel have tried and been successful to a large extent in 'indianizing' the English language. Having remoulded its style and diction, they have given a completely Indian taste and appeal to English while using it for their poetic endeavours. The Indianness of their poems has been recognized and admired globally. Yet, somewhere we find a strain of their being distanced from the mainstream public domain of India. Sometimes, this distancing is of a physical nature whereas at other places we find it to be more of a psychological, sociological or spiritual nature. For example, a few poets may actually leave

India for better financial or intellectual promises. But even those who continue to live in India despite all their bitterness and repulsion for the various negative aspects of Indian life are not reconciled with it. The bitterness of their heart, expressed in ironical statements in their poems, makes it quite distasteful or at the least unappealing for the majority of the average Indians. In short, we can also say that the majority of Indian English poets suffer with a problem of belongingness, in regard to their native land, culture and tradition. It can also be considered as moving away from the centre or the heart of the mainstream culture and traditions.

The above spoken problem is recognized and called by many diverse terms like, 'Diaspora and marginalization'. Diaspora, which is a Greek term, used in the old testament of the Bible, stands for being 'scattered' or 'dispersed'. Its origin lies in the Greek word "diaspeirein". While "Dia" means across, "Speirien" stands for "sowing or scattering of seeds." As explained by Om Prakash Dwivedi: "The term 'diaspora' is of Greek origin which literally means a scattering or dispersion of a group of people to a foreign land" (Qtd. by S. Mangaiyarkarasi 164). It alludes originally to the dispersion of Jews during the post-Babylonian period. It was also used for the large scale flight of the Jews to escape Roman persecution in the beginning of the Christian millennium as well as for the large number of Jews taking refuge in Europe and America, during the Nazi holocaust. However, at present, this term is free of any Jewish connection and is used for any age group of people, irrespective of the racial, religious, cultural or national background; distanced from their own native land. It should not be confused with the phenomenon of 'migration' which is more or less, a matter of self-decision to quit one's own country for better prospective of life or profession in abroad. Though there are many similar traits in both, yet the degree of suffering and trauma is generally found to be in greater proportions, in the case of the 'Diaspora' groups. While migration has no strictly technical definition, 'Diaspora' can be defined in a most lucid manner by the eminent Diaspora critic, Anand Mulloo. In his words: "By Diaspora, we mean dispersion of people who left their homeland through compulsion, through slavery, indentured labour, through expulsion or voluntary emigration in search of asylum, or of better livelihood abroad" (*Voices of the Indian Diaspora* 129).

Though these people leave behind their social circles and identities of their native past, to forge new identities; they find that the situation is not upto their expectation. Due to the stamp of their native culture, religion and language, they face certain invisible barriers to their assimilation with the social circles of their new homeland. The noted critic William Safran, has enlisted all these difficulties in the following manner: "1) they, or their ancestors have been dispersed from a specific original "centre" to two or more "peripheral" or foreign regions; 2) they retain a collective memory, vision or myth about their original homeland– its physical location, history and achievements; 3) they believe they are not and perhaps cannot be- fully accepted by their host society and therefore feel partly alienated and insulated from it" (*Perspectives on Indian Diaspora* 44).

The problems stated above are the factors which create the physical or the outer aspects of the 'Diasporic' phenomenon. It is because of these that the groups concerned are separated from their native lands, with all apparent ties, severed and obliterated. But, it is only the first half of the phenomenon.

The other half consists of the inability of the diasporic groups to merge into their 'host' society or the social circles of their new homeland. The factors which represent or consist the inner or the psychological aspects of Diaspora form the second half of it. These factors are: "4) they regard their ancestral homeland as their true, ideal home and as the place to which their descendants would (or should) eventually return- when conditions are appropriate; 5) they believe that they should, collectively, be committed to the maintenance or restoration of their homeland and its safety and prosperity; and 6) they continue to relate, personally or vicariously, to that homeland in one way or another, and their ethno-communal consciousness and solidarity are importantly defined by the existence of such relationship" (Safran ibid, 44).

The above referred to conditions hold back the 'Diasporic' groups' assimilation with the main-stream social circles. This in turn, gives rise to the phenomenon of 'marginalisation' of these groups. Having moved away from their cultural roots, they are pushed to the margins of their national sphere. But as they are unable to adjust themselves or rather 'adopt' the foreign culture and soil, they remain at the 'margins' of the 'host' country also. The diasporic groups are not allowed to mix with the social fabric of the new homeland due to their indigenous characteristics like complexion, ethnicity, and culture and in some cases, religion also. The eminent critic M.K.Naik in his critical review, upon the theme of identity in Salman Rushdie's novel *Midnight's Children,* comments: "Identity is in turn shown as a sham, as mistaken and confused, fractured and fragmented, merged and super-imposed, subjected to oblivion and dwarfed and reduced to animal level, totally lost and as barren and sterile" (46). A very effective solution to this type of desperate and complex situation is suggested by one of the most illustrious proponents of the Postcolonial theory- Homi K Bhabha. This solution was the process of 'Hybridization'. According to it, the colonized or the subjugated native can empower their position in a foreign society or country by imbibing some of the characteristics of the new environment or rather by getting 'adapted' to it. However, in this process, the native should not lose his own indigenous culture, which would in such a case render him rootless without any true and authentic identity.

'Hybridity' to be exact, is a compromise between the two ends- namely, native 'ethnicism' and the colonialist 'westernism'. Bhabha suggests that hybridity imparts some of the empowering features of the colonizer to the colonized. According to Bhabha, with a change in the socio-political conditions, there must be compulsorily a change in the representation of the cultural values and traditions. However, it is not an adulteration or defiling of the original culture or tradition. Rather, adaptation with the prevalent conditions, give it an edge to assert itself in a better manner. In the words of Bhabha himself: "The representation of difference must not be hastily read as the reflection of pre-given ethnic or cultural traits set in the fixed tablet of tradition. The social articulation of difference, from the minority perspective, is a complex, on-going negotiation that seeks to authorize cultural hybridities that emerge in moments of historical transformation" (*Location of culture* 2). In this manner, hybridity can become the most effective strategy against the oppression and subjugation of the colonizers. Yet even this unique method, fails to solve the problems of the more complex groups, classified under the collective term "Subaltern". This term generally covers the suppressed and the subjugated sections of the society, who are the easiest victims of exploitation by the elite or the ruling classes. Used first of all by the Italian intellectual Antonio Gramsci, it became the basis of the 'subaltern' theory of the noted proponent of postcolonialism; Gayatri Chakraborty Spivak. According to this theory, the so-called lower ranks of the society, which consist mainly of the workers, daily –wage earners, labourers, social outcastes and the women, are always at the risk of being suppressed and exploited. Even the very idea of 'third world', comprising of the under-developed nations and races (having a non-western culture) is nothing else but a result of the biased colonialist representation. Thus, the 'subaltern' theory speaks about the mechanism of exploitation and subjugation of some specific social sections, either directly through the colonialist rule or through some procedure initiated by it.

The women, according to Spivak, are the most unfortunate victims of the process of postcolonialism. They are dually colonialised, both by the colonialist rule and by the Patriarchical structure of their own country. Having been suppressed to a state of perpetual silence, they are now unable to express or speak for themselves. They have to conform to the dictates of their patriarchical society. Furthermore, the women of the western countries, who instead of experiencing the feeling of being colonized, have rather enjoyed the position of a colonizing master, try to enforce upon them the concepts of freedom, self-respect and individuality, without taking into concern the sensibility of the latter. Feminist criticism took a new turn with the publication of Simone de Beauvoir's critical master piece *The Second Sex*. There he has given his views upon the real causes of female subjugation. The chief reason for the enslavement of the women in this world is the notion that has been impressed upon their mind by men, that: "...the world is masculine on the whole, those who fashioned it, ruled it and still dominate it today are men" (298). The artificiality and irrational nature of the concept of women, as is generally and traditionally accepted, can be summed up in his words from the same book: "One is not born but becomes a woman"(ibid, 298) Thus, the main aim of the feminist movement is to seek rectification of all such fabricated myths about the inborn inferiority of the women and the superiority of the men. Its goal can be described best in the words of Shirin Kudchedkar: "It aims at making women the subject of her own story and not the object of male desire and male satisfaction or a whipping block for male frustration. Women come to realize the inauthenticity of the lives lead and struggle to discover for themselves their own impulses, reactions, desires and needs" (34).

In this context, one can also co-relate Indian English Literature of the postcolonial period, with that of the impact of post-modernism. Identical to the feminist way, the post-modernist trend also concerns itself with the 'de-colonization' of the hitherto accepted trends and conventions. It takes into account not only the outdated traditions of Patriarchy, racial hierarchy etc., but also the modern trends of Marxism, capitalism, etc. It interrogates the concerned subjects with the most strict and practical approach, and declares the shortcomings of each in the most lucid yet subjective manner. It gives stress upon humanism, rationality and scientific temperament, in judging the various matters and aspects of this world. As all these tendencies, more or less, go against the conventional and orthodox structure of the largely tradition-bound Indian society, the poets who believe and practice them throughout their poetic career, find themselves removed from the centre to the margins. In other words, they find themselves 'dislocated' from the centre of their native or national culture, which is the very basis of an individual's national identity.

These more or less dislocated poets can be categorized under three distinct groups:

a. The first group consists of those English poets, who have remained in India, accepting all the adverse conditions to fight from within, through their revolutionary poems. The prominent figures in this group consist of Nissim Ezekiel, Jayanata Mahapatra, Keki N. Daruwalla, Adil Jassawala and others.

b. The second group is formed of those poets who have opted to settle abroad but try to maintain their Indian roots by constantly writing poems upon India and Indian subjects. They believe in influencing Indian outlook and system from the outside. This group also has eminent poets like A.K. Ramanujan, R. Parthasarathy, Sujata Bhatt and others.

c. The third group is made up of the poets, who for economic purposes stay most of the time in West but still frequently visit India to renew their cultural bonds and roots in the Indian soil. This last group that shuttles relentlessly between India and the West has famous figures of Indian poetry like Shiv K. Kumar, Vikram Seth and others in its fold.

All these above mentioned poets suffer in one or the other way due to the problem of physical or ideological dislocation from their homeland and its mainstream culture and tradition.

The first group of poets though they remain in India, become ideologically dislocated, due to their radical and revolutionary views along with their rationalist approach to all the traditions, customs and conventions whether social, religious or political. Thus the poets of this group like Ezekiel and Jayanta Mahapatra become dislocated due to their aversion for outer forms of religion, worthless traditions and corruption in the socio-religious sphere, and Kamala Das faces the same fate for her highly bold and even for going to the extent of obscene picturization of sexual desires. In the second group, A.K. Ramanujan faces double dislocation. First due to the same reason for which Ezekiel and Mahapatra stand dislocated. And secondly due to his own physical dislocation from India. The third groups of poets like Shiv K. Kumar have a much more difficult situation, on account of their not belonging to either of the sides. They, for fame, prosperity and other facilities opt for West but feeling nostalgic are inclined to their roots. They try their best to remain connected with India. Their condition becomes somewhat like a no-where-man due to their double jeopardy.

The only solution to counter this problem is to 'relocate' oneself. Relocating Indian English Poets means resituating them in the Indian context, to fix them to their native roots like the native culture and tradition. This demands the Indian English poets to acclimatize native tradition in English language, without distorting or disfiguring it. Poets like Jayanta Mahapatra, A.K. Ramanujan and Kamala Das evoke native tradition and myth in their poetry. They lay emphasis on history and time. They belong to the category of poets who are deeply ingrained in the Indian tradition. On the other hand, Nissim Ezekiel and Shiv K. Kumar lay emphasis on contemporary reality and recreate characters in their own situations. A.K. Ramanujan as a diasporic poet has observed the native Hindu tradition and family, keeping in view the changing stance of the society. Living abroad, he looked back on the India he had left behind and the family in our society with all its changes that have over-taken them in course of time. In the poetry of these poets, the commonly found elements are:

(1) History (2) Myth (3) Corruption of various kinds (4) Superstitions (5) Crossing boundaries of (dismantling of) family bonds (6) Political situations (7) Displacement (8) The impact of modernization or globalization on Indian society.

In representing them in their poetry they frequently employ the poetic styles of irony and parody in an effective manner. In their effort for relocating themselves, they have created a new idiom, the Indian English idiom, in their poetry. This not only helps them in joining their roots but also distinguishes them from other third world poets who also write in English. Lastly, the use of typical Indian themes, symbols and metaphors gives their poems an Indian liveliness and makes them acceptable to the Indian literary circle without much difficulty.

Nissim Ezekiel, the foremost modern Indian English poet, is a very important figure in the history of Indian English poetry. With the publication of his first volume of poetry *A Time to Change* in the year 1952, he heralded a new age in the History of Indian English Poetry. He changed the traditions; vocabulary and aesthetics followed by his predecessors and introduced a spirit of realism into the till-then romantic and imaginative English Poetry in India. Though originally not an Indian with his roots in this soil, he has adapted himself wonderfully to this country and has become an inalienable part of it. He looks upon India, its various virtues and vices with a keen interest. His poems give a graphic picture of the everyday Indian life with its numerous colours, smells and sounds. Contrary feelings like admiration and disgust, pride and sorrow, faith and scepticism, spiritualism and materialism make his poems unique. His poems are marked with frankness, detachment and objectivity. Born and brought up in the highly westernized urban suburbs of Bombay, he has got a good experience of all the bright and dark aspects of urban life in a metro. Though there were no bonds of culture, history, or religion to bind him to India, he felt a deep closeness to her. The fact that he identifies his existence in context to the Indian ground justifies him as a naturalized outsider, who almost forgetting his own individual identity, seems to assimilate his identity with that of India. Here, he seems to be using the technique of 'hybridity' by which a foreigner or outsider can successfully assimilate himself or herself with the social fabric of the new homeland. For this, he has to develop a genuine sensibility and understanding towards the customs, traditions, myths, folklore and socio-political conditions of the country concerned. Leaving all personal, cultural, religious or even linguistic reservations, one has to interact, experience and imbibe the essence of one's socio-cultural and political milieu. In short, one has to rather make himself an integral part of the soil in order to claim it as its own. In a manner, he has to 'hybridize' himself to the local soil, to gain acceptance. In this context, he can, however, confidently conclude that the poet has completely hybridized himself by accepting all the fundamental roots of Indian culture like its myth, history, religion, socio-political scenario and contemporary problems.

His enormous use of pure Indian words and symbols along with the Indian colloquial English for his poems, gives a pure Indian taste to them. Though sometimes dejected with the people's attitude and corruption in his country, he seems to be in harmony with them. Though he had doubts about his own religious traditions, he is full of praise for the ancient Indian knowledge of the Upanishads. Thus in various ways the poet joins him with the Indian background and his attempt to become a part of it also meets with much success.

The main fact which sometimes seems to alienate Ezekiel is his not being a Hindu. As the question put upon by N.K.Ghosh: What prevents Ezekiel "from revelling in the non-personal notions of a poem- worthy India, its glorious past, its mysticism, cultural or historical nostalgia"(233). As he is not a Hindu he is unable to connect himself with the glory and tradition of the ancient India. However as he is born in modern India, he has a very deep affinity with it. The words of Ghosh also echo the same fact, that Ezekiel's "Primary concern is not the India which appeals to the west, but the India to which he can, and does, truly belong" (ibid, 233). It is rather this modern, urban and rather westernized India with which the poet connects himself to have roots in the soil. Like Jayanta Mahapatra, in whose poems 'Odisha' represents India with all its culture, history, heritage of sufferings and corruption, 'Bombay' in Ezekiel's poem stands for all the faces of modern India, whether pretty or repulsive. His mixed emotions of deep love and disgust for the island city are reflected in the poems "Island," and "A Morning Walk," respectively. In the first poem he seems to be deeply attached to the city:

How delight the soul with absolute

> Sense of salvation, how
> Hold to a single willed direction?
> I cannot leave the island
> I was born here and belong
> (*Collected Poems* 182).

In complete difference to the first poem, in the second one he gives a very dark and repulsive description of the city:

> Barbaric city, sick with slums,
> Deprived of seasons, blessed with rains.
> Its hawkers, beggars, iron lunged,
> Processions led by frantic drums,
> A million purgatorial lanes,
> And child-like masses many tongued,
> Whose wages are in words and crumbs
> (*Collected Poems* 119).

Though not an ardent admirer of the rural landscapes like Jayanta Mahapatra, the poet nevertheless dislikes the busy life of the city; polluted, mean and selfish. In one of his poems bearing the name "Urban," he gives the details of the grim conditions in the big cities in India. The inhabitants of such places are unaware of the beauty of nature and know only the waste he sees in the city. He becomes unaware of the soothing experiences of the dawn and the dusk due to the overshadowing sky scrapers surrounding him. Neither he feels the warmth of the sun nor the life giving rains as "his landscape has no depth or height", (*Collected Poems* 117). The agony of the city dweller seems to pour out from these words:

The city like a passion burns
He dreams of morning walks, alone
And floating on a wave of sand.
But still his mind its traffic turns
Away from beach and trees and stone.
To kindred clamour close at hand (117).

Yet, the poet can't live without the city. He wants to stay in it and become a part of it. He has a deep attachment to it and he doesn't want to achieve anything at the cost of leaving it. Therefore, he proclaims:

I don't wish to go any higher
I want to return
As soon as I can,
To be of the city,
To feel its hot breath
(City Song 42).

The poet though generally represents India through the symbol of Bombay; still there are some of his poems dealing with his outlooks about India, its society, customs and the present conditions it is facing. In his poem "India," the poet gives a very touching and pathetic picture of India's poverty:

Always in the sun's eye,
Here among the beggars,
Hawkers, Pavement Sleepers,
Hutment dwellers, slums
Dead souls of men and goods,
Burnt out mothers, frightened

Virgins, wasted child
And tortured animal,
All in noisy silence
Suffering the place and time
(In India 131).

Originally as he is a refugee and hence in a sense is a foreigner to this land, his outlook towards this land is formed from his different kind of experiences he had during the various stages of his life. The sum of all those experiences from the moment of his birth to the realization of his affinity with India and especially Bombay, is given in his famous poem "Background, Casually". The first stanza is full of the existentialist gloom that seems to cast its shadow throughout the life of the poet. The very term 'Poet-rascal-clown' implies the fact how meaningless the poet himself thinks of his life. When the poet arrives for education at the Roman Catholic school, there he faced not only the anti-Jewish feelings common in Christians but also physical abuse from Muslim boys and racial discrimination of the Hindu boys. The Jews not only faced discrimination but they themselves had very reserved views about the Hindus, with whom they lived. They disliked certain Hindu habits like talking too loudly or knocking the doors too heavily. This entire mutual wrong outlook was discarded by the poet for when all conventions and traditions were meaningless.

As a responsible poet, Ezekiel also, like Eliot observes and analyses the various defects due to which the Indian society remains backward. He cites various examples of corruption practised by the government officials. During the time of natural calamities like floods or cyclones, when thousands of people suffer from loss of home and property, starvation, insecurity, diseases and cold, they have a good time in exploiting the government funds in the name of providing relief to the victims of the floods or cyclones. When enquired about the condition of the respective areas under their administration or supervision, their altitude is as presented by the poet:

> Meet any official
> he claims his district
> subdivision or block is the 'worst-hit'
> and pass on a hand-out
> with statistics of relief work
> (The Truth about the Floods 185).

The poet gives a vivid description of the affected people with images of "Paddy fields with knee-deep water" (Floods 17) and "all the house had collapsed" (Floods 24). However unconcerned with their plight, the government officials eat away a major portion of the funds meant for their sustenance and rehabilitation. The officials enrich themselves while the victims face even death due to disease and starvation. Due to this, villagers refuse even to interact with the reporters mistaking them for government officials. Among the voluntary relief workers also there is no true dedication or sympathy for the poor victims as is reflected from the example of the student workers who even in this serious times, carry along with them their transistors and film song cassettes, while the villagers express their pain for various problems they face in the following way:

> The villagers (...)

slapped their bellies
and whined:
'I have not eaten for three days'
"my husband has been washed away"
"my son is dying"
"I cannot find my daughter"
(The Truth about the floods 185)

There are also other social evils like the abuse of women, child marriage etc which till now has not been eradicated in an effective manner. The poet gives the example of the maid-servant working in his house, who was regularly beaten by her husband, only for the show of male authority:

At twelve or fourteen, married off
to the usual brute
she has a child,
and tells my mother every time
her husband beats her
for the fun of it.
(Servants 6-11)

He is perfectly aware of the various superstitions and evils which have crept into the elegant spiritual systems of ancient India. In his another popular poem "Night of the Scorpion," he gives detailed account of the great fuss made by the superstitious rural folk when the poet's mother is bitten by a scorpion. The village had strange ideas like, with every movement of the creature, his poison would spread in the body of the victim; the poison would reduce evil Karmas of the victim done in past and this suffering would help in decreasing the misfortunes of the next birth. The scene becomes more comic with the father of the poet, a rational man trying every valid and absurd method of curing the bite, by trying "every curse and blessing, powder, mixture, herb and hybrid" (131). He even went to the extent of pouring paraffin on the bitten toe and setting it afire with a match. A holy man was also brought to cure her through spells and incantations. The poet in another poem "The Visitor," gives the example of the common superstitions, prevalent in India that if the crow caws before your house, a visitor is soon expected:

> Three times the crow had cawed
> At the windows, baleful eyes fixed
> On mine, wings slightly raised
> In sinister poise, body tense
> and neck craned like a nagging woman's
> Filling the room with voice and presence (137).

In his poem titled "Guru," and "Healers," he gives an account of the so called spiritual men befooling the orthodox, superstitious and especially the uneducated masses of India. In the first poem he gives a very disheartening description of a godman:

> ... the saint is still a faithless friend,
> obstinate in argument.
> ungrateful for favours done,
> hard with servants and the poor,
> discourteous to disciples, especially men,
> condescending, even rude
> to visitors (except the foreigners)

and over scrupulous in checking
the accounts of the ashram.
He is also rather fat (191).

The poet at the end of the poem is forced to comment that "If Saints are like this, what hope is there then for us?" In the other poem "Healers," he satirizes those spiritual healers who prescribe the same method for all sufferings and difficulties. However, one should not make haste in giving the decision that the poet is religiously biased. The poet though a Jew himself, liberally praises the ancient Indian wisdom and philosophy in the poems like "Tribute to the Upanishads," and "Very Indian poems in Indian English,". His faith in Mahatma Gandhi and the concept of Ram-Rajya are also proof enough of his admiration of Indian spirituality.

The poet has much admiration for the wisdom of the ancient sages of India. He is pained to see the young generation of India neglecting this great treasure inherited from their ancestors and trying to copy the habits and the ways of the west. While the West itself is seeking peace and solace in Indian spiritualism, scriptures and traditions, the Indians themselves are forgetting it. He points the present condition as follows:

> ... Ancient Indian Wisdom is 100% correct
> I should say even 20% correct.
> But Modern generation is neglecting-
> Too much going for fashion and foreign thing
> (The Patriot, 237).

He is also quite at ease with the myths and traditions of the Hindu community. He has no intentions to change their gullible and liberal attitude towards other religions. Though, according to the poet, the language sometimes acts as a barrier in communicating with the different social groups and communities; the basic human emotions transcend all such barriers. The poet speaks out his views in the following manner:

> I lack the means to change
> Their amiable ways,
> Although I love their gods.
> It's the language really
> Separates, whatever else
> Is shared…
> (Minority Poem, *Collected Poems* 236).

His knowledge about the Hindu myths and pantheon can be confirmed even by his early compositions like the "Passion Poems," where in poem number six and eight, he shows his acquaintance with both the amorous plays of Radha-Krishna and the unshakable austerities of Lord Shiva.

The poet is also concerned with the trauma of displacement faced by the refugees as he is aware of his own near to refugee position. In his "Minority Poem," he presents the difficult situation between his community (the Jews) and the Indians, both of whom are unable to shake off their biased outlook towards each other. In "Poem of the Separation," he presents a very complex mixture of the poet's feeling of separation from his love and the plight of the Kashmiri refugees, ousted from their homeland. The poet thus perfectly aware of the pain of being separated from one's roots tries to belong to India and become a part of it, by showing active interest in all its matters, traditions, phenomenon and facts. His liberal admiration of whatever is good in India shows his love for India in very clear terms. Therefore, in his poem "Background, Casually," he says:

> ... The Indian landscape sears my eyes.
> I have become a part of it
> To be observed by foreigners,
> They say that I am singular,
> Their letters overstate the case,
> (*Collected Poems*: 179).

At the end of the poem, saying that he has made his commitment to stay in India, he concludes with the sentence: "My backward place is where I am" (181).

So, from all the analysis done above on the poems and views of Ezekiel, we can undoubtedly call him a poet successful to a great extent in rooting himself in the soil and traditions of India and thus, in relocating himself. In the words of Dr. K.Balachandran, "Ezekiel is essentially Indian in his sensibility, without losing his national identity his writings appeal internationally. As a painstaking craftsman his poetry is simple, introspective and analytical. Highly disciplined and unpretentious with skillful use of language in a conversational style and mastery of irony with simple dictions and perfect control over his emotions, he occupies an important place on the top of the modern Indo-Anglian poets and his 'Indianness' no doubt has brought him this much coveted crown. (Qtd. Rukhaiyar 92).

Jayanta Mahapatra, the poet representing Orissa with all its history, culture and myths, is one of the most prominent figures in the sphere of modern Indian English Poetry. Dilip Chitre describes him as "Mahapatra …. is traditional in his poetic bias despite the contemporariness of his articulation. His verse is free and moves slowly and smoothly. It is almost languid in its metaphysical poise until suddenly he transforms elemental visual images of Indian nature and traditional rural life into memorable metaphors. Mahapatra is what the Indian poet writing in English is supposed to be: an interpreter of a unique, complex and exotic culture through its landscape and people" (Rukhaiyar 2002: 150). Probably no other poet in India, writing in English at present, is able to draw a picture of the historical, cultural and social India, as detailed and lively as he. Though, it is true that in the past and even in the present, there are many poets who create lively pictures out of words, but there is a great difference between them and Jayanta Mahapatra. The pre-independence poets had an idealistic vision of their motherland which was not real in the physical sense. On the other hand most of the modern poets either follow somewhat the same way or draw a naked picture of present ill condition of India, which generally is highly unattractive for the readers. In stark contrast, Jayanta Mahapatra's art depicts both the sides with equal calibre. It is true that generally most of his poems are related to and depict various facts and conditions of Odisha, but, Odisha in his poems stands as a symbol for the entire India. For him, India is a land of contrasts. To assert this fact, he again and again uses highly unpleasant images of India, by the side of its pleasant images. He doesn't attempt to link the present in anyway with the past. Instead he tries to show the truth of both in a way that can be felt only by a true native of the soil. In all his writings, whether concerned with the past or present, the poet shows a painful and gloomy tone in describing different facts about Odisha. The reason for this is not hard to guess as from the very ancient times, the land of Odisha has faced great trouble from nature and men. Floods and cyclones are nothing new for Odisha and wars and conflicts of the worst kind have left their impression upon the land. The people of Odisha, in fact seem to have inherited only pain and misfortune from history, nature and politics. The poet seems to re-affirm his location in the context of Orissa by revealing all the sufferings the land has undergone and is still undergoing. He actually wants to reduce these pains by giving a healing touch of sympathy to the wounds of the land and its people.

The poet is a firm believer of realism in its hardest form. He believes that as a poet his responsibility to the society is by showing it its negative aspects by portraying them in a sensitive manner. Due to this his poems abound with such images which arouse pain, guilt or repulsion. His poems though sometimes speaking of natural beauty give their attention mainly to facts like dirt, beggars, poverty, starvation, moral degradation, communal conflicts, hypocrisy and social evils like prostitution etc. Like other writers, he is not the one who sitting in an atmosphere of comfort and security, writes only what he imagines. He is a true realistic poet, whose poetry also uses highly realistic symbols and images. One may complain that there is no pleasant aspect in his poem but in the view of the poet with a history of pain and the present misfortunes, it is impossible to have any thing pleasant in the poems. This outlook is reflected in his poem "Song of the River," (Waiting 21), where he says:"There is no song of

India" (Song of the River). The extent of the melancholy of the poet can be measured by the fact that he is doubtful of even poetry itself as a means of reforming any thing or matter. His scepticism about the poet's role, assumed by the idealists as highly contributing to the upliftment of a nation, can be observed in the following lines:

> The worn out face of India holds the weak of
> dumb,
> solitary poets who die alone,
> silenced by the shapelessness of live alive,
> (Possessions 26).

Still, the poet feels that his weapons can be only words and he uses them in a sharp inflicting manner to vent his anguish and anger upon the various political, social and economic evils that exploit and torture the poor masses of the land. His poems speak of his experiences gained not by an occasional visit, but by long stays in the concerned surroundings studying every minute detail of it. As a poet, he thinks that the legacy which he should leave behind should be a poetry reflecting the pains and sufferings of the masses and the causes from which they grow. In his poem "Saving Ourselves," he says:

> There is only this failure I must pass on to you
> the bruise of iron cuffs on the wrists that watch
> the grimace of India's drawn face,
> the pain of the shadows from the fallen trees of
> our conscience (21).

In the masterpiece creation of poet *Relationship* (1980) he invokes his motherland through a number of native images, in a highly evocative manner:

> I know I can never come alive
> if I refuse to consecrate at the alter of my origins ?
> where the hollow horns blows every morning
> and its suburban sound pick its way
> through the tangled moonlight of your lazy sleep (...)
> as the earth glistens with old mountains
> and moaning rivers... (18).

The origins about which the poet talks are nothing else than his firm roots in India and Odisha. During his explorations of the land's infinite sides, he is unable to find facts which would help in glorifying the land. Still he is unable to forsake it. Instead he feels a certain pride of his roots in the land. His poetry thus presents a very strange combination of his proud declaration of his roots as well as the lamentation on the condition of the country:

> The leaves of the dark trees of India
> are gasping for breath
> across the green air (...)
> I can only hear the hum of silent, shut-in-machinery
> *(Disposed Nests* 48).

The immense pain felt by the poet on seeing his beloved land starving with hunger and oppressed by a host of socio-economic and political evils, is ventilated in his poem "A Dark Wind,":

> India, like the decapitated old temple by the river,
> its mouth open and staring,
> all its bewildering hunger born into Sorrow (7).

The poet's struggle for relocation makes him write dispassionately about all the short comings and defects of the land to which he belongs. Yet, in spite of all negative aspects, the poet feels deeply attached to all those things which represent Odisha or India. Declaring, his intention of remaining in Odisha, like Ezekiel's decision of remaining in Bombay, he draws a very realistic picture of the difficult conditions one may have to face, if he decides to live in Odisha:

> Something here, perhaps fatal spirit,
> Something that recalls the centuries of defeat.
> To live here
> antlered in sickness and disease,
> in the past of comprehended totems,
> and the spilt blood of ancestors
> one would wear like an amulet
> (Living in Orissa 11).

Though the poet draws the picture of his land with the colour of hunger, misery and pain, yet he at the same time seems to be full of surprise at the endurance of the people who bearing all difficulties quietly spend a serene simple life.

A true description of a particular nation or a land is never complete without giving some details about its history. Though

Odisha has many special events of history to its credit, yet no other event associated with Odisha has such far-fetching effect as the Kalinga War, fought against the invasion of the Mauryan emperor, Ashoka. The war fought in 261, B.C., was one of the bloodiest battles fought in the ancient India. Traditions say that the river Daya became red with the blood of the dead soldiers. Thousand of people died, much more were injured or imprisoned. The loss of life and property was beyond calculation. This carnage and sufferings were so powerful that even the victorious conqueror Ashoka was overwhelmed by it. He then decided to quit war forever and follow the path of peace and virtue propagated by Lord Buddha. Becoming a devout Buddhist missionary, he helped in the propagation of Buddhism to far-off countries and engaged himself in various charitable works for the whole life. Due to this his name has become immortal, not only in Indian but world history also. Even Odisha has started taking pride in its relation to Ashoka's change of heart. But the poet has a totally different view of all these facts. According to him, whatever Ashoka did later didn't matter as much as the great sufferings of the people of Odisha. In his fifth volume of poems *Waiting* (1978) he has clearly stated it in his poem "Dhoulagiri," thinking the amount of bloodshed and suffering, Odisha had to face:

> … the measure of Ashoka's suffering
> does not appear enough.
> The place of his pain peers lamentably
> from among the pains of the dead
> (Selected Poems 22).

The amount of anger in the poet towards Ashoka, vents itself upon the people of Odisha also, who forgetting all the cruelties have started praising and honouring all the things and memories associated with him:

> … forgetting the cruelties
> of ruthless emperors who carved peaceful edicts
> on blood-red rock,
> forgetting our grooms and cries,
> the smells of gunsmoke and smoldering flesh,
> forgetting the tactics and the strategy
> that led to the founding of the infinite distance
> inside our watery skulls (*Relationship* 1).

Being unable to forget it by having some pleasant memories, he again engages himself in continuing the story in another poem:

> What can ever wash the air of its gashed voices ?
> It is hard to tell now
> what opened the anxious skies,
> how the age-old proud stones
> lost their strength and fell
> and how the waters of the Daya
> stank with the bodies of my ancestors
> (The Uncertainty of Colour, *Random Decent* 23)

However, it doesn't mean that he blames the past events for all the evils of the present, as some may be tempted to think from his views in his poem "Of Independence Day," (*A Whiteness of Bone*). His main concern is the wellbeing of the present generation as is reciprocated in "The Abandoned British Cemetery at Balasore,": "… for the elaborate ceremonial of a coming generation to keep history awake,/ stifle the survivor's issuing cry"(30).

The present for which the poet gives stress, also appears as dark as the past in his own poems. He seems to hold the view that history is only constantly repeating itself. The only difference being that in the past all the oppressors come from outside, now they come from the inside especially in the form of political leaders. In *Dispossessed Nests* the poet writes:

> … the Calender hatches India's history
> A lifeless story
> Chewed on by the country's leaders (30).

In his poem "Possessions," (*Shadow Space* 24), he paints a very disgusting picture of these types of leaders who decide the fate of the country and keep their name untarnished, even after failing to fulfill promises made during the time of election or even when the country's population starves for lack of food. At such times the poet is reminded of Mahatma Gandhi, known as the father of our nation. He was a true political leader, sacrificing everything he had for the sake of nation without any desire for honour, wealth, power or comfort. In his various poems he seems to ask Gandhiji, how he felt on seeing the present condition of our country for whose freedom he fought so bravely. In the earlier stage, the poet seems not to be sure of the utility of Gandhian ideals but at later stages shows a deep respect and interest of the poet towards them. In one of his collection of poems titled *Bare Face,* there is a long poem "Requem," which the poet has dedicated to Gandhiji. In this he describes the various aspects of Gandhiji like selflessness, concern for his country and countrymen, bravery and the tragic end he faced despite his dedication to non-violence. Most of the sections of the poem show in a sense a deep pain and disappointment. Only the fifteenth section referring to the time of Buddha when he lived and preached his message of peace and equality. This poem however describes the irony of both Buddha's teachings and Gandhi's ideal. Both are forgotten in the land they originated.

His other poems dealing with the present are also not any brighter in their attitude. He speaks of the plight of women in many poems of his various volumes. He in fact strikes a resemblance between the women, who also are the mothers of men and the nation, visualized as mother India by the patriots. In his "Story at all the Start of 1978," (*Waiting*), he describes the pain of both in a poetical manner by which all the lines apply to both.

The poet views the women kind as an eternally suffering group whose conditions have never changed during the several ages gone by. Even in art, the poet finds their sorry state of affairs as depicted in "In a Time of Winter Rain," (*Bare Face*). The poet goes on recounting the various evils which are suffocating our country. In his poems like "Hunger," (*A Rain of Rites* 44), "Nightfall," (*Waiting* 3), "A Country Festival," (*Waiting* 4) and "Deaths in Orissa," (*A Whiteness of Bone*), he gives a grim description of the physical and moral degradation due to starvation and poverty. In his eighth volume *Dispossessed Nests,* the poet laments the lack of unity in the country due to which various communal conflicts are hampering its peace and progress. In the same manner, in his twelfth volume *A Whiteness of Bone,* in the form of a number of poems including "The Hill," the poet narrates the tragedy of December 1984 in Bhopal where thousands of people were killed due to the poisonous gas that leaked from the chemical pesticide plant. He elucidates the gravity of the event by giving the example of the death of the five year old Leela, the numerous children orphaned by the gas leak and the thousands of people suffering from various physical disorders due to the effects of the poisonous gas.

For the above described misery, the poet also criticizes the superstitious nature of our people. In his volume *Dispossessed Nest*, the poem no.32 known as "Shantytown," gives not only a very repulsive and horrible picture of the slums and the life there in our country, but also the easy-going, careless and superstitious nature of the poor sections of our society:

> For if any thing happens,
> their dreams of belief tell them that their gods
> and their government shall take care of them (54).

In his poem "The Stoneage," he remarks that in this land, the dark past has not gone away. All the superstitions, taboos and savage laws and customs still exist strangling the voice of free thought and free life:

> Beneath the bloodied walls of history
> nothing can happen more dreadful
> than stones turned to gods through prayers
> stones, whose eyes have had no expression in them
> stones, like governments, who have no honour at all
> stones, whose long arms easily batter and kill
> a young woman accused of adultery
> (*Random Descent* 47).

All these circumstances, make the poet feel disgusted with not only the country and its people but with himself also. The sense of defeat and helplessness makes him remark:

> … Why is it so hard to realize one day
> that you are meaningless ? That one
> is not even living for one's own sake ?
> (Possessions, *Shadow Space* 25).

He loses his faith upon poetry as a tool for revolutionary changes and reformation. In his view he is only doing a futile work with no benefit either for him or the society.He is also sceptical about the bright future our freedom fighters had dreamt of and about which the present politicians give false promises. He thinks that though it is now more than half a century of our obtaining freedom, yet it is not at all fruitful, as we have not achieved the desired goals and there is little hope to do so in near future:

> ... Would all this endless waiting of belief
> ever change anything ?
> or if someone wrote another poem today
> on drug-taking or sexual deviation,
> would it shut out
> the epiphany of history ? (. . .)
> This time is not an easy one
> for us who cannot forget ourselves
> why wait to be free of history
> when you are now in it ?
> (Waiting, *A Whiteness of Bone* 34-35)

Still, despite all the hopelessness, misery, failure and disappointment, the poet, taking inspiration from the land itself to live on despite all the difficulties, decides to go on with his work, with a hope that at least in the distant future, the country would achieve its redemption:

> I must move ahead (…)
> in my eagerness to catch hope against hope,
> towards the hiding place
> under the roots of a fallen country
> (The Time of What Is, *Shadow Space* 67).

Thus, finally we find that Jayanta Mahapatra has achieved his relocation by finding his roots in an honest manner. Making Orissa his focal point, he has got the mark of a true native poet rooted in his tradition. Though his way becomes different from other poets who do so by eulogizing their mother land, it can only be taken as his unique and genuine individual style of expressing his affinity to the land. In the opinion of K. Satchidanandan: "Jayanta sings not with the murderer but with the murdered and shares the bread of his poverty not with the cunning master but with the silent slave, the hapless orphan, the half-starved tiller, the half-awake rural craftsman, the tenacious survivor of a thousand calamities . . . He only moves from night to night; the empty window in his lonely wall is his pet possession …. Mahapatra's whole oeuvre reveals his extreme sensitivity to the larger issues that concern mankind in general and our society in particular (Qtd. by Syamala Kallury, The Indian Imagination… 60). The best proof one can give for his firm roots is his unfaltering love, concern and respect for motherland despite all its dark aspects.

He though feeling dejected at times, doesn't want to escape the situation. Like Ezekiel, his determination to stay in his native grounds gives the authority, force and beauty that is found in his numerous volumes of poetry.

Kamala Das, and her contributions to modern Indian English Poetry need no introduction. She is not only the first female poet of the modern trend; being one of the four founding poets of the genre, but by far the best one also. Possessing a dynamic, prolific and an evergreen spirit, she has written some of the best verses in English. In her poetry one gets a very truthful picture of the feminine desires and psychology. Her life is almost of an epic-scale. Born in the Malabar region of Kerala, she moved on to the metro-cities like Bombay, Calcutta etc., either with her father or husband. She even remained for a time period in Sri Lanka or Ceylon. Her experiences of very great phenomena like the freedom struggle in India, the partition of India, the Bangladeshi Holocaust and the starting of the conflict between the Tamils and the Sinhalese in Ceylon, give a sharpness of thought and clarity of vision in her poetry. Though she has written only three volumes of poetry; *Summer in Calcutta* (1965), *The Descendants* (1967) and *The Old Playhouse and other Poems* (1973), she has written many others which are to be found in books like *Tonight* and *This Savage Rite* (1979), in which she has collaborated with Pritish Nady. Having born and spent a part of childhood in highly traditional and orthodox atmosphere, she has moved forward to study, marry, experiment, write and live in the most urban areas. Due to this there seems a never-ending conflict in her poems between her traditional Dravidian roots and the modern urban culture in which she is presently living. Her poem has an intricate mixture of the expression of her own private feelings as well as her universalized observance of her pains which are felt by others also. Hari Mohan Prasad and Chandra Prasad Singh seem to understand her in a very clear manner as is evident from their writing: "Her Poetry has often been considered as a gimmick in sex or striptease in words, an over exposer of body or 'snippets of trivia'. But the truth is that her poetry is an autobiography, an articulate voice of her ethnic identity, her Dravidian Culture" (Qtd. by K.V. Surendran 176). Like Ezekiel, she also follows a modern and rationalist approach to every matter she observes. Her unconventional thought and the way of expressing it may very well raise eyebrows in the orthodox sections of the society. Still no one can challenge the truth her poems reveal about the real condition of the Indian women, their desires and the tragedy of their lives. In her poems, actually it is the unsatisfied and tortured Indian women whose voice and desires are heard and felt in various forms.

Her poems show a deep attachment to Indian roots despite her modernized outlook. In her first volume itself she narrates her childhood in the Nalapat house, her arranged marriage to a stranger, her sexual exploitation by her husband, her resolution to become unconventional in all the ways and the reaction of her relatives to this type of attitude, in her famous poem "An Introduction,". Her highly intimate reminiscing of the childhood plays she had played with her elder brother, with whom the poet shared a very close emotional relationship, is reflected in her poem "To a Big Brother (about to be married)." Further in the same volume, she presents all the smells and colours to be seen at a roadside market in Calcutta, in the poem bearing the same title as the volume. Apart from all these poems, there is the poem "Someone Else's Song," in which she universalizes her voice by using a normal scene of rural India as a symbol.

There is also a poem with the name 'The Dance of the Eunuchs," in which she presents a very colourful and lively description of the Eunuchs dancing in their colourful costumes like women. This scene also is very much easily found in India as traditionally the eunuchs play a great role in many festive occasions by dancing and singing, which is deemed to repel evil spirits and omens. In the same manner there are many other poems in which description of the locality or other such native scenes are used in abundance by the poet as symbols to express her pain, confusion and anger.

In her third volume *The Old Playhouse and other Poems* (1973), there are many fine examples of poems dealing with Indian subjects, facts and matters. There are two poems, "Blood," and "Nani," respectively which deal exclusively with the private experiences of the poet during their stay in the ancestral house. The first poem "Blood" gives a very Indian description of a joint family where the elderly religious and orthodox grandmother loves and narrates stories to her grandchildren. The poet had a very deep attachment with her great grandmother who narrated her stories of how, when she was young, she went to the Shiva Temple every Monday riding an elephant, all the jewellery, cosmetics and dresses she owned and her early marriage which resulted in her early widowhood due to the death of her husband just after one year. The old lady had great attachment to tradition. She told the grandchildren that their family has the most pure kind of blood while all other low castes have impure blood. She also felt a very deep pain for the decaying old ancestral house with ancient snake shrines in it. Old with age, sick with arthritis and grieving for the house, she died. At her death, the poet felt as if the house was also expressing its grief by the various movement and sounds made by the windows, pillars and dark rooms:

> For I thought saw the windows close
> Like the closing of the eyes
> I thought I heard the Pillars groon
> And the dark rooms heave a sigh
> (Blood, *The Old Playhouse and Other Poems* 18).

The second poem "Nani," narrates the tragic suicide committed by the housemaid working in the Nalapat house during the poet's childhood. The poet had deep closeness with her also as she many times entertained the children of that house. Unfortunately, someone seduced her and made her pregnant, due to which out of shame and fear of public censor, she committed suicide. Incidents of this sort are also common in rural India, where poor women are frequently seduced, raped or sexually abused by the lusty males of noble or rich families and are forced to commit suicide on becoming pregnant. The revolutionary attitude of the poet against the orthodox and fanatic religious elements is also shown in another poem "Inheritance," in which she debunks these types of fanatic notions among the religious people:

> ... Oh God
> Blessed be your fair name, blessed be the religion
> Purified in the unbeliever's blood, blessed be
> our sacred city, blessed be its incarnated glory ....
> (Inheritance; *The Old Playhouse and Other Poems* 20).

However, one shouldn't make haste in the decision that the poet seems to be an atheist. No, she has a deep faith in God. Even when she was undergoing her various adulterous affairs, she constantly prayed to lord Krishna, the divine lover, as slowly she was coming to realize the unending hunger of mortal sexual love. Therefore she clamoured for the divine spiritual love which brings peace and bliss to one's mind and heart. There are many poems which are either direct invocation to Lord Krishna or are Radha's or Meera's longing for and experiences with Krishna. There are some others which simply narrate various parts of the Radha Krishna myth. These poems like "Radha Krishna," "Radha," "Ghana Shyam," and "Prayer to Unfamiliar Gods," express the desire for true love for which the poet desired without any success. However there is one poem titled "Maggots," also which throws the dark shadow of disgust and suffering resulting from sexual love, even upon the pair of divine lovers like Radha and Krishna. This feeling of death shadowing every moment of life is very frequent in her poems. In her view, death is inevitable so it is better to live this life to the full. She also, like ancient Hindus, believes in soul's indestructibility as is reflected in the following lines:

> ... Where would
> death be then, that meaningless word
> when life is all that there is, that
> raging continuity that
> after the wise once recognize as God ?
> (Anamalai Poems IV: 109).

Some critics like M.L. Sharma go to the extent of declaring her as an amorous devotee of Lord Krishna by taking examples from her Radha-Krishna poems. But one should consider and analyse her poems deeply before reaching that decision as the amount of carnal desires, obscene picturization of sexual intercourse and frequent use of taboo words, show her real attitude. Still one can safely consider from these poems that the poet is very well rooted to her myth and traditions though apparently there may be some misgivings and misunderstandings.

Religious dilemma and spiritual confusion are two of the major characteristics, integral to the poetry of Kamala Das. As we have observed till now, she had a strong antipathy towards the repressive traditions of Hinduism, which to her was a form of Aryan subjugation continuing till now. The true Dravidian culture, she loved, is no more existent. Thus, in her quest for solutions and solace, she turned towards Islam, which is famous for its equanimous treatment to all human beings, irrespective of caste, colour, creed etc. In fact, Islam is a purely casteless religion, where all opportunities for socio-economic or religious development, are open to all, irrespective of sex, colour or social background. Moreover, the biggest incentive that Islam offered to the poet was the equality of rights, position and security guaranteed to the women. The exclusive rights conferred by Islam upon women, greatly enticed her to the study of the Holy Quran. With the progress in her study, of the holy text, her conviction regarding the emancipative capability of Islam became more and more firm. Even the 'Burkah' or 'Purdah', appeared to her as a most efficient measure of safety for the women against the preying eyes of the male-dominated society. All these convinced her strongly to break away from her own socio-religious traditions and embrace whole-heartedly the protective and redeeming power of Islam. Ultimately she converted to Islam in 1999.

The early few years of her post-conversion life were full of peace, contentment and religious fervour. She felt as if she had finally achieved what she had craved for through the years of her life she had lived till now. Her mind was at great peace as her fear regarding bodilessness in the after-life was completely allayed by the authority of the holy Quran. Islam is one of the few religions in this world, which promises a physical body even in the after-life. This relieved the poet of her fear of losing her body with death. Yet, due to her strongly independent and rational bent of mind, she could not ignore the presence of the various conventional and suppressive elements even in the liberal and humanitarian fold of Islam. Though disillusioned, she had reached a stage too far to desert Islam. She continued as a devout Muslim, but kept herself aloof from any type of religious involvement. Instead, she dedicated the rest of her life to the work of social welfare and the upliftment of the exploited sections of the Indian society. Till her last breath, she worked incessantly for the betterment of women, children and backward classes.

Thus at last we see that all the volumes of poetry of Kamala Das are replete with Indian themes, subjects, symbols and scenes. Not only has she herself remained firm with her roots but has also shown the way to her juniors so that they can follow their roots along with keeping in tune with the impacts of globalization and modernization. Her most notable service to Indian English poetry is perhaps her contribution to the development of Indian English idiom like her contemporaries Ezekiel and Jayanta Mahapatra. Though maximum of them are taboo, obscene or not generally used words, yet her use of such words has added to the vocabulary of typical Indian Poetry. On her contribution, Bruce King praises her for the "Indianisation of English" through her individual use of vocabulary idioms, choice of verbs and syntactic constructions.

His comment is as follows:

> It is important in the development of a national literature that writers free themselves from the linguistic standards of their colonizers and create a literature based on local speech, and this is especially important for woman writers".
> (Qtd. by Rukhaiyar 105)

So, from the study of all the above given examples, facts and views, we can justly proclaim that Kamala Das has very honestly clung to her roots and maintained them despite various upheavals in her life.

A. K. Ramanujan, the fourth of the five poets to whom goes the credit of modernizing Indian English Poetry, was the first of the modern Indian English poets to settle abroad permanently. In his view it was from the comfortable and secure position in west that he can influence India through his thoughts and views expressed through his poems. Still he never forgot India. Reminscing again and again upon his experience in India, he formed his base for composing poetry on Indian subjects, mostly those, with which he had at one or another time, interacted. His personal experiences develop to take the form of collected or shared experience. As observed by Nagrajan:

> Most of the poems in the new volume, as in the
> first, have their origin in recollected personal
> emotion. They deal with the Poet's memory of
> his Relations and the ambiguous freedom that life
> away from them confers (Qtd. by Rukhaiyar 129).

His poetic creations can thus be claimed to have originated from his 'Diaspora' consciousness, which keeps a man mentally and spiritually attached to his homeland in spite of being physically separated from it. The critic Pramod Kumar Nayar has defined the diaspora sensibility as a combination of nostalgia, rootlessness, split-consciousness and "multiple identities and solidarities or a reassertion of 'native' cultural identity" (197). It is this unique sensibility, which makes the poet contemplate and analyse every possible aspect of the memories he comes with from his motherland. It also makes him speculate upon the various traits of culture and tradition that he inherits from his ancestors and which as a legacy he is supposed to pass on to his successors. Therefore, the poet, time and again goes back to his experiences in his own motherland. He meditates upon the underlying essence of all the experiences he had, the traditions and customs with which he was introduced, the myth and the folklore which he came to know and above all the contemporary realities, which he himself observed.

Apart from his experiences on the private and public level, he constantly refers to the various myths, superstitions, beliefs, corrupt spiritual systems and other defects in various spheres of India. His extensive search for his roots in Indian and especially in the Dravidian Culture seems to have borne good fruits in his poems referring to the South Indian places, myths and symbols. In the view of M.K. Naik: "It is perhaps his long sojourn aboard (he has been living in the United States for almost two decades now) that explains Ramanujan's presistent obsession with his Indian past both familial and racial, and it is this obsession that constitutes a major theme in all his poetry" (Qtd. by Rukhaiyar 130).

However, the fact is that Ramanujan is actually joined to his roots with the help of his highly subjective memory. These memories of the past create an inner world within him which sometimes abruptly jumps into the present in the form of anxieties, fears and new insights. His poems like "Still Life," "Love Poem for a Wife-I," "Small Scale Reflections on a Great House," and "Conventions of Despair," further substantiate this point, with their contents clearly indicative of being created by the poet pondering deeply in a contemplative manner upon his past, its effect on the present and its relevance in the present context.

There are many poems in his various volumes starting from *Striders* (1966) to *The Black Hen* (1995) which constantly allude to various cultural facts, native scenes, religious beliefs, myths and other such facts native to the poet's South Indian-Dravidian-Tamil identity. His poems like "Small town, South India," and "Small Scale Reflections on a Great House," directly or indirectly refer to his own experience of South Indian urban and rural atmosphere. While the first poem describes vividly all the common characteristics of a South Indian town along with the types of people generally to be found there, the second one gives in detail all the memories of the poet associated to his father's house at his native place. In this poem, he presents a very lively picture of what the house looked like when he was living there and who all lived there. About his Hindu roots, he does not seem to have a very encouraging stand. His poems like "THE HINDOO: he doesn't hurt a fly or a spider either," "THE HINDOO: he reads his GITA and is calm at all events," "THE HINDO: the only risk," and "Second Sight," give a rather sarcastic and ridiculous description of the conventional Hindu practices, attitude and concepts. In the three "HINDOO" poems, he presents the conventional Hindu as a hypocrite, a careless and heartless creature whereas in "Second Sight," he seems to make fun of the concept of the intuitive sight deemed as a great spiritual and mystical faculty in India for knowing the truth in its absolute reality. Not only Hindu but he refers to facts related with other Indian religions also which have originated in India itself. In his poem "Pleasure," he gives a terrifying account of a naked (Digambara) Jain monk trying to dissuade his mind from obscene sexual thoughts by pouring honey allover his body and standing upon an anthill of red ants with fiery stings. This type of methods of liberating or cleansing one's mind of evil or obscene thoughts through serious physical torture is a very well known concept in India from the very ancient times, popular especially among Hindus and Jains. However, due to the radical and rational outlook of the poet, he rejects that bodilessness can lead to freedom of desires. Quoting from Indian mythological sources, he argues that bodilessness instead makes desires also as boundless just as Kama (The Indian Cupid) when burnt to ashes by the rage of Lord Shiva, became all pervasive. Furthermore, the love-god in the bodiless state is far more comfortable than the human beings, as is indicated by the following lines:

> All symbol, no limbs, a nobody all soul,
> O Kama, only you can have no use
> For the Kamasutra.
> Ashes have no posture
> (*Collected Poems* 72).

His deep knowledge of Hindu religion and myth is reflected in his various poems like "Prayers to Lord Murugan," "A Minor Sacrifice," "No Amnesiac King," and the "Mythologies," series while the "Mythologies-1, 2 and 3 narrate popular legends from the Puranas and history with the purpose of teaching some vital moral facts. The poems like "No Amnesiac King," and "A Minor Sacrifice," recount respectively the tale of love of Shakuntala and Dushyanta and the death of king Parikshita by snakebite, to avenge which his son started a sacrifice to destroy all snakes. Similarly, the section 'Heredity' from the poem "Excerpts from a Father's Wisdom," speaks of the special dice fashioned by Shakuni from his own father's bones:

> Even gambling dues
> Are bred in an ancestor's bone
> (*Collected poems* 42).

All of these tales are part of the ancient Indian Sanskrit epic 'Maha Bharata' and are found in slightly altered or exaggerated forms in other Puranas also. Being born in a Shri Vaishnava family, there seems to be some impression upon his mind of the Vaishnavite cult also, though its form has become rather heterodox due to the effect of modernization on the mind of the poet. This is proved by the study of such poems as "Mythologies-1," Mythologies-2," "Zoo Gardens Revisited," and "Moulting,". In the two "Mythologies" poems the first one is an invocation to the Lord Krishna recounting the incident of how Putana trying to kill him by making him suck at her poisoned nipples was herself killed when Krishna sucked away her life. The second one narrates though in an alluding manner about the incarnation of the man-lion (Nara Simha) form of the lord to kill the demon King, Hiranya Kashipu, who had received the boon not to be killed in the sky or on the earth, at indoors or outdoors, by animal or man and by any type of weapon that is manufactured. In "Zoo Gardens Revisited," the poet calls and describes the lord in the given manner:

> ... Lord of lion face, boar snout, and fish eyes,
> killer of killer cranes,
> shepherd or rampant elephants ...
> (Zoo Garden Revisited, *Second Sight* 154).

In the above description the poet simultaneously invokes all the incarnations like the man-lion, boar (Varaha), fish (Matsya) and Krishna, in which the lord appeared in different ages to redeem the good and innocent. In "Moulting," also he calls the lord as "....... Lord of Snakes and eagles" alluding the facts of the lord sleeping on the coils of the great divine cobra, Sesha and riding on the divine eagle, Garuda. This reference also indicates the all-sustaining nature of the Lord by the power of natural balance in this world. It is due to this reason, that even the most opposing factors and creatures, like the snakes and eagles, are equally sustained by the Lord. In yet another poem "Difference," we find him immersed in a mystical contemplation of Lord Vishnu, whose name according to Sanskrit etymology means, 'the all-pervading one'. In quite a radical tone, he speaks of the idolatrous practices of the Hindus in a satirical manner. Yet, suddenly he gets a vision of Vishnu who, blue as the sky is infinite and all pervading like it. Trying to comprehend the divine form in its entirety, the poet at last accepts his defeat. In his own words, identical to a true devotee's expression of complete incapability and submissiveness, he says:

> But I know I've no way at all of telling
> The look,
> If any, on his face, or of catching
> The rumoured beat of his extraordinary heart.
> (*Collected Poems* 173).

All these above descriptions, without any doubt indicate towards Lord Vishnu, the presiding deity of the Vaishnavaite Cult, who is famous in Hindu mythology for taking various incarnations. It also indicates towards the strong affinity shared by the poet with the Vaishnava cult, with which, he in fact, had a family bonding.

In his seemingly spiritual poems and those dealing with mythologies and legends, one can also notice his close affinity to his Dravidian tradition. In his famous poem "Prayers to Lord Murugan," which like Ezekiel's "Hymns in Darkness," is a very unique and modern form of prayer, breaking all conventional methods of praying, he prays to the highly popular – Dravidian deity of youth, beauty and fertility, Murugan or Subrahmanya Karttikeya, as his Aryanised form is generally known now-a-days. In this poem his asking for the destruction of all the illusory myths created by not only the British colonists but by the Orthodox Indian Sanskrit scholars also, may remind one of the Tamil separatist movement which started when after the drafting of our national constitution – Hindi was declared as the national language. This also shows his deep and even orthodox clinging to his roots. Other poems which refer to South Indian and especially Tamil legends are "Mythologies-3," and "Fear no Fall,". In the third poem of the "Mythologies" series the poet gives a narration of Mahadevi Yakka, the great Tamil female devotee of Shiva. On the first night of her married life she instead of indulging in sex with her husband sat to meditate upon Lord Shiva. Unable to control his desire of enjoying her beautiful body, when her husband touched her, she fled from the house and found the great Lord, the centre of her devotion was standing in wait for her, riding on his divine bull. Yet, another poem "Fear No Fall," from his last volume *The Black Hen* (1995) draws its source form the legend of the famous Tamil Saint Arunagiri – Nathar. Known as Arunagiri in his youth, he was corrupt and licentious of the worst kind. Due to this reckless life of debauchery and other vile practices, his whole body became infected with various venereal diseases. One day tired of this cursed life, he tried to end his life by jumping from a high place. But an old man saved him and curing him of all his diseases, asked him to sing a song in praise of Murugan. Finding him unable to sing, the old man who was none other than Lord Murugan himself gave the first line and vanished. The young man then became a true saint and dedicated his life to meditate upon and sing praises of Lord Murugan.

One can also find his knowledge of common folklore in his poem "No fifth Man," which narrates a tale very common throughout India. Apart from these poems his modern rationalist approach towards the conventional matters can be seen in poems such as "The Guru," and "A River,". The first poem like Ezekiel's "Guru," is a satire upon the stereotype godmen found in multitudes now-a-days. The poem also suggests giving them a taste of their own medicine by applying their absurd advices upon themselves. In "A River," he condemns the poetic virtues of the River Vaigai flowing near the city of Madurai. While the ancient Tamil poets described it as plentiful and beautiful, the poet brings before us the opposite picture. The river becomes full only in the rainy season. In summer it is reduced to a mere trickle. Also, when it becomes full it causes great damage to life and property in the villages situated near its banks. The great tragedy that occurs due to the floods is indicated by the washing away of the cows called Gopi and Brinda, and a pregnant woman expecting twins with no dissimilar physical characteristic. In this way, he also like Ezekiel and Mahapatra, breaks away from the false or worthless conventions whether in the social or religious, or in the literacy sphere.

Finally, one can also see a very native type of English in his poem with use of native terms, concepts and symbols which contribute in expanding the volume of the Indian English vocabulary. Like Mahapatra's contribution of highlighting Oriya aspects into English poetry, his contribution is spectacular in bringing very authentic Dravidian elements into Indian English poetry. His poetry can be assessed in Tagi Ali Mirza's words: "Ramanujan's work bears the impress of all great poetry turning the ephemeral into the permanent articulating the predicament of whole people in verse which at one and the same time is charged with emotion and has the detachment of great art" (Qtd. by Rukhaiyar 129).

Thus we can very well conclude by contemplating over all the above facts and examples, in a serious manner that Ramanujan though doubly dislocated due to his physical dislocation from India, is very well attached to his local roots of culture and tradition and thereby succeeds in the criteria of being relocated to one's own roots. Last but not least, we find that the Indian English poets have successfully persevered through a most strenuous internal and external conflict. At great odds in regard to determine their real identity, they have spent the major part of their lives either in search of it or in forging a new one, ultimately, we find them moving towards the 'centre' from the 'peripheral' or 'marginal' states of their existence. This shows that they have prevailed over all hurdles in their path to achieve a new identity with regard to their cultural roots.

WORKS CITED

Beauvoir, Simone de. *The Second Sex.* Trans. H.M.Parshley. London: Four Square Books, 1949. Print.

Bhabha, Homi K. *Location of Culture. London:* Routledge, 1994. Print

Bhadra, Gautam. *Subaltem Studies X: Writings on South Asian History And Society.* New Delhi: Oxford University Press, 2000. Print.

Das, Bijay Kumar. *The Poetry of Jayanta Mahapatra.* New Delhi:1992. Print.

Das, Bijay Kumar. *Twentieth Century Literary Criticism.* New Delhi: Atlantic Publisher and Distributers, 1998. Print.

Das, Kamala. *The Old Playhouse and Other Poems.* Bombay: Orient Longman Limited, 1973. Print.

Das, Kamala. *Summer in Calcutta.* New Delhi: Everest Press,1965.Print.

Das, Kamala. *The Descendent,* Calcutta: Writers Workshop, 1967. Print.

Dwivedi, A.N.*Kamla Das and her Poetry.* Delhi: Doaba House Bookseller and Publishers,1983. Print.

Ezekiel, Nissim. *Collected Poems.* New Delhi: Oxford University Press,1989. Print.

Ghosh, N.K. *Essays on Nissim Ezekiel.* Ed. T.R. Sharma. Meerut: Salabh Prakashan, 1994. print.

Kallury, Syamala and Anjana N. Dev. "Jayanta Mahapatra's India: Because I cannot grow A Rose, I Plant the Seeds of the Thistle." *The Indian Imagination of Jayanta Mahapatra.* Ed. Jaydeep Sarangi and Gauri Shankar Jha. New Delhi: Sarup and Sons, 2006. Print.

King, Bruce. *Modern India Poetry in English*. New Delhi: Oxford University Press, 1987. Print.

Kudchedkar, Shirin. "Feminist Literary Criticism: The Ground Work." *Journal of Literary Criticism*. 8:1(June 1996): 34. Print.

Kottiswai. W.S. *Post modern Feminist Writers*. New Delhi: Sarup and Sons, 2008. Print.

Mahapatra, Jayanta. *Dispossessed Nests*. Jaipur: Nirala Publications, 1986. Print.

_____. *Random Descent*. Bhubaneswar: Third Eye Communications, 2005. Print.

_____. *Selected Poems*. New Delhi: Oxford University Press, 1987. Print.

Mishra, Soubhagya K. The Largest Circle- A Reading of Jayanta Mahapatra's "Relationship" *The Literary Endavour* IX (1987-88):30. Print.

Mulloo, Anand. *Voices of The Indian Diaspora*. Delhi: Motilal Benarsidas,2007. Print.

Nabar, Vrinda. *The Endless Female Hunger: A Study of Kamala Das*. New Delhi: Sterling Publisher Pvt Ltd., 1994. Print.

Naik, M.K. *Studies in Indian Poetry in English*. New Delhi: Sterling Publishers, 1987. Print.

Naik, M.K. "Nissim Ezekiel and Alienation." *The Journal Of Indian Witing In English*. 14(1986): 49-57. Print.

Nagrajan, S. "A.K.Ramanujan" *Studies in Indian Poetry in English*. Ed. U.S.Rukhaiyar. New Delhi: Sarup and Sons, 2002. Print.

Nayar, Pramod Kumar. *Postcolonial Literature:An Introduction 1st Edition*. New Delhi: Dorling Kindersley Ltd., 2008. Print.

Paul, S.K and Amarnath Prasad. *Indian Poetry in English: Roots and Bloosoms*. New Delhi: Sarup and Sons, 2007. Print.

Prasad, Amarnath and S.K. Paul. ed. *Feminism in Indian Writing in English*. New Delhi: Sarup and Sons, 2006. Print.

Ramanujam, A.K. *Collected Poems*. New Delhi: Oxford University Press, 2005. Print.

Rukhaiyar, U.S. and Amarnath Prasad. *Studies in Indian Poetry in English*. New Delhi: Sarup and Sons, 2002. Print.

Sarangi, Jaydeep and Gouri Shankar Jha. ed. *The Indian Imagination of Jayanta Mahapatra*. New Delhi: Sarup and Sons,2006. Print.

Singh, Kanwar Dinesh. *Feminism and Post-Feminism: The Context of Modern Indian Women Poets Writing in English*. New Delhi: Sarup and Sons,2004. Print.

Souza, Eunice de..ed. *Nine Indian Women Poet An Anthology*. New Delhi: Oxford University Press, 1989. Print.

Surendran, K.V. *Indian Writing Critical Prespectives*. New Delhi: Oxford University Press, 2000. Print.

Upadhaya, Onkar Nath. *Perspectives on Indian Diaspora*. New Delhi: Sarup Book Publishers, 2014. Print.

CHAPTER 4

CENTRE AND PERIPHERY AS A THEMATIC CONCERN WITH THESE POETS

The introduction of 'Postcolonialism' ushered a new age of introspects and retrospects into the literary circles of the modern world. It led to a deep psychological and socio-cultural analysis of not only the colonizers but also the colonized subjects. It became a mouthpiece for the erstwhile colonies to address their grievances and views regarding the self-proclaimed welfare work of their colonizing masters. It also held to them the stage from which they could answer back to all the biased allegations and claims made by the West regarding the East. The 'postcolonial discourse' as it is stated, gave scope to all sections and groups of the societies which had borne the yoke of slavery, silently for centuries. It touched various intimate aspects of the colonized native societies and tried to find out the answers to their problems. As per the variations in the nature of their problems, various theories came into existence to interpret and solve these problems according to their own view points. So, starting from the 'Psycho-analytical' approach of Franz Fanon to the 'Orientalism' of Edward said, there was a spree of theories which emerged on the scene to define the problems of the native population and the solutions to it from the viewpoint of the natives. However, along with the problems of the colonial rule, some new problems also grew up in the postcolonial period. One such was the problem of 'marginalisation'. In the words of Gayatri Spivak: "The study of colonial discourse, directly released by work such as Said's, has .... blossomed into a garden where the marginal can speak and be spoken, even spoken for" (Spivak 1993, 56)

'Marginality' as a concept is characterized or distinguished by some basic elements like uncertainty of identity, feelings of inferiority, scorn for one's own culture and society. As such elements are the major themes of the postcolonial Indian English poetry; there is no surprise in the fact that it is branded as a 'marginalized' literature. Furthermore, with the end of the British rule, the exclusive honour and position, enjoyed by English came to an end. The centre of literary activities in India was thus occupied by the national language i.e. Hindi, as well as other vernaculars. The position of English was pushed to the margins, as now it was the language of the educated or elite sections of the Indian masses. Even there, it was distanced from the Indian ethos due to the western influences like urbanization, unconventionalism and rationalism etc. All major and representative poets of the postcolonial Indian trend have a marked antagonism against the various cultural and traditional elements of the Indian society. Many of them belong to the minority communities like Jews, Christians etc. Others, who belong to the Hindu community are quite unconventional or atheistical in their outlook and approach. Having no deep understanding of the Indian culture and spiritualism, their literary creations became unappealing to the Indian masses. It is only the elite and educated 'Pro-western' sections of the Indian society, who somewhat appreciated their writings. Thus, the postcolonial Indian English poetry became marginalized due to the following social reasons also. The African anthropologist, Diop comments in this regard: "Flight from one's own language is the quickest short-cut to cultural alienation"(Qtd. by Parker and Starkey 5).

Among all the proponents of the Postcolonial theory, the most descriptive analysis of the concept of 'marginalization' is credited to Gayatri Chakravorty Spivak. In her position, it was a case of triple marginalization in the western world. Deepak Kumar Singh has tried to explain and elucidate her situation in the West in the following manner: "In her role of a woman, of an Asian and an immigrant, in the first world, Spivak found the experience of marginality to be a common factor. Inclusion in the main stream, closeness to the centre was possible on given conditions" (Qtd. by Upadhaya 101).

As stated above, the inclusion of the peripheral individuals is done in a politically motivated manner. Some selected individuals are patronized, accepted or assimilated into the inner circles but not as a reconciling gesture but rather as a further alienating gesture. The granting of British citizenship to individual Indians like Nirod C. Chodhury and Salman Rushdie, who apparently have a rather anti-Indian taste, is a direct indication of the antagonistic attitude of the colonizers towards the colonized. It is mainly this antagonism of the colonial masters that the colonized subjects revolt against and try to repudiate. We can sum up the essence of the above stated situations in the following words: "whereas racist colonial regimes and their discourses have asserted that 'Humanity is not one' and privileged the white and the male, postcolonial writers have insisted that the colonized belong to 'the same world and are not absolutely other', and have vigorously affirmed the rights of the silenced to be heard" (*New Casebook*, Parker 6).

In the Indian context, there is no dearth of the causes leading to the marginalization of the Postcolonial Indian English poets. Various factors like alienation from one's socio-cultural ethos, estrangement from the surrounding milieu and a rather objective and scientific approach towards all matters, inspired by western rationalism contribute towards this. All such factors are sufficient enough to make the majority of Indians feel apprehensive of the actual validity or benefit of accepting the postcolonial Indian English poetry. However, in the context, the great mystic intellectual of India, Sri Aurobindo, tries to assuage this fear for the Indian Writing in English in the following words: "It is not true in all cases that one can't write first class things in a learned language. Both in French and English people to whom the language was not native have done remarkable work, although that is rare. (...) I think, as time goes on, people will become more and more polyglot and these mental barriers will begin to disappear" (Iyengar 6). Yet, in this age of rationality, one cannot completely believe upon idealistic visions, much less than prophetic ideas of extraordinary intellectuals. On the rational or practical level also, it seems necessary that a mutual reconciliation should be brought upon to end this linguistic bias. As the present scenario demands, one can refuse neither 'English language' nor 'English contribution to science and technology'; if one sincerely desires to express himself and thrive on a global sphere. So, it becomes inevitable for all the 'marginalized' trends or genres of literature to strive for the centre, as there only lies the true achievement of universal recognition.

Bhabha invents the idea of 'Hybridity' as a viable solution to these problems. In his view it is basically the differences of culture that creates the major part of the marginality problems. For Robert J. C. Young, 'Hybridity' is linked to the problem of marginalization in the following manner:

> Hybridity works in different ways at the same time, according to the cultural, economic and political demands of specific situations. It involves processes of interaction that creates new social spaces to which new meaning are given. These relations enable the articulation of experiences of change in societies splintered by modernity, and they facilitate consequent demands for social transformation (Postcolonialism: A Very Short Introduction 79).

Therefore the solution of the problem lies in a harmonious synthesis of the culture and literature of both the colonized and the colonizer. Each side should come forward in an honest manner so as to understand and learn from each other. Marginalization should not be a thing to be wept upon but to stand and overcome it. He denounces the false spelndour of the marginality studies in the following words:

> The marginal or minority is not the space of celebratory or utopian, self-marginalization.

It is a much more substantial intervention into those justifications of modernity-progress, homogeneity, cultural organicism, the deep nation, the long post that rationalize the authoritarian, 'normalizing' tendencies within culture in the name of national interest . . .
(*Nation and Narration 4).*

However, there are still some points at which doubt lingers. To debunk the idea of 'modernity' is a very heavy price for the common third-world people and they may not be interested in such theories. Still, the present times are witnessing a much active and healthy interaction between the centre and periphery and the trauma of marginality is fast becoming the facts of history. The present scene, in Bhabha's words is: "America leads to Africa; the nations of Europe and Asia meet in Australia; the margins of the nation displace the centre; the peoples of the periphery return to write the history and fiction of the metropolis" (*Nation and Narration* 6).

In the context of the literary tradition of India, the present modern Indian English poetry also has fallen under the area of marginality. Due to various reasons, though English is the most popular and readable language in India after Hindi, English literature as a whole and Modern English Indian poetry especially consist only of the peripheries of the Indian literacy circle both due to quantity and quality. Various critics, both from home and abroad, while praising the modern Indian English poets, accept the fact that their contribution both to Indian and world literature remains highly marginalized. A famous critic and a modern Indian English poet himself, R. Parthasarathy holds the view that compared to the whole poetic tradition of India, the contribution of the English poets remains and will remain marginal. Another prominent Indian critic of Indian English poetry, Shantinath K. Desai, puts before us a stronger and defined opinion:

> One of the characteristics of a marginal or peripheral body of literature is that it is such a loose entity that it can easily become part of other intersecting circle. Thus Indian writing could easily become a part of Anglo-Indian writing, then of English literature, then of commonwealth literature and of course it is always part of Indian literature – though marginal (Indian Writing in English: The predicament of marginality 32 to 33).

He continues his argument by pointing towards the effect of marginality upon the choice of homeland of the modern Indian English Poets. They either move abroad to live there as exiles otherwise they continue to live in India itself but feeling like a stranger in their own home. Their view towards the events happening around is generally detached and their style is ironic, existentialist and historical. While some like Ezekiel feel existentialist anguish, others like Kamala Das are haunted by the guilt conscience, identical to the American confessional poets. Most of them abandon writing poetry after the publication of their first volume and adopt other occupations. Those who continue writing poetry receive the Sahitya Akademi awards for whatever contribution they make to Indian English literature. Thus in this way Shantinath K. Desai presents his own view upon the nature of marginality in context to modern Indian English Poetry.

Another critic, Bruce king in his *Modern Indian Poetry in English* presents yet another opinion in relation to the topic of marginality. According to him, after independence the poets of India faced the challenge that they could never write poetry in English as good as written by the British or American. However, while some orthodox sections of the elite demanded nationalist literature in English, both in subject and style; the poets largely chose subjects and style which were not up to the taste of not only common Indian masses but also that of orthodox and nationalist elite sections of Indian society. One cannot however blame the poets for this as their temperament was formed entirely by their English laden upbringing. Most of them were born in well-educated middle class families where English was commonly spoken. They also received their education in good English medium schools, colleges and universities and often went abroad for higher studies. Thus brought up in an environment of English language, literature and culture, they felt a natural intimacy with them instead of their own native or national culture, tradition, language and literature. After studies also, most of them travelled abroad either in search of knowledge or jobs. While some of them settled there permanently others returned with determined tastes and choices. Some poets like Nissim Ezekiel returned early disillusioned of the so-called western greatness, while some like Dom Moraes stayed in foreign countries for a long time. Yet, some more like Deb Kumar Das and A.K. Ramanujan became permanent exiles. In this way, more or less all of them were influenced or overcame by the west. They were alienated not only by their upbringing and education but also by their radical views about their own religious and cultural traditions. Many of them can be purely branded as rebels to their religion and community.

The T.S. Eliot of modern Indian English Poetry, Nissim Ezekiel is a highly important figure in the field of Indian English Literature. Like most of his contemporaries, he also had to face the marginality complex. However, there are some facts which make his problem of marginalization more complicated and assume a highly varied form. They are:

i) As a descendant of the Bene-Israel Jewish tribe, that had taken refuge in India many centuries ago, he lacks any real Indian roots, making him a natural outsider.

ii) As he is not a Hindu, he is unable to take inspiration from ancient India. He therefore turns to modern India, especially the almost westernized city of Bombay. In this way, he also gets alienated from the mainstream Indian Culture.

iii) An existential anguish in him caused by the lack of faith in religion, philosophy and tradition. This further alienates him from his own social existence.

The above facts illustrate the uniqueness of Ezekiel's confusion over his inability to connect himself with the conditions that give him a social identity. He feels a sense of isolation that makes him a stranger in his own city and community. His early poems throw light upon the various causes which slowly created this alien consciousness in his mind. They show his consciousness of being a permanent expatriate in India. But later on, his poems take the theme of his choice to stay on in India. It is his struggle between the dual impulses which keeps his poetic imagination between the two ends of his cultural past and his highly modern and rational surroundings in America. The critic Kurup comments in this context that: "If his Jewishness denies the poet a background he might have shared with his Indian society, his recognition of his place and status gives him an ensured ground underfoot from which to operate with an unqualified deftness" (Qtd. by Raghunath sahoo 63).

Particularly, in his famous poem "Background Casually," he has recounted various experiences of his own, which made him realize his marginalized existence in the society. In the beginning of the poem, telling about his birth, he speaks himself of as a 'poet-rascal-clown'. This first line itself speaks of the negative attitude of the poet towards his own wretched existence. The above mentioned line of the first stanza also describes the emaciated health of the poet in his childhood and his inability to learn even the most common games of children. The following two stanzas show its predicament of studying in a highly hostile environment in a very lucid manner:

> I went Roman Catholic School,
> A mugging Jew among the wolves.
> They told me I had killed Christ,
> That year I won the scripture prize.
> A Muslim Sportsman boxed my ears.
>
> I grew in terror of the strong
> But undernourished Hindu lads,
> Their prepositions always wrong,
> Repelled me by passivity.
> One noisy day I used a Knife
> (Collected Poems 179).

Not only did he face religious prejudices in his childhood but also was tortured by an inner sense of scepticism towards his own religion. During his higher studies at London, he also underwent the trauma of sexual isolation from which he recovered due to an affair with a woman, but the affair also didn't last long. Finally dejected with his various failures, he returned to India but here also he didn't feel at home. However he got married and tried different jobs but became unsuccessful in them. This reminded him of his ancestors of whom everyone except one followed their traditional occupation of crushing oil seeds. The exceptional one joined the British army and fought for them. The poet thinks himself to be inspired by him though he never thought of joining the armed forces. All these experiences inspired poetic ability in his mind. But for a time period, he wasn't sure of it. After some time, he was able to strike the required balance between his failure in work and the troubled thoughts in his mind and decides to make the best out of them in his poetry. At last he also exclaims that though foreigners think him to be isolated from his Indian surroundings, yet he is a part of it. Though others may decide to leave it, he has decided to live here and here only. This shows that now finally the poet has come up with a commitment and has also adapted himself to this country despite all isolation, irritation and prejudices.

Along with, "Background Casually," there are a lot of other poems which throw light upon this process of alienation taking place within the mind of the poet. The poems like "In Emptiness," "Communication," "Minority poem," and collection of poems like *The Unfinished Man* published in 1960 and *The Exact Name* in 1965 stand exactly in the same category and help the readers have a view of the tumult taking place in the mind of the reader. In the Poem "In Emptiness," the poet confesses his helplessness over giving over totally to the faculties of only reason or emotion either. In "Minority Poem," he in the guise of poetic words, speaks out the sum of his feelings towards the racial prejudice, he faces in the city of Bombay. However he is not only pointing out the native citizens, who in his words 'will never give up their mantras, old or new', but also his own community members, about whom he says:

> And you, uneasy
> Orphan of their racial
> Memories, merely
> Polish up your alien
> Techniques of observation,
> While the city burns
> (*Collected Poems* 236)

In the poem titled "Song Desolation," the poet reaches the height of isolation by isolating himself from his own existence. His deep existential anguish seems to pour from the following words:

> Write, I have nothing to say,
> confess it to the cold domestic room,
> Worked the long day,
> Noticed nothing bloom (103).

Likewise, in his poetic volume *The Unfinished Man,* each poem in itself is an expression of his marginal position in context to not only his country, city, community but also his own self. All the poems, like "Urban," "Enterprise'" "A Morning Walk," and other such are full of the same sense of being separate from everything and everybody and also the inability to communicate with them successfully. In the last poem, entitled "Jamini Roy," he seems to be envious of the poet of the same name, as he is firmly rooted in his tradition and doesn't suffer with the marginalization complex. In the words to Ezekiel:

> He started with a different style,
> He travelled, so he found his roots.
> His rage became a quiet smile.
> Prolific in its proper roots (125).

In another volume, *The Exact Name,* he seems to struggle to get hold of the main stream Indian Culture from which he feels isolated. His poems in this volume like "Philosophy," "Night of the scorpion," "In India," and "Perspective," etc. show not only the sense of isolation like the previous volumes but also the will to gain a place in the centre of the cultural arena.

In spite of all these expressions of discomfiture and a strong sense of alienation, we cannot deny that a very persistent Indian consciousness prevails throughout the length and breadth of his poetry. Any reader, going through his poems, can't fail to observe that all his images of wretchedness, poverty and squalor are undoubtedly derived and inspired from the Indian landscapes. All his poems depicting the pathetic state of Indian cities like "Island," "In India," "At the Hotel," "A Morning Walk," and "In The Theater," etc. have the unmistakable mark of Bombay on them. Similarly, his poems on the rural conditions of India like "Night of the Scorpion," "Rural Suite," "In The Country Cottage," and "The Truth about the Floods," are all true to the rural scenario of India. In the poem "On Bellasis Road," he presents the predicaments of an average Indian prostitute, who is dependent for her daily sustenance upon such people, who in turn are themselves daily wage earners:

> She doesn't glance at me,
> Waiting for her
> Hawker or mill-worker,
> Coolie or bird-man
> Fortune-teller,
> Pavement man of medicine
> Or street-barber on the move
> (*Collected Poems* 189).

The multi-faceted corruption in India frequently figures in his poems like "Guru," and "The Truth about the Flood," with poems like "The Railway Clerk," presenting before us the dilemma of the middle class people due to financial constraints. "The Truth about Dhanya," and "Ganga," are similarly, poems upon our biased negative thoughts and outlook towards the poor lower sections of our society.

All the above stated facts undoubtedly are enough to induce existentialist anguish and a sense of alienation from such an unwanted and repulsive milieu. The poet himself, unhesitatingly, expresses such feelings in his poems like "Poem of the Separation," "For Satish Gujaral," and "A Small Summit,". In the last poem, he blatantly speaks of his intensity of alienation felt with the country in which he was born:

> Do I belong, I wonder
> To the common plain? A better thought.
> I know that I would rather
> Suffers somewhere else
> Than be at home
> Among the accepted styles
> (Collected Poems 153).

Yet, despite all the wretchedness and alienation, the poet gradually seems to develop a strong affinity and sympathy with his surroundings. His poems like "Tribute to the Upanishads," and "From very Indian poems in Indian English," speak about his evolution or rather to say 'hybridization' of the poet on the socio-cultural and spiritual spheres of Indian ethos. In other poems like "Background Casually," and "Minority poem," he confesses that he has now achieved a state of symbiosis with the land and as well as the people of India. Even many of his minor poems like "Passion poems," prove his interest in and knowledge of Hindu religion, myth and culture. All these jointly point to the fact that the poet has ultimately left his marginal position to merge with the centre. This discovery of roots or rather of one's own identity, by the poet has been well summed up in the words of Garman: "The acceptance of the Indian reality is an important characteristic of Ezekiel's poetry. He is not caustically critical of the Indian cities like Nirad C.Chaudhori. But his poems contain an image of urbanity. Ezekiel seeks his identity in the country and its incongruities" (Qtd. by C. Annalatha Devi, *Indian Poetry in English: Roots…* 145)

Thus, in observation of all the above given facts, we can see that Ezekiel in his literary pursuit was actually marginalized due to the problems of language, culture and other such fundamental problems. Yet, like all other poets of repute he has struggled to overcome what he lacks and to a large extent he has also been successful in it. Therefore we can only say that Ezekiel is a poet who though was earlier marginalized, has well overcome it through his continuous and earnest struggle.

After Ezekiel, the greatest modern Indian English Poet, who comes to the mind of those, well-read in the history of Indian English literature from its starting to the present, is none other than, Jayanta Mahapatra. He has, though born in the backward state of Odisha, been able to earn fame in the most distant lands, wherever English Poetry is read. His contribution to the Indian Poetry is manifold as his poetry not only forms a new vocabulary of Indian English terms but also a new set of Indian and especially Odia symbols. His poetry abounds not only in humanist, social and spiritual concerns but also with facts about the history, culture and geography of Odisha. After publishing his first volume of poetry *Close the Sky Ten by Ten* in the year of 1971, he has been relentlessly busy in producing volumes of poetry, one by one, each one unique in its artistic skill, beauty and power of impression. Like most of his contemporaries, he also is endowed with a deep concern for human values, rationalism and liberalism in the sphere of society and religion. He is a first rate free thinker with an open mind and alert ear for all types of matter. He is unreserved in any sphere concerned with humanity, society or religion, as can be well proved by his poems on these things. His poems make the history, geography, culture, natural beauty and social conditions of Odisha appear before one's own eyes of imagination. Though a true modernist with deep rational outlook, he is very strongly attached to his native land, culture and religion in a way which seems much stronger than even A.K. Ramanujan's. His writings with their evocation of Odisha in her various forms and faces, remind one of Judith Wright's views upon the relation of a poet with his own country: "Before One's country can become an accepted backgrounds against which the poet's and novelist's imagination can move unhindered, it must be observed, understood, described as it were, absorbed. The writer must be at peace with his landscape before he can confidently turn to its human figures" (Qtd. by Devindra Kohli 54-70).

However, this affinity to one's own land and landscape with its myths and tradition should not lead a person to make the opinion that the poet is of an emotional temperament like Keats and Shelley. Rather the approach of the poet to his surroundings is that of a scientist who observes everything in a strict analytical manner. In fact, to do justice to him, we can say that he has his own unique and special outlook which scrutinizes every matter and thing in an equal manner. All these characteristics of him thus combine to make him a glowing star in the sky of Indian English poetry and the pride of Orissa.

Though there is no doubt about the vitality and vigour of his poetry, yet there are some facts which like in the case of all his contemporaries, haunt him also. His choice for English as his creative medium, his highly un-orthodox views upon crucial social matters, and his thoughts estranged from the general public, tend him towards marginalization, like most of his co-poets. There are a vast number of poems in his fourteen volumes of poetry; all of them in an equivocal manner speak of the way in which the poet feels himself marginalized from the centre of his social sphere. This marginalized consciousness has stuck to him from as early as 1976, the year in which he published his fourth volume of poetry *A Rain Of Rites*. In that volume there are some particular poems like "Dawn at Puri," "Sunburst," and "Hunger," which speak of the radical views of the poet which exclude him from the general crowd. The first poem starts with the description of a skull upon the holy sands of the famous temple-town of Puri. The skull acts as a symbol of death in whose shadow the widows described in the poem live constantly. They are merely breathing corpses as they have been made bereft of all joys, desires and imaginations by the society from the day of the death of their husband. It is as if they have also died with their husbands in an informal manner and are waiting only to get a formal death certificate. This poem in fact satrises the holiness associated with the life led by these unfortunate women. The second poem titled "Sunbrust," heavily criticizes the traditional and orthodox repression of sexual desires in the young generation whereas the older generation engages itself in various vulgar traditions like making animals have sex in the open where everyone can see it. This poem is a denouncement of the hypocrisy prevalent in the Indian society, by the poet. In the third poem "Hunger," it narrates the sad tale of a poor fisherman who is forced to push his own young daughter into the hellish profession of prostitution. In his poem "The whorehouse in a Calcutta Street," the poet describes the rampant exploitation of women leading to the deadening of their emotions and the mechanization of their sexual response.

Like a girl holding on to your wide wilderness,
As though it were real, as though the renewing voice
Tore the member of your half-women mind
When, like a door, her words close behind:
'Hurry, will you? Let me go,
And her lonely breath thrashed against your kind.
(*A Rain of Rites* 18)

Such abuse of women's dignity is also practiced in most of the slums in India, where survival demands a rather heavy price in term of sacrificing one's self respect. The poet portrays their predicament in the most touching manner in the poem "Slum,":

The familiar old whore on the road
Splits open in the Sugary dusk,
Her tired breasts trailing me everywhere:
Where the jackals find the rotting carcass
And I turn around
To avoid my fiery eyes in the glass; there stands
Only a lonely girl, beaten in battle, all mine,
Sadly licking the blood from my crazed smile
(*The False Start* 29).

In this manner, the poet has depicted the pathetic condition of the whores or prostitutes. They are both forced into this profession and victimized by the men. Though coveted for the insatiable aggressive lust of the masculine section, they are never accepted into the folds of the society in any manner. Their predicament has been summed up by the critic Neha Misra in the following words: "women have been marginalized and kept on the periphery, blamed and harassed, used and abused. Even for writers, she was only an object and never the subject. Literary misogyny compelled her to remain a non-entity. Impotent and disagreeable, she was over flooded with the rusty life of no importance"(203).

It presents the sad condition of the poor sections of our society whose poverty leads them to the lowest depths of moral degradation. Yet another poem "Dhauli," from his fifth volume *Waiting* (1976) stands apart for its exclusive outlook held by the poet. While the whole of India glorifies the battle of Kalinga which turned the heartless emperor Ashoka into a kind and religious Buddhist missionary, no one ever thinks of the pains caused by the battle to Odisha and its people. Today, even Odisha also seems to have forgotten the tragedy of the battle and seems to take pride in its occurrence on its land. However, separate from all this, the poet is in no mood to forgive Ashoka, as is reflected from the last stanza of the poem:

> ... the measure of Ashoka's suffering
> Does not appear enough.
> The place of his pain peers lamentably
> From among the pains of the dead
> (*Selected Poems* 22).

Though there is no scarcity of such poems, yet nothing seems to stand equal to his poetic masterpiece *Relationship* (1980). This poem in its starting calls Odisha as the land of 'forbidding myth'. This term symbolizes that the people of the land are now not at all interested in keeping up with all the glory of their myths and traditions. The poem which in very lofty words describes the ancient Odisha; rich by its commerce spread all over the world, beautiful both by its natural beauty and temples made by great sculptors and formidable due to its brave warrior sons. The poet is pained with loss of glory of his motherland. His acute pain can be gauged by the following lines:

> It is hard to tell now
> what opened the anxious skies
> how the age old proud stones
> lost their strength and fell
> and how the waters of Daya
> stank with the bodies of my ancestors
> my eyes close now
> because of the fear that moves my skin
> (Dhaulagiri, *Waiting* 14)

The last line deserves special attention as it speaks of the difficult conditions through which the poet is struggling. The people of his own land are reluctant to remember and feel proud, much less than trying to retain back, the old golden days of Odisha.

There are many poems in his other volumes like *Life Signs* (1983) in which a poem "The Lost Children of America," speaks of the moral and spiritual degradation of our country to which people from all over the world come to receive spiritual guidance. His latest poetic volume *Random Descent* published in 2005 abounds in such poems which give us a direct view of the pained and troubled mind of the poet. A large number of poems such as "Shadow," "Freedom," "One Evening, One Day, Standing in Corner," "The Stones," "Declining God,"

"Because I am the One," and "The Land That is Not," are glowing examples of the causes and effects of the poet's marginalized status. In the poem titled "Freedom," the poet gives his view that the present Odisha is not the place where his mind and heart actually reside. In his words:

> At times, as I watch,
> it seems as though my country's body
> floats down somewhere on the river.
> left alone, I grow into
> a half-disembodied bamboo,
> its lower part sunk
> into itself on the bank
> (Freedom 32)

This anguish further like the existentialists proceeds further to criticize and even decline God himself. In his poem "Declining Gods," the poet seems severely opposed to the existence of anything called 'God':

> A God of concrete walls can't want
> what he doesn't know exists. But pain's blood is
> human.
> The metaphor is always adrift
> in the waters of the strong telling the weak what
> to do
> (Declining Gods 66).

All these feelings at last seem to culminate in his poem "The Land That is Not," in which he gives a detailed description of the horrible situations of our country torn by communal hatred, corruption and other myriad vices. His opening line is enough to declare his decision:

> The land some love to call holy
> is not the one I want to live in
> (The Land That is Not 70).

Still, one should not surmise from the poems referred till now, that the poet has no affinity with his country or his people. On the contrary, he possesses a most genuine spirit of patriotic sympathy, which makes him co-relate himself with all the pains, sufferings, tragedies and loss occurring in the lives of the millions, who are his fellow citizens. His strong feelings of sympathy for these unfortunate masses are duly expressed in these lines:

> And they are close to me, I know
> Those silent people, uninvolved, who do not use
> the calendar,
> Who parade with the eyes of lonely mountains,
> Who grow like tough coarse grass from cracked
> pavements
> Who wake me up in the cold mists of night
> And my frightened glance comes and goes
> Like a silence flattened against the shaken time.
> (*A Father's Hours* 38).

With such a strong affectionate feeling for the poor, marginalized, backward and suppressed sections of the Indian society, he can in no manner be stated as a 'marginalized' poet. The critic Dilip Chitre rightly comments: "His (Mahapatra's) verse is free and moves slowly and smoothly. It is almost languid in its metaphysical poise until suddenly, he transforms elemental visual images of Indian nature and traditional rural life into memorable metaphors. Mahapatra is what the Indian poet writing in English is supposed to be; an interpreter of unique, complex and exotic culture through its landscape and people" (199).

Thus, we can sum up from all above examples and observations that due to his modernist approach, revolutionary ideology and radical views, the poet in spite of his firm roots in his culture and traditions stands truly marginalized. Even his best poems representing Oriya culture and tradition have in them a spirit of revolt against the much accepted norms of the traditional society of Odisha. Though physically the poet is present in the modern Odisha, yet in truth his heart and mind still cling to the ancient Kalinga shining with glory, rich in wealth and fabulously powerful.

Kamala Das, as we know is one of the most prominent figures in the sphere of modern Indian English Literature. Her contribution to the English poetry in Modern India is very much comparable to Ezekiel or Jayanta Mohapatra and yet owns a uniqueness of its very own kind. She started a very new trend of feminist poetry that was for the first time not idealistic or romantic like the former colonial poets. Instead, it was very much realistic and had the capacity of showing the very depths of the psyche of the Indian women and Indian society. Her poems grasp a very large number of subjects with a very deep analysis of them. They present a very minute and detailed observation of various matters such as the backwardness in Indian society, the prejudices against the Indian Women, the forced repression of the desires of the

Indian women, the regional conflict in India, the controversy upon the importance of English and the corruption breeding under the splendour of the metro cities. However, in spite of all these references to India, her writings show a distinct marginal tinge, due to the highly unconventional and bold observation of the poet. She as a poet has for the first time used such vocabularies which till now were never used in the conventional Indian English poetry. The uniqueness of these words are that not only they are quite odd and unconventional but also highly vulgar. The words such as 'menstrual blood', 'flesh', and 'bones and mire' cause a nauseating effect on the readers and hearers. The explicit pasteurization of love-making and copulation makes the Indian readers with a conventional mindset to feel outraged. Except for some of her highly exclusive poems related with Krishna and other subjects, almost all her poems display these features due to which her poetry moves far away from the mainstream Indian poetry. The major characteristic of her poetry is that it reveals the corrupt, decaying and morbid aspects of the present society with such liveliness that the orthodox readers, who always try to avoid and overlook even the mention of such things get involved. In her major poems like "An Introduction," "The Looking Glass," "The Invitation," and "The Freaks," she paints very bleak and gruesome pictures of the conditions in real life that Indian women have to face even today. For knowing all such facts which cause the marginal aspects of her poems, let us make a further deep study.

Indian women have remained as a puppet or property in the hands of patriarchy or male dominated social system. Her rights to education, marriage by her own will or to claim share in paternal property were never given emphasis. As a conscious human being, capable of deciding her own course of life, her existence was never given the freedom of expression or action. Even her rights were strictly curbed on the basis of the scriptural authority of the texts like *Manu Smriti*, *Shukra Neeti* and various other Dharmashastras. The predicament of women in India especially that of the Hindu women, can be surmised by the very fact that not only was she bound by rules throughout her life but her death was also generally decided by the male patriarchy. The texts like *Garuda Puranam,* greatly extolled the spiritual merit that a woman obtains by becoming 'Sati' or immolating herself on the funeral pyre of her husband. If at all a woman lived as a widow, she was considered as something unholy or ominous. Her diet according to the scriptures was devoid of all taste and nourishment. In fact, she was indirectly expected to starve herself to death gradually by malnutrition. How she was denied even the right to life can be proved by the practice of female infanticide, still rampant in most of the Indian states. All this was the cause which led to the formation of Kamala Das as a heterodox, anti-conventional poet. In her own words she has stated: "I needed to disturb society out of its complacence. I found the complacence a very ugly state. I wanted to make woman of my generation feel that if men could do something wrong; they could do it themselves too. I wanted them to realize that they were equal. I wanted to remove gender difference" (Qtd. by Devika M.P. *Indian Poetry in English...* 111-112).

Though people refer to Kamala Das as a poet of sex, sensuality and feminine interests, the major part of her poetry is about the sub-ordination, exploitation and subjugation of the Indian women as well as the other backward or marginalized sections of the Indian society. She is aware of the fact that women on a scientific level have no separate existence from men as both are the two sides of the same coin. Yet, it is on the socio-economic and political levels, she wants the empowerment and self-sufficiency of the women. In the words of R.K. Mishra: "In the realms of post-modern literature, Kamala Das occupies a very significant position as a rebel against the tradition of marginalization of women in Indian society. She is widely acclaimed as a revolutionary poet for having raised in poetry her voice rebelliously against the patriarchal dominance which is the causal factor for subordination of women to men in Indian society" (260). In a number of her poems like "The Millionaires at Marine Drive," "Ode to a Lynx," and "The Freaks," she has revealed the hypocrisy and insincerity of the emotional expressions of the males. For example, in the poem" The Millionaires at Marine Drive," she discloses in a rather outspoken manner of the unthinkably vulgar opportunist tendencies of the Indian male mind. There she says how on the solemn occasion of her grandmother's death, many male persons (mostly her own relatives) tried to grope her body in the most indecent manner on the pretext of consoling her or expressing their sympathy to her. The following lines are potent enough to shock the sensibility of any person regarding the concepts about Indian male psychology:

> ... all the hands
> The great brown thieving hands groped beneath my
> clothes, their fire was that of a arsonist's,
> warmth was not their aim...
> (*Collected Poems* 197)

In short, she was the first female poet of India to shake the very foundations of patriarchal dominance in the sphere of Indian English literature. Side by side, she also prepared the ground for a pro-feminist revolution on the socio-political level, leading to the gradual empowerment and emancipation of the Indian women.

Kamala Das as an individual shows highly controversial personality with revolutionary ideas about sex, extramarital relationship and others, which are considered as taboo subjects for Indian women. She thinks that perfect sexual pleasure is the most truthful expression of actual love. In her view, this sexual gratification of love is more necessary than showing faithfulness to the uncaring husband. In her own personal life she considers the show of love from her husband as "a gilded/ empty container, good for show" (Captive 17). Thus, frustrated by this she asks as if to all the womankind on the earth:

> Woman, is this happiness, this laying buried
> Beneath a man ?
> (The Conflagration 20).

How much she hates the docile submission of the wives to their husbands in the traditional Indian way can be ascertained by these lines, from her famous poem "The Old Play house,":

> Cowering
> Beneath your monstrous ego I ate the magic loaf and
> Became a dwarf.
> I lost my will and reason, to all your
> questions I mumbled incoherent replies (1).

The above effects finally result into the death of the joyful spirit of the poet which she describes in the same poem in the following lines:

> There is No more singing, no more a dance,
> my mind is an old play house with all its lights
> put out
> (The Old Playhouse and Other Poems 1).

In the poem "The Stone Age," she outrightly accuses her husband for exploiting her sexually and killing her individuality:

> You turn me into a bird of stone, a granite
> Dove … (51).

The above expressions of a deeply distressed mind such as Kamala's show the trauma, most of the Indian women from traditional background face.

The experience, faced by the poet at last makes her understand what is the real tragedy in a human life. In her own words:

> The tragedy of life
> is not death but growth
> the child growing into adult
> and, growing out of needs …..
> (Composition, *The Descendants* 29).

This fact can be verified by her other poems as "Blood," and others which the poet seems to have written in a nostalgic mood resulting from her unsuccessful adult life. In those poems she fervently misses the innocent and happy moments of her childhood at her ancestral home.

Her search for love, after its failure with the ordinary humans, transcends to the divine realm. She tries to satisfy her thirst for love by meditating upon the divine lover Krishna of the Hindu mythology. In her poems like "Radha," "Radha Krishna," "Lines addressed to a Devadasi," and "Ghanshyam," she has tried to feel the passion of love and devotion, felt by Radha, the fiancée of Krishna or Meera, the great female devotee of Krishna. All these poems speak about the deep and true experience of love for which the poet's soul longed. However the negative and tragic outlook of the poet about the ultimate result of the sexual union taking place between two lovers shows its impact upon her Radha-Krishna concept also. In her poem "The Maggots," from her poetic volume *The Descendants* (1987), she speaks of the tragic state of Radha on the day when Krishna left her forever:

> At Sunset, on the river bank, Krishna
> loved her for the last time and left.
> that night in her husband's arms Radha felt
> so dead that he asked what is wrong
> do you mind my kisses love, and she said
> no, not at all, but thought, what is
> it to the corpse if the maggots nip ?(10).

The above lines make it clear that now the poet has come to a conclusion that however true the lovers may be, still sexual union leads to nothing but a sense of futility. Though this theme is also expressed in her other poems such as "Convicts," and many others of such type, what makes "The Maggots," important is that Kamala Das here, in fact, demeans the divine love play of Radha and Krishna, which no other poet whether ancient or modern, had done before her. These unique attempts of the poet are sometimes branded as heretical or blasphemous. These poems also reveal the alienation of the poet from the general Hindu outlook of religion and divinity. Though it is a known fact that the poet has a firm belief in God, she is also well known for her ridicule to the outer forms of religion and the various social systems and rules sanctioned by it.

Apart from all these examples, perhaps the best example one can give to assert the way the poet became marginalized or rather she made herself marginal is, her poem "An Introduction," from the first volume of poetry written by her, *Summer in Calcutta* published in 1965. In this poem, the poet presents a detailed description of the various facts which clashed with the various conventions laid by her family or society. She had a great liking for English but others discouraged her from it on the ground that she should not give importance to a foreign language. On gaining puberty, she was quickly married to a youngman of sixteen. This man never caused her any physical pain but his gross sexual hunger and other vices caused her immense mental pain. His psychological invasion on her personality shattered her womanliness and she threw away the usual and traditional characteristics of forbearance, humbleness and fidelity found in most of the Indian women in general. After the birth of her first son, she took a new form. Determined to do away with her feminine characteristics, she started wearing male garments and made her hair short. Irritated by this all her relatives and others such started advising her to dress as a girl, behave like a married woman, take up household chores like embroidery, cooking and supervising the servants. These experiences of her, has been recounted in her poetry, in the following manner:

> Dress in sarees, be a girl or be wife,
> …Be embroider, cook or a quarreler
> With servants. Fit in, belong, said the categorizers
> Be Amy or be Kamala. Or, better still be
> Just Madhavikutty.
> (Best of Kamala Das 12-13).

They also told her not to sit upon walls or peep through windows as they were taboos for women. They tried to make her confirm to the traditional role of a married woman. They kept reminding her against behaving independently, unmindfully, desiring for sexual pleasures and crying aloud in an embarrassing manner on being jilted in love. She however, craving for true love, loved another man and developed an extra marital affair from which she derived immense pleasure but not true satisfaction. Still she never felt guilty upon this, as in her view it was not only her but every woman's natural longing for love. She feels amazed upon the false ego of the people around her and especially of her husband. As he remains too busy in his own work, the poet is forced to go alone to a place she wants however odd that may be or however late be the time. She feels herself a strange mixture of contradictions – an adulteress yet feeling ashamed, laughing yet crying in heart, a sinner yet innocent and a one who is loved but also betrayed. She then transcends to the plane of universalism and says that her own joys and sorrows are not different in any way than felt by her other fellow human beings. In fact like all others she also is bound to a personal ego and has an identity she has herself created.

By a detailed study of the above facts and contemplating upon them we can perceive that Kamala Das's marginalization is the result of a culmination of her revolutionary attitude and views about the society, tradition, religion and other subjects which are taboos for a traditional Indian woman like sex, infidelity, extra-marital affairs and adultery. Her poems are like announcement of a war against the orthodox systems of the society. Each of her poems strikes like a bomb shell upon the orthodox systems of the society. Each of her poems strikes like a bomb shell upon the hollow traditions and rules followed by the Indian society for more than a thousand years. She seems to have become disgusted and fed up of all these and have decided to give no place to them in her personal life. Her thinking, attitude and actions; everything goes against even the most essential of the traditions held sacred by the Indian society. As the very same is reflected in her poems, it is but natural for the Indian readers not to show any major interest for her poetry. Thus along with the prejudices and problems of writing in English, all these factors also contribute to the process of her marginalization from the centre of mainstream Indian literary circle.

A. K. Ramanujan, is the only expatriate poet of the five founders of the modern Indian English Poetry. While the other poets like Ezekiel and Shiv K. Kumar, returned to India, disillusioned by their experience of the West, he decided to remain in the West even after fully realizing its true nature. With all the remarkable contribution made by him to Indian English Poetry and his highly unique and fascinating personality, he has emerged as a role model for the Indian expatriate poets. Even after leaving India for so many years and living in America for a long time, adapting himself to its culture and customs totally different from India, India and Indianness don't seem neglected in his poetry. As a modern poet he observes all Indian facts and subjects in a very sharp, radical and rational manner. Though referring frequently to the joint-family system, various religious beliefs, customs, traditions and myths, he presents them in an unconventional manner, due to which all these popular and much well-known subjects appear new even to the Indian native readers. The tone in most of his poems appears not only sceptic and repulsive in some cases but also atheistic and heretical. He often involves himself in various conflicts, arguments, ironies and ambiguities. There seems to be in him a habit of going against age old conventions and traditions and to present the facts in their naked reality, stripped of all the beauty conferred by the ancient traditional poets. These facts along with English in which he writes his poetry, bring him within the criteria of marginality, as all these things tend only to remove him from the general or main stream Indian literature. Minutely observed, his place seems to be on the margins of the Indian literary circle, even after his praiseworthy contribution to the enrichment, development and standardization of modern Indian English Poetry. Upon this, the critic S.K.Desai comments: "Ramanujan's expatriation is a marginal affair and his alienation is a myth created by critics. Though, he lives in Chicago, he is all the time preoccupied with India, one of his continuing projects being collection of folk tales, proverbs, riddles which bring him to India once at least in two years. (Qtd. by Rawat 22).

Analyzing Ramanujan's poetry, a reader may become surprised or even shocked in the way he presents a particular thing in a totally different way. For example, in his poems related to Indian society, he mostly talks of the South Indian Kannada or Tamil Brahmin society. Most of these are reflections of his personal experiences he had in his childhood. In no case, one should mistake these personal narrations as a general fact. One more problem which makes his poem highly complex is that they don't have a clear theme, pivotal point or fixed direction. They start in one manner, make progress in another way and end in a quite different form from the previous two. For example the poem "A Leaky Tap After a Sister's Wedding," in the poetic volume *The Striders* (1966) starts with the mention of a leaking tap, proceeds to the sisters of the poet, one of whom has attained the age to marry, further proceeds to the description of a wood-pecker and ends with a reference to a writhing snake, the poet saw, caught in a crow's beak. In the same volume, a poem titled "A River," displays the poet's aversion against blind traditionalism. He criticizes the ancient Tamil poets for praising a river ignoring all its physical shortcomings or ill effects. In his poem, he draws the true picture of the river, which dries to a trickle in the summer and when it is in floods, it causes great damage to the life and property of the villages situated near its banks. In the words of Ramanujan:

> It carries away
> in the first half-hour
> three village houses
> a couple of cows
> named Gopi and Brinda

and one Pregnant woman
expecting identical twins
(*Collected Poems* 38).

The poet accuses the followers of the traditional poets for blindly following the mistakes of their predecessors. The best example, however of these types of anti-conventional poems is the "Prayers to Lord Murugan," in which the poet prays the ancient Dravidian deity Murugan, now Aryanised as Subrahmanya, in a very unique and modern way. In the poem he asks the God to deliver him from the various false theories made both by the orthodox Indian Sanskrit scholars and the self-motivated British Colonists, about India and its civilization. The last stanza in fact shocks us with its seemingly heretic tone:

Lord of answers,
cure us at once
of prayers
(*Collected Poems* 117).

Another characteristic which influences the poet's works to become marginalized is the heavily overlaid sexual tone, which in traditional India is considered obscene. Though Ezekiel and especially Kamala Das also specialize in writing highly sexual poems, what gives Ramanujan his uniqueness is his seemingly incestuous attitude in matters of sex and marriage. In his poetic volume *Relations* (1971) a poem entitled "Love Poem for a Wife, I," seems to criticize the modern system of marriage in India, in which generally two strangers tie the knots for a whole life, without properly acquainted with each other. This he seems to dislike as in his opinion it leads to a loss of closeness in the old age. He thinks that the ancient systems of oral marriage fixed by the elders of the families and child marriage as practiced by the traditional Hindus were a good solution for this problem:

> Or we should do as well-meaning Hindus did,
> betroth us before birth,
> forestalling separate horoscopes
> and mothers' first periods,
> and wed us in the oral cradle
> and carry marriage back into
> the namelessness of childhoods
> (*Collected Poems* 67)

The poem further proceeds giving examples from the personal experiences of the poet who faces difficulties becoming a part of his wife's family due to the lack of proper emotional exchange. He even goes to the extent of referring to the ancient Egyptian royal tradition where kings generally married their own sisters:

> … Probably
> only the Egyptians had it right:
> their kings had sisters for queens
> to continue the incests
> of childhood into marriage (67).

In one more poem of the same volume, titled "Any Cow's Horn Can Do It," the poet gives highly sexual and even to some extent obscene depictions. The second stanza may even sound outrageous to the general Indian readers:

> Any reminder
> of her youth's market places
> Crawling with feeling hands, eyes
> Groping for the hidden books
> That hold together little girls
> And she will glow green fire
> From all nine wells of a woman's
> Shame (Any Cow's Horn Can Do it)
> (93).

Further in the same poem, the poet makes a very lewd comment treating unexpected pregnancy as normally as common household quarrels over petty things:

> Any old quarrel over novel,
> Movie, or a suspicion
> of pregnancy is enough
> to make wife, sister, or girl friend
> walk silent from room to room
> (93).

These lines show a very amazing and relaxed view point of the poet towards the subjects considered normally as taboos by the Indians in general.

Any one truly interested in the works of Ramanujan, cannot miss the strange way in which he uses mythology and other concepts of Indian culture. His invocation of God in his various poems such as "Prayers to Lord Murugan," in *Relations*

(1971) and "Mythologis – 1, 2 and 3," of *The Black Hen* (1995), either God is invoked in a novel, rational way or else various mythologies have been mechanically narrated without clearly indicating the points to which the readers should communicate. There are some other poems also which give us an insight into the strange mindset of the poet. For example, there are two poems in his third volume of poetry *Second Sight* (1986) titled "Zoo Gardens Revisited," and "Moulting," respectively, which show the strange prayers made by the poet to God. In the first poem, observing the pitiable condition of the various animals and birds in the zoo, the poet calls upon God to redeem those poor creatures. There he refers god as having the face of a lion, a snout of a boar and the eyes of a fish. This makes a composite form of some of the most famous incarnations of Lord Vishnu. As he is considered the presiding deity of the act of sustenance or preservation in this world, the poet as if, reminds him of his duty to preserve the animals mentioned in the poem. One may be appalled by his request to devour the animals (referred to in the poem as 'lambs') but that the poet intends no harm to them can be proved by his next sentence praying the lord to devour the concerned animals as a whole. Further, he clearly requests God not to eat them up but rather make them safe in his belly, which again, according to the Hindu myths, is the very source from which the entire creation with countless life-forms sprung up into existence. In another poem titled "Moulting," he refers to the process of moulting as a symbolic representation of rebirth or spiritual realization. Here, the most intricate detail, which catches our attention, is his reference to God as "Lord of Snakes and Eagles"(*Collected Poems* 176). As explained earlier, this alludes to Lord Vishnu. We see multi-layers of meaning in this apparently mythical allusion. While snake here may stand for spiritual regeneration (as depicted in the Indian scriptures as the mystic awakening of the serpentine Kundalini power) the eagle may very well stand for death. The Lord reigns supreme over not only these two but the entirety of human life. The poet therefore asks his son to be covered by an hour's shade, which pertains to the shield of divine grace against death before the ultimate realization. He also prays that the Lord himself would act as the thorn, fixing on which, his son would be able to wriggle out from the sheath of ignorance or rebirth. Last but not least, his poem "A Devotee's Complainant," from *The Black Hen* volume leaves no doubt in the minds of the readers who come across the nonsense mention of Hindu details like Lakshmi, Saraswati and Shiva.

Apart from all these facts, the best proof one can give of Ramanujan's marginalization is his own admission of the fact. In the group of the five founders of modern Indian English poetry, no one else makes such a clear statement of his or her sense of being marginalized. Though Ezekiel and Jayanta Mahapatra give much indication of the fact through their various poems, no one has made a direct comment upon it. It is only in Ramanujan's poetry that we come across such statements along with the use of the exact terms such as circles, centre, marginal and disconnection. Also his feeling of marginalization can be traced back to his first volume of poetry *The Striders* (1966) in which there are two poems which clearly reflect the feelings of the poet in this prospect. The first one "Self-Protrait," presents the feeling of absence, in the private as well as the public sphere, by the poet. This is illustrated by the very first line:

I resemble everyone
But myself …
(Self Portrait 23).

The second poem bears a name suggestive of the trauma experienced by the poet, which is a common feature of those who feel marginalized. The "Conventions of Despair," clearly describes the state of the poet's mind in the following lines:

I should smile, dry-eyed,
and nurse martins like the Marginal Man,
but, Sorry, I cannot unclear
Conventions of despair
They have their pride.
I must seek and will find
My particular hell only in my Hindu mind
(34).

Along with the above two poems, there are some others also which give the same impression upon the minds of the readers. In his third volume of poetry *Second Sight* (1986), there are three exclusive poems which directly speaks of the feeling of being marginalized. The very first poem itself, "Elements of Composition," in the volume, makes it clear in the ending lines:

… And even as I add,
I lose, decompose
into my elements,
into other names and forms
past, and passing tenses

without time,

Caterpillar on a leaf, eating,

Being eaten (Elements of Composition 123).

The following lines in fact speak of the process through which the poet has become marginalized, in the garb of the process of decomposition. Like decomposing human body whose elements take a totally different form after released from it, the poet's whole identity has altered due to different facts and circumstances. Like a dead person, now the poet feels a total loss of his original identity. This sense of loss develops into the feeling of the need for reconnecting oneself back to the old ground from which one has been uprooted. This is illustrated by the first lines of his poem "Connect," from the same volume:

Connect! Connect! Cries my disconnecting

madness, remembering phrases.

... But my watchers are silent as if

They knew my truth is in fragments

(178).

The above lines give a very clear view of the difficult situation in which the poet finds himself. He has become virtually dead in the prospect of his native culture and identity. However, the third poem "Looking for the Centre," is a highly ambiguous one, whose exact meaning is very difficult to contemplate. A reader is puzzled by the starting lines:

Looking for the centre these says
is like looking for the center
for Missing children

which used to be here, but now has moved
downtown to a new building
(Looking for the Centre 184)

Thus, one is bound to become confused of the exact mental condition of the poet. He sometimes seems to suffer from the sense of marginalization in very acute terms but other times seems very relaxed about it. "A Report," from his last poetic volume *The Black Hen*, seems to be a warning against hankering after native culture and identity, which can lead to racial conflicts and cause tension and fear between various communities. We can safely conclude that he is a poet who admits his marginalized position; but doesn't want to make any fuss over it. Like Ezekiel, who has made his commitments with the city of Bombay, Ramanujan also has seemed to have achieved the perfect state of adaption in respect to his present place.

At last we can conclude that all the principal poets, who have contributed to the formation and development of modern Indian English poetry stand marginalized due to a large number of facts. However, closely observed, one also notices that in truth, all these poets have become successful in breaking most of the limitations that marginality puts upon them. Their successful search and grounding of their roots, adaptation to the traditions of India, keeping in tune with the process of modernization and their immense popularity both in and outside India, have brought them much near to the centre. Therefore, these poets seem not marginalized in the exact sense, but struggling and searching for their roots and true identity, which is blurred by the colonial aftermath and the influence of the modern 'universalist' approach.

WORKS CITED

Bhabha, Homi K. *Nation and Narration*. London: Routledge, 1992. Print.

Desai, Shantinath K., "Indian Writing in English: The Predicament of Marginality" *IJES,* Vol. XXVI, New Delhi:Sahitya Akademi,1987. Print.

Devi, C.Anna Latha. "Vignettes of indian life: An analysis of the Selected Poems of Nissim Ezekiel." *Indian Poetry in English: Roots and Blossoms.*Ed. S.K.Paul and Amar Nath Prasad. New Delhi: Sarup and Sons, 2007. Print.

Kohli, Devindra. "Landscape and Poetry", *The Journal of Commonwealth Literature.* 13.3, April 1979.,54-70. Print.

Iyengar,K R Srinivasa. *Indian writing in English.* Sterling New Delhi: Sterling Publishers,1996. Print.

Mishra, Neha. "In the Shackles of Convention and Destiny: Women in the Poetry of Jayanta Mahapatra. *Indian poetry in English: Roots and Blossoms.* New Delhi: Sarup and Sons, 2007. Print.

Mishra, R.K. "Poetry of Revolt Against Marginalisation of Matrirchal Section in India: A Thematic Study of kamala Das's Poetry." *Indian literature in English;Critical Views.* Ed. Satish Barbudhe. New Delhi: Sarup and Sons, 2007. Print.

Parker, Michael and Roger Starkey. Ed. *Postcolonial Literature.* London: Macmillan Press Ltd., 1995. Print.

Rawat, Anniruddh. *Episteme of Desire: The Poetry of A.K.Ramanujan.* New Delhi: Adhyayan Publishers, 2012. Print.

Ramanujan, A.K. *Collected Poems.*New Delhi: OUP, 2005. Print.

Spivak, Gayatri Chakravorty. *Outside in the Teaching Machine.* London:Psychology Press,1993. Print.

Sahoo, Raghunath.*Tension and Moral Dilemmas in Nissim Ezekiel's Poetry.* New Delhi: Sarup and Sons, 2012. Print.

Upadhaya, Onkar Nath. *Perspectives on Indian Diaspora.* New Delhi: Sarup Book Publishers, 2014. Print.

Young, Robert J.C. *Postcolonialism: A very short Introduction.* New York: OUP, 2003. Print.

CONCLUSION

Historically Indian English Poetry dates back to the year 1827 when Henry Derezio published his first book of verse, *Poems*. Between 1827 and 1947, we have poets like Toru Dutt, Aru Dutt, Michael Madhusudan Dutt, Harindra Nath Chattopadhaya, Sarojini Naidu, Manmohan Ghose and Sri Aurobindo who have written poetry following the British Romantics and Victorians. Of these poets only three of them stand out- they are Toru Dutt, Sarojini Naidu and Sri Aurobindo. With the advent of Post- independence era which is synonymous with Post-Colonial period, Nissim Ezekiel gave a new direction to Indian English Poetry. No wonder Bruce King calls him the founding father of Modern Indian English Poetry in his book *Indian Poetry in English*. Two other poets namely Kamala Das and A.K.Ramanujan published in 1960s along with Nissim Ezekiel. Truly speaking modernism in Indian English poetry began with the publication of Nissim Ezekiel's *The Unfinished Man* (1960), *The Exact Name* (1965),

Kamala Das's *Summer In Calcutta*(1965), and Ramanujan's *The Striders*(1966). In a way these poets have started acclimatizing indigenous tradition and contemporary Indian life in English language.

The sea change came in the mid 1970s when R.Parthasarathy as the editor of Oxford University Press started publishing new books of poetry by his contemporaries and edited the most significant anthology, *Ten Twentieth Century Indian Poets* (1976).When the country sulked under Emergency, Indian English Poetry flourished. All important poets like Ezekiel, Ramanujan, Parthasarathy, Daruwalla, Shiv K.Kumar, Jayanta Mahapatra were published by Oxford University Press. Poetry become a favourite form in the 1970s and 1980s. During this time Sahitya Academy, New Delhi started giving annual prizes to Indian English Poets. Most of the poets mentioned above were given Sahitya Academy Awards for their books of verse in the 1980s.

As the migratory movement gained momentum in the late 80s and 90s, most of the poets started visiting either UK or USA to give their poetry readings in different universities. Here Indian English Poetry came in close contact with Australian, Canadian poetry, Caribbean poetry and poetry written in English in the third World countries. Here comes the question of Postcoloniality as three Austrarlian Critics Bill Ashcroft, Gareth Griffith and Helen Tiffin have underlined the importance of poetry written in the former British colonies as a form of protest and reiteration of identity, Indian English Poets trod the line. The Indian English Poets while facing challenge from their counterparts in Australia, Canada, New Zealand, West Indians, deliberately created a new Indian English idiom in order to assert their Indian identity. Postcoloniality for them became a form of assertion of identity and therefore they have tried to nativise the themes in their poetry. Being conscious of the postcolonial condition, Indian English poets sought to write poetry with India in their bones. Nativism became a medium and method to come to terms with postcoloniality. Assimilation of the native tradition with the ever charging world under the impact of globalisation made their poetry acceptable to the West. This is a significant achievement.

Indian English poets too faced a serious challenge at home thrown by the Bhasha writers. The Bhasha writers called them inauthentic propagandist and argued that these poets cannot represent India as they are marginalised. This seems to be a little bit misplaced. The locale of Indian English poetry is the whole of India and it is not confined to any particular state. Educated Indians all over the country read their poetry and it is also prescribed as a course in several Universities. It is not correct to say that Indian English poets do not represent India because they write in English. It is not true that the writer chooses the medium but always the medium too chooses the writer. One writes Literature in that language in which he has literary competence. That language may or may not be his mother tongue. That is exactly the case with Indian English poets. These poets successfully face the double challenge: One at home (Bhasha writers) and two abroad (the Third World writers and the Anglo-American writers). Indian English poetry is not marginal because the readers of Indian English poetry outweigh the readers of any regional language literature except, perhaps in Hindi.

Indian English Poetry is robust and reflective of current Indian situation. Most of the poets now write topical poems about contemporary reality. Indian English poets have succeeded in creating a new Indian English 'idiom' in their poetry. In a way they have fulfilled Raja Rao's desire to write poetry in their own way. They have successfully overcome the Anglo American tradition. In the age of neo-colonialism, these poets have earned national and international acclaim for their poetry. Thus, notwithstanding the charges of the Bhasha writers, the Indian English poets have moved to the centre and blurred the periphery or the margin.

So, ultimately we find that the tradition of Indo-Anglican poetry, which started as a mere reflection of the British English poetry, has developed into a genuine and individual trend, universally accepted and regarded. It has not only withstood the charges of being a mere offshoot of British English poetry by the western critics but also the allegation by the supporters of the 'Bhasha' or Indian vernacular literatures that "... the Indian English poetry has no indigenous cultural roots and hence its flowering is merely imitative and derivative- a synthetic creation of the colonial encounter". (Qtd. By Thakur 49). This latter allegation raised its head and gained momentum during the post-independence period due to the strong anti-British and pro-nationalist feelings. But many Indian English poets like Nissim Ezekiel, Jayanta Mahapatra and Kamala Das along with others like R.Parthasarathy, Dom Moraes and Bibhu Padhi, proved them wrong. However, most of these post colonial Indian English poets were harshly critical and disregardful of their predecessor, i.e. the colonial poets like Sarojini Naidu and Sri Aurobindo Ghosh. A modern Indian English poet like K.N. Daruwalla made a very rude remark in the following words: "I have read only one poem each by Toru Dutt and Sri Aurobindo Ghosh, and have no intention of reading any more." (ibid, 52)

To reconcile these warring factions of Indian intelligentsia and to put an end to all these biased mud-slinging, the great scholarly critics of India like K.R. Srinivasa Iyenger, M.K. Naik and C.D. Narasimhaiah, came to the forefront of this literary battle. M.K. Naik in a very liberal yet logical manner, traced the origin of the Indian English poetry from the colonial period to its following in the post-colonial period. From his study beginning with Toru Dutt and ending with Kamala Das and from Henry Vivian Derozio to A.K Ramanujan, he ultimately sets a criteria for' Indianness' in modern Indian English poetry. In his words: "The modern Indian poet in English is truly Indian, when he draws his artistic sustenance from this heritage. He may not totally accept it; but he cannot altogether ignore it. He is all the time aware of it as a point of reference-as the still point of his turning world"(72). He also refutes the notion that authentic and standard English poetry can be written only by such poet, who leaving India, settle in the countries where English is the natural tongue of the people. Referring to A.K. Ramanujan, who left for America physically but emotionally and spiritually come more closer to India by constantly reminiscing and contemplating upon it, he comments: "This does not mean that the Indian poet must go into exile in order to discover his roots" (ibid, 74).

Another luminary of the sky of Indian intellect, K.R. Srinivasa Iyengar has shown that how all the five major post-colonial poets of India have helped in creating a genuine poetic trend in English. In his book *The Indian Contribution to English Literature,* he has remarked: "The best Indo-Anglian poets have given us something which neither English poetry nor any of our regional literature can give; in other words, they have effected a true marriage of Indian process of poetic experience with English formula of verse expression" (*Indian Writing in English* 4). He has shown the appropriateness and validity of choosing English as the medium of creative expression for modern Indian poetry. He also explains the basic characteristics, outlook and approach of the modern Indian poets belonging to the post-colonial trend. He justifies their unconventionalism, novelty of style and revolutionary thought-process. Thus in short, he seems to be in total agreement with Prof. Naik, in the latter's following observation: "Finally, what is the achievement of the modernist school? These poets have certainly learnt well all the lesson taught by their British masters, but it is significant that they have produced their best roots: as Ezekiel does in *Hymns in Darkness*, Kolatkar in *Jejuri* and Mahapatra in *Relationship*." (*IJES* Vol. L.2013 56).

The first and foremost of the Indian poets who has in fact, laid the foundation-stone of the great edifice of modern Indian English poetry is the great urban poet, Nissim Ezekiel. He can even be called as the father of the modern English poetry in India. Like Eliot in the west, he was the one to give the present form and essence to Indian English poetry. He occupies the first position in the series of the modern English poets not only due to his emergence in this field earlier than the others but also for his competence and skills. His poetry is imbibed with an appeal that touches the heart of readers. Many poems of his, even have a therapeutic approach. In such poems the poet observes a particular condition or problem with an ironic attitude and detached out-look. Though the present situation inspires hopelessness yet the poet advises to keep hope. In this context also one can compare him with T.S.Eliot, whose poems like Gerontion, present a similar theme and scenario. Ezekiel also seems to be influenced by Eliot in his sense of responsibility as a poet, towards the country and society he is living in. Not only the sense of responsibility but a deep sense of belongingness in respect to his native surroundings is the element which gives the special flavour to Ezekiel's poetry and which was subsequently followed by all the others poets.

Ezekiel was also gifted with a great power of narration. In the manner of all the post-colonial poets, he also refers mostly to the present conditions of his country and society. His dexterity can be seen in his drawing inspiration from even the most ordinary day-to-day life, situations, incidents and happenings. As pointed out by B.K..Das "He takes a situation, examines it and describes it in such a way that it immediately assumes a kind of social significance. Then, he turns his personal emotion into 'structural' emotion which finally becomes artistic emotion" (Bharucha and Nabar 128). By his acute poetic dexterity, he gives a universalized form to his feelings of agony and depression. However, his foremost contribution in the context of Indian English poetry is the introduction of a new Indian English 'idiom' which was further developed by various other poets. This new idiom played a very vital role in Indianizing English for the purpose of using it in creating literature upon typical Indian subjects. For example, in his poem "Guru," he gives a most lively description of the spiritual hollowness of the self-professed Godmen. Though, in India such frauds are pseudo-divine figures, the poet proclaims his complete lack of faith in them in the following manner:

Witnessing the spectacle
We no longer smile.
If saints are like this,
What hope is there then for us?
`(*Collected Poems*192)

In yet another poem "Healers," he vents the same ridicule for these people. But spiritual corruption is only a singular aspect of the multi-faceted scenario of problems prevailing in India. He is equally outspoken about the various socio-political and economic problems that are relevant in the present situation of India. Still one should not think that the poet feels repulsed or fed up of India. Rather, he has developed a most unique intimacy and feeling of belongingness, not only with the land of India but also with its religious, cultural and philosophical heritage. His poems like "Tribute to the Upanishads," "The Patriot," from "Very Indian Poems in Indian English," and "Passion Poems," indicate towards his gradual acceptance of the Indian philosophical, mythical and religious traditions. His deep understanding of the state of a 'Jivan-Mukta' i.e. 'an alive liberated soul', as described in the Advaita philosophy of the 'Vedanta', can be observed in the following lines:

The secret locked within the seed
Becomes my need, and so
I shrink to the nothingness
Within the seed
(*Collected Poems* 205).

In the other poems, like "Minority Poem," and "Touching," from "Songs for Nandu Bhende" ; we can surmise the slow yet steady march of the poet towards a voluntary rooting on the soil of the native Indian ethos. It is this strong emotional bonding with India that ultimately leads him to say:

> Confiscate my passport, Lord
> I don't want to go abroad.
> Let me find my song
> Where I belong
> (*Collected Poems* 123)

Thus, we can unhesitatingly proclaim Ezekiel as the poet of modern Indian English poetry.

Jayanta Mahapatra, is the second prominent figure of the Indian pentagon of modern English poetry. The entire essence of his poetry, in fact even of his very existence seems to be built up of native elements. The glorious past, the natural beauty, the traditions, and even the present vices of the modern times, nothing remains untouched by him. He can be termed more as a regional poet as it is his birthplace, Odisha which is generally the subject of his poems. Though the poet's national sentiments can be viewed in many of his poems, still nothing inspires him more than Odisha. In his masterpiece *Relationship* (1980), he openly declares his love and dedication for it:

> …I want to finish my prayer
> that began like a thin rustling in a mango tree,
> a prayer to draw my body out of a thousand years
> and reflect the earth's lost amplitudes,
> the bridal footprints of fantastic peacocks
> dancing in the rain
> (*Selected Poems* 43).

His poems serve as a mirror to the readers reflecting the geography, history, natural beauty, beliefs, art and prevailing socio-economic conditions of Odisha. His poetry is replete with a wide and extensive variety of images. These images give a special charm and force to his work. Various images like that of ancient temples containing a 'shivalingam' and guarded by two stone lions at the entrance to those referring to the oppressed womanhood in India, all adorn his poetry like gems studded in gold.

Most of his poems refer to Odisha and the past ages. Yet, the poet also shows his concern for the present day problems. His volumes like *Dispossessed Nests*, *A Whiteness of Bone*, *Random Descent* and *Shadow Space* are testimonies of the pain he experiences by observing the numerous evils infecting Indian society. While he pours the anguish of his heart for the suffering of the underprivileged people in poems like "About my Favourite Things," (*Shadow Space*) and "Defeat," he also shows the same emotion for the anti national activities like the Khalistan movement in his poems like 'A monsoon Day Fable,'. His seventh volume *Random Descent,* a collection of forty-nine poems presents an abundance of such tragic feelings experienced by the poet. Especially, poems like "Happening," even take a universal shape due to his concern for the misery of the entire humanity. In *Dispossessed Nests* (1984) poem number 8, 20 and 32, also reflect the same emotions. The 'Poem Number 20' is of special importance due to the doubt and pain expressed by the poet in the closing lines:

> ...was everything you did,
> Gandhiji, only an act you put on for posterity?
> With India, our India, barely worth raping?"(34).

In this way, his other latest volumes also convey the message of the ever continuous plight of humanity whether in the national or universal context. The efforts of saints like Buddha and leaders like Gandhi also have fell short of bringing peace and understanding to the world. In such a context, what is his role as a mere poet ? This is expressed by Jayanta Mahapatra in the following lines

> But what use is a poem, once writing so done?
> Words looking for what, in the dark of the soul ?
> like the sound of a match striking, then over,
> I know that much. When all else has failed,
> the poem' words are perhaps justified.
> (Last Night the Poem 127)

There is a strong rebellious tone in Mahapatra's poetry, whose origin can be traced in his radical views regarding traditions, myths, conventions and history. For example, in his volume *Temple* (1984), he speaks in an ironical tone about the sufferings of Sita and Parvati (considered generally as divine ideals for Indian Hindu womanhood), equalising them to normal women of everyday life. Similarly, he ridicules the dubious divinization of women, while exploiting, subjugating and degrading them in the worst possible manner. His strong aversion to religious rites, which have become symbols of exploitation, ignorance and superstition, can be summed up from the following lines:

> Our rites have become burdens
> Given to us like curses upon our souls,

And hope has become God, difficult to see
(*Bare Face* 41).

Yet, it should not be blindly taken as his total disregard for the Indian traditions. In many of his poems like "The Temple Road, Puri," (29) and "In the Chariot Festival at Puri," (32) of the volume *Waiting,* we find him having a rather veiled sense of admiration for the cultural environment and spiritual enthusiasm, characteristic of such festivities. Even a large part of his poetry seems heavily influenced by the doctrine of 'Rasa', which is a most integral and inevitable part of the Classical Sanskrit Poetics. This is also testimony to his internal longing to find his ground in the culture and tradition from which he has been distanced due to the conversion of his grandfather. All his concern, observation and analysis of the problems and conditions prevailing in both Odisha and India, proves his internal affinity and genuine sympathy for the Indian soil and milieu. This ultimately leads to his firm and stable establishment within the socio-cultural folds of Indian scenario.

Though India was initiated into the world of English poetry by a female poet, Toru Dutt, it was only in the twentieth century that it became representative of the Indian feminine ethos. This time also, it was a female poet, Kamala Das, who revolutionized the convention-bound feminine expressions of Indian women in poems. With almost suicidal zeal to shatter all age-old traditions, conventions and restriction, she became a torch-bearer for the feminist movement in India. Being unusually sensitive and reckless, she had felt agonized during her childhood due to the socio-cultural conventions prevailing both within and outside her ancient Nalapat house. In her childhood days, she had witnessed the pathetic situation of both the low-caste women, i.e the sexual exploitation of her maid, 'Nani' and the upper-caste women, i.e. the neglect suffered by her widowed great grandmother; in the Indian society. Her marital life further aggravated this tragic sensibility due to the dominating, lustful and rather indifferent attitude of her husband. All this made her revolt against the age-old Indian tradition of meekly submitting to the whims of the husband, whom conventions deify as the very manifestation of god for a wife. Even, a lover also fails to satisfy her craving for love and true sympathy. In her poem "Freak," she ridicules the lover by metaphorically comparing him with a dark cave, devoid of the light of love:

> He talks turning a sun-stained
> Cheek to me, his mouth, a dark
> Cavern, where the stalactites of
> Uneven teeth gleam, …
> (The *Old Playhouse and Other Poems* 8)

She rails at the licentious, unfeeling and hypocritical nature of the average male section of the Indian society. Though all her lovers sexually abused her body to quench their lust, they do this with a self-assumed spirit of kindness, as is expressed in these lines:

> To forget, oh, to forget…and they said, each of
> Them, I don't love, I cannot love, it is not
> In my nature to love, but I can be kind to you (…)
> (The Sunshine Cat 25).

She glorifies love and even advocates unrestrained expressions of it in forms of pre-marital and extra-marital relationships. However, she seeks a realization (of a mystical nature) through the experiences of physical love, by which she can transcend the realm of lust. India has a long and ancient tradition of employing the sexual instinct, its power and joy, to unlock the doors of divine realization as well as that of salvation itself. In the Tantric traditions of both Hinduism and Buddhism, it has led to the development of a unique and most elaborate philosophy, iconography and ritualism. All these not only divinize the sexual impulse but also advocate its divine potentiality to lead an individual to the highest level of spiritual consciousness. The feeling of a most profound and sublime transcendence is reflected in the poet's own poem "Radha," where she claims to lose her own existence into the sweet sensation of Krishna's love. Her poem "Vrindavan," holds the mystical sporting place of Krishna as a goal to be achieved by every woman, who is unhappy, unsatisfied or is bereft of love:

> Vrindavan lives on in every woman's mind,
> and the flute, luring her
> from home and her husband...
> (Only the Soul Knows How to Sing 101)

In this regard, she seems to echo the views of the medieval Sahaja (or Sahajiya) Vaishnava mystics, known for their sexo-aesthetic rituals as well as the modern existentialist German poet, Rainer Maria Rilke. Though, not against the institution of marriage, she does not support the subjugation or exploitation of women in any manner. She has the same feeling for the poor and the lower sections of the society like the daily-wage earners, the untouchables, the eunuchs and prostitutes, who as per the 'marginalist' theory of Gayatri Chakraborty Spivak come under the broad category of 'Marginalized Classes'. Her nostalgia for the ancient classless, casteless and convention free Dravidian Culture, is yet another aspect of her versatile poetic sensibility. It is actually her indigenous sensibility that gives the unique appeal to her poems. For example, she epitomizes Lord Krishna as the ideal lover, but this ideal lover is no way a good natured and sympathetic gentleman, typical of the Renaissaince or medieval English poetry. Instead, he is treacherous, heartless, selfish and uncaring. Her description of Krishna's sexual charm may well horrify many a tradition-bound Hindus:

> Of what does the burning mouth
> Of Sun, burning in to day's sky
> Remind me. Oh yes, his mouth and ….
> His limbs like pale and carnivorous
> Plants reaching out for me
> The sad lie of my unending lust
> (Love 10).

With such intense feelings of desperation and dissatisfaction, it is not hard to realize the rebellious overtone of her poetry. Her strong and sincere enthusiasm for breaking conventions of oppression and exploitation makes her take the most daring steps that were ever taken by Indian women. After the death of her husband, she went through a study of Islamic religion to compare its socio- religious aspects with that of Hinduism. Finding her desired answers, she lost no time in converting to what seemed to her 'a dream religion for women'. For this, she was threatened with death also, but she remained undaunted till her last breath. Throughout her life, she spoke and fought for the suppressed, the subjugated, the exploited and the marginalized. Finally, she ended a long life full of strife and turbulence on 31st May 2009. Her rebellious spirit is aptly summed up by the critic K.Satchidanandan, according to whom: "She [Das] refuses to glorify the historical past... She rejects the patriarchal value system that is based on egoism, greed for power, expansion, hero-cult, violence, war, mindless exploitation of man and nature, the misuse of intelligence and the supremacy of reason and theory over sensitiveness and experience" (Qtd. by Jayakrishnan Nair 103).

The most prominent themes and the most frequently concurring subjects in her poetry are the acute feeling of having lost her real self-identity and the most sincere and desperate effort to retrieve it, by any possible manner. The poems such as "Too Early the Autumn Sights," "Substitute," "The Sunshine Cat," "Captive," "Composition" and "The Old Playhouse" seems to be shedding tears and sighing heavy breaths from every single word of theirs. Specially "The Old Playhouse," presents the situation in a most moving style:

> ... There is
> No more singing, no more dance, my mind is an old
> Playhouse with all its lights put out.
> (The Old Playhouse and Other Poems 1).

The theme of a spiritual revival and a resurrection of her feminine consciousness is reflected in a number of poems such as "Ghanashyam," "An Introduction," 'A Widow's Lament," and "I shall Some Day". Even in one of her early poems "After the Illness," we find this strain of conscious realization growing in gradual manner. There, the poet after a serious term of sickness contemplates upon her cravings for love in spite of her decimated physique:

> ... There was
> Not much flesh left for the flesh to hunger, the blood had
> Weakened too much to lust, and the skin, without health's
> Anointments, was numb and unyearning. What lusted then
> For him, was perhaps the deeply hidden soul?
> (The Old Playhouse and Other Poems 50).

Here in the lines quoted above, the poet in a typically Indian manner contemplates over the source of all desires and passions in a human body. She feels that even after her physical strength had weird off, her lust had not grown weak. This leads her to accept the presence of an entity called soul, whose existence hither to she had been denying. This also seems to be her first step towards spiritualism, as true spiritualism always starts with the acceptance of the 'spirit.'

Among the four postcolonial Indian poets, A.K. Ramanujan holds a unique position, in terms of both, interest as well as importance. He is the only one in the group to have left India in search of a more empowered expression of his self-identity. Yet, his nostalgia made him as attached to the soil of India as the 'bard of odisha' i.e. Jayanta Mahapatra. Belonging to a highly learned and orthodox Brahmin lineage, he grew up with the staple diet of Kannada, Tamil and Sanskrit along with English. These classical languages of India made him well-versed in the literary, cultural, religious, and philosophical traditions, which are associated with them. The strong fascination of the poet for the beauty, variety and antiquity of the Dravidian culture doesn't die even after leaving India. He in fact, made it his profession and became a professor of Dravidian linguistics in the University of Chicago. Throughout his stay in America, his consciousness constantly revelled in the traditions of Dravidian Culture, history, and mythology. His innovativeness rejuvenated the aesthetic appeal of ancient classical Tamil Poetry, with the help of English. Both his original works as well as translations show his unique capability of grafting the Tamil aesthetics and ethos on the bough of English language. His poetry has variety and bears the distinct stamp of Indianness on account of his assimilation of the native Indian poetic tradition, particularly, the tradition of Tamil and Kannada poetry to his English poetry.

His early works are reminiscences and recollections of his experiences in India during the early years of his life. They narrate his childhood experiences, his interaction with the members of his family, the environment of his house, the myths he learnt about from his elders and the traditions and lore, with which he grew up. Some of his early poems, worthy of mention like "Snakes", "Still Another for Mother", "Lines to a Granny", "A Leaky Tap After a Sister's Wedding" and "KMnO4 in Grandfather's Shaving Glass" are all products of his meditation upon his early past in India. They all speak of his childish innocence, adolescent curiosity and the exuberance of thoughts at early youth. What gives these poems a unique taste of their own is unaltered expression of the poet's feelings.

He has not tried to give them an analytical and critical colour. Rather he gives them a simple narrative style, which adds to their charm and appeal. The critic Vandana Dutta rightly catches the strain of his poetry in these words: "No Wonder, a large bulk of Ramanujan's poetical works deal with the Indian past. Memories of childhood cover the whole range of his imagination. In a number of poems, there is an accurate representation of certain instances (Qtd.by Rawat, *Episteme of Desire...* 20).

The poetry of Ramanujan is a unique confluence of fact and myth, psychology and spiritualism, and the past and the present. There one can find a western prototype of stark realism, unheeding of any tradition or convention. Side by it, there is the well-known mysticism of India, which again goes beyond all traditional system. For example in his poems like "Old Indian Belief," he laughs at the unscientific concepts that Indians have about Snakes. While on one hand, he refers to the once-upon-a time glory of the great Mughals in his poem "The Last of the Princes", he also speaks there of the wretched and extremely degraded position of their descendants at present. While one can get a whiff of Freudian psychology in his poems like "Looking for a Cousin on a Swing", there are poems like "One More on a Death- less Theme", where one gets the poet contemplating upon death like a true Indian mystic. Science and tradition are like the two poles of his globe of poetry- separate yet complimentary to each other. In his poems, like "Death and the Good Citizen," and "One More on a Deathless Theme," he speaks simultaneously about both scientific facts and myths or traditions. In his poem, "Astronomer," he gives a rather curious introduction of his father, who was as well versed in scriptural lore as he was educated in western science:

> Sky-man in a manhole
> With astronomy for dream,
> Astrology for nightmare
> (*Collected Poems* 134).

His "mythologies" series "Zoo Gardens Revisited," and "Moulting," are not only testimonies to his deep knowledge of Indian Hindu mythology but also to his remarkable flexibility by which he can co-relate them with new and innovative styles and theme.

The South-Indian or Dravidian imagery, symbolism and mythology are replete in his poetry. While he desperately prays Lord Murugan, one of the most prominent deities of Dravidian culture, for redeeming it from both the Aryan as well as Anglican subjugation in "Prayers to Lord Murugan". He also refers to the boon of fearlessness granted by the god to saint Arunagirinathar in the poem "Fear no Fall." The reference to the famous South Indian image of Lord Shiva in the form of 'Nataraja' or the cosmic dancer king is successfully brought out in the following lines of the poem "Compensations,"

> Surpassed only by the last
> Miracle of grace, the three-eyed
> Whirlwind of arms, dancing on
> A single leg though he can dance
> On many, kind returning god
> Of Indian deluges
> (*Collected Poems*110).

His all encompassing nature of Indian vision can be surmised from his description of the strange penance or expiation of a naked Jain monk, who are commonly found in the state of his birth, Karnataka. This poem "Pleasure" speaks of his genuine affinity with the ethos of every socio-religious and cultural element belonging to the South-Indian or Dravidian soil.

However, the poet is not a blind follower of conventions as one can observe in his "The Hindoo," poems. He is a liberal minded person with a scientific outlook as well as a deep pro-mystical insight, typical of his own poem "The Second Sight". Many of his poems like "Foundlings in the Yukon" (*Collected Poems* 197), "Some Indian Uses of History on a Rainy Day" (ibid, 74-75), and "A Lapse of Memory" (ibid, 76) point to his strong feeling of nostalgia and alienation on the foreign soil. His realization of his having been uprooted from his own soil, becomes more pronounced in the following lines of "Chicago Zen,":

Now you know what you always knew
The country cannot be reached
By jet... (*Collected Poems* 187).

Yet, we find that the poet struggles incessantly for the search of his true identity. Ultimately, we find that he comes to a realization that his Indian spirit is ever present within him in the form of his Dravidian roots.

Last but not least, one finds a spirit of genuine Indianness in his use of English. Unlike most of the colonial poets of the past, his words breath out the fragrance of Indian soil, culture and ethos. As observed by H.C.Harrex: "A.K.Ramanujan used language with a surgeon-like precision, realizing that the secret of life is more likely to be found in the smallest rather than the most cosmic particles of existence ... we should note under language that Ramanujan has evolved a personal pliant English which retains its normal power of rational analysis yet is also internalised to achieve a resonance of Indian feeling and Hindu impulse" (*JIWE* 1980, 155). In his poem "The Conventions of Despair", he declares his everlasting affinity and relation with the Indian soil, culture and spiritualism despite all geographical barriers. The critic P.K.J.Kurup pays him a most deserving tribute in the following words: "It is to the credit of Ramanujan that he could reach out from such a predicament to a state of creative freedom by means of cultivating a uniquely personal idiom...... Such a poetic process not only helps him achieve a remarkable precision and subtlety in describing the indescribable but it also helps his poetic self, pre-occupied with the desire to discover his roots, to catch the subtle nuances of vibrations of his Hindu sensibility" (183-187).

The poetic texts of all the poets concerned have become an apt site for the interaction and interface between the self and the society manifested through variegated contending voices. These contending voices symbolise the various stances in the cultural hierarchy of norm-givers and norm-receivers. Besides the poetic tension in the poems of the poets under study are grounded on binary oppositions ever striving for a resolution. This self and society, culture-identity interface, though found in all the four poets, is rather more significant and conspicuous in the poetry of Kamala Das.

All these poets are grouped together by some common traits. First of all, all of them were rebels against the prevalent tradition of colonial poetry. Instead of only eulogizing Indian heritage, culture and practices, they also revealed the real and dark aspects of its present conditions. However, each of them still deserves individual attention, due to their individual talent and preferences. While Jayanta Mahapatra claims his allegiance to the state of Odisha, Ezekiel confesses his affection for the city of Mumbai. Ramanujan declares his loyalty towards the ancient Dravidian culture and language, while Kamala Das concerns herself mainly with the suppressed female section of Indian society. There are however, some traits of continuation of tradition in the form of references to Vedantic thought, Indian mythology and folklore, and Indian imagery to be found in their poetry. Most of them have also maintained the nine fold aesthetic tastes (i.e., the Nava-Rasas) in their works. All these establish their identity and affinity to the Indian soil, culture and consciousness, beyond any possible question of controversy.

WORKS CITED

Bharucha, Nilufer E. and Vrinda Nabar. (Eds.) *Mapping Cultural Spaces:Post-colonial Indian Literature in English.* New Delhi: Vision Books, 1998. Print.

Das, Kamala. *The Old Playhouse and Other Poems.* Hyderabad: Orient Longman Limited,1986. Print.

Ezekiel, Nissim. *Collected Poems.* New Delhi: OUP, 2005. Print.

Harrex, S.C. "Small Scale Reflections on Indian English Language Poetry." *The Journal Of Indian Writing in English.* Vol-VIII: 1-2.1980. 155.

Iyengar, K R Srinivas. *Indian Writing in English.* New Delhi: Sterling Publishers Pvt. Ltd., 1996. Print.

Kurup, P.K.J. "The Self in the Poetry of A.K. Ramanujan." *Contemporary Indian Poetry inEnglish.* New Delhi: Atlantic Publishers and Distributors, 1991. Print.

Mahapatra, Jayanta. *Relationship.* Cuttack: The Chandrabhaga Society, 1982. Print.

————————. *Dispossessed Nests.* Jaipur: Nirala Publications, 1986. Print.

————————. *Selected Poems.* New Delhi: Oxford University Press, 1987. Print.

Naik, M.K. *Studies in Indian English Literature.* New Delhi: Sterling Publishers Pvt. Ltd.,1987. Print.

Nair, Jayakrishnan. "The Eunuchs' World of Vacant Ecstacy: Kamala Das's Wasteland." *Indian Poetry in English: Roots and Blossoms.* (Ed.) S.K. Paul and Amarnath Prasad.New Delhi: Sarup and Sons, 2007. Print.

Parthasarathy, R. *Ten Twentieth Century Indian Poets.* Delhi: Oxford University Press, 1986. Print.

Ramanujan, A.K. *Collected Poems.* New Delhi: OUP, 1995. Print.

Rawat, Anirudh. *Episteme of Desire: The Poetry of A.K.Ramanujan.* New Delhi: AdhyayanPublishers and Distributors, 2012. Print.

Thakur, Akhileswar. "Problematics of Tradition in Indian English Poetry." *IJES.* Vol-L, No-50. 2013. Print.

BIBLIOGRAPHY

PRIMARY SOURCES:

Das, Kamala. : *Summer In Calcutta.*New Delhi: Everest Press. 1965. Print.

_____. *The Descedants.* Calcutta: Writer's Workshop. 1967. Print.

_____. *The Testing of The Sirens.* New Delhi: Sterling Publishers 1976. Print.

_____. *My Story.* New Delhi: Sterling Publishers. 1976. Print.

_____. *The Old Playhouse and Other Poems.* Hyderabad: Orient Longman Ltd., 1986. Print.

_____. *The Anamalai Poems.* New Delhi: Sterling Publishers, 1990. Print.

_____. *Only The Soul Knows How To Sing.* Kottayam: D C Books, 1996. Print.

Ezekiel, Nissim. : *A Time to Change.* London: Fortune Press, 1952. Print.

_____. *Sixty Poems.* Bombay: The Author, 1953. Print.

_____. *The Third.* Bombay: The Strand Book Shop, 1959. Print.

_____. *The Unfinished Man.* Calcutta: Writers' Workshop, 1960. Print.

_____. *The Exact Name.* Calcutta: Writers' Workshop, 1965. Print.

_____. *Hymns in Darkness.* New Delhi: Oxford University Press, 1982. Print.

_____. *Latter-Day Psalms.* New Delhi: Oxford University Press, 1982. Print.

_____. *Collected Poems 1952 – 88.* New Delhi: Oxford University Press, 1989. Print.

Mahapatra, Jayanta. : *Close the Sky, Ten by Ten.* Calcutta: Dialogue Publication, 1971. Print.

_____. *Swayamvara and other Poems.* Calcutta: Writers' Workshop, 1971. Print.

_____. *A Father's Hours.* Calcutta: University of Georgia Press, 1976. Print.

_____. *A Rain of Rites.* Athens: University of Georgia Press, 1976. Print.

_____. *Waiting.* New Delhi: Samkaleen Prakashan, 1979. Print.

_____. *The False Start.* Bombay: Clering House, 1980. Print.

_____. *Relationship.* Greenfield, New York: Greenfield Review Press, 1980. Print.

_____. *Life Signs.* New Delhi: Oxford University Press, 1983. Print.

_____. *Dispossessed Nests.* Jaipur: Nirala Publications, 1986. Print.

_____. *Selected Poems.* New Delhi: Oxford University Press, 1987. Print.

_____. *Burden of Waves and Fruit.* Washington D.C: Three Continent Press, 1988. Print.

_____. *Temple.* Sydney: Dangaroo Press, 1989. Print.

_____. *A Whiteness of Bone.* New Delhi: Penguin Books, 1992. Print.

_____. *The Best of Jayanta Mahapatra.* Calicut: Bodhi Books, 1995. Print.

Mahapatra, Jayanta. *Shadow Space.* Kottayam: D.C Books, 1997. Print.

Ramanujan, A.K. *The Striders.* London: Oxford University Press, 1966. Print.

_____. *Relations.* London: Oxford university Press 1971. Print.

_____. *Selected Poems.* Delhi: Oxford University Press, 1977. Print.

_____. *Second Sight.* New Delhi: Oxford University Press, 1986. Print.

_____. *The Collected Poems of A.K. Ramanujan.* Delhi: Oxford University Press, 1995. Print.

REVIEWS:

Kumar, Prema Nanda. Rev. of *Modern Indian Poet Writing in English: Jayanta Mahapatra,* by Laxminarayana, Bhat P. *The Journal of Indian Writing in English,* Vol-29,Jan.2001:68-70.Print.

Kumar, Sukrita Paul. Rev. of *Expressive Form in The Poetry of Kamala Das,* by Anisur Rahman.*The Journal of Indian Writing in English,* Vol-12, Jan. 1984:51-52.Print.

Kumar, Sukrita Paul. Rev. of *Form and Value in The Poetry of Nissim Ezekiel,* by Anisur Rahman.*The Journal of Indian Writing in English,* Vol-12, Jan. 1984:51-53.Print.

Parvathi, B. Rev. *of Perspectives on the Poetry of A.K.ramanujan,* by Bijay Kumar Das.*Critical Endeavour,* Vol-20, Jan.2014:416-417. Print.

Viswanathan, S. Rev. of *Perspectives on the Poetry of A.K.ramanujan,* by Bijay Kumar Das.*Critical Endeavour,* Vol-20, Jan.2014:416-417. Print.

INTERVIEW:

Jha, Rama. "A Conversation with A.K.Ramanujan".*The Humanities Review.*3.No 1. (Jan-Jun 1981).7.

Shankarnarayan,T.N. and S.A.Krishnaiah. "Interview with Prof. A.K.Ramanujan".*Indian English Poetry:Critical Perspectives.* Ed. Jaydeep K.Dodiya. NewDelhi: Sarup and Sons, 2009. Print.

De Souza, Eunice. *Talking Poems: Conversation with Poets.* New Delhi: Oxford University Press, 1999. Print.

SECONDARY SOURCES:
ANTHOLOGIES AND BOOKS:

Abidi, S.Z.H.	*Studies in Indo-Anglian Poetry.* Bareilly: Prakash Books Depot, 1978. Print.
Ahmed, Aijaz.	*In Theory: Classes, Nations Literatures.* New Delhi: Oxford University Press, 1992. Print.
Aldan, Daisy, ed.	*World Poetry in English.* New Delhi: Sterling Publishers, 1981. Print.
Baral, Saranga Dhar.	*The Verse and Vision of A.K-Ramanujan.* New Delhi: Sarup and Sons, 2008. Print.
Barbuddhe, Satish.	*Indian Literature in English: Critical Views.* New Delhi: Sarup and Sons, 2007. Print.
Bhadra, Gautam, Prakash, Gyan and Tharu, Susie. Eds.	*Subattem studies X: Writing on South Asian History and Society.* Delhi: OUP, 2000. Print.
Bharati, Shivram.	*Indian writing in English In the Twentieth century.* New Delhi: DPS Publishing House, 2010. Print.

Bharucha, Nilufer E. and Vrinda Nabar. Eds. *Mapping Cultural Spaces: Post-colonial Indian Literature in English.* New Delhi, Vision Books, 1998. Print.

Boehmer, Elleke. *Colonial and Postcolonial Literature.* Oxford: Oxford University Press, 1995. Print.

Das, Bijay Kumar. Ed. *Perspectives on the Poetry of R.Parthasarathy.* Bareilly: Prakash Book Depot, 1983, 1997. Print.

_____. Ed.*Contemporary Ind-Enmglish Poetry.* Bareilly: Prakash Book Depot, 1986. Print.

_____. *Critical Perspectives on 'Relationship' and Later-Day Psalms.* Bareilly. Prakash Book Depot, 1986. Print.

_____. *The Poetry of Jayanta Mahapatra.* Calcutta Writers' Workshop, 1992. Print.

_____. *Modern India English Poetry.* Bareilly: Prakash Book Depot, 1992. Print.

_____. Ed.*Critical Essays on Poetry.* New Delhi: Kalyani Publishers, 1993. Print.

_____. *Aspects of Commonwealth Literature.* New Delhi: Creative Books, 1995. Print.

_____. *Critical Essays on Post-colonial Literature.* New Delhi: Atlantic Publishers, 1999. Print.

246

_____. *Critical Essays on Post–Colonial Literature.* New Delhi: Atlantic Publishers, 2007. Print.

_____. *Twentieth Century Literary Criticism.* New Delhi: Atlantic Publishers, 2000. Print.

Das, Bijay Kumar. *Post modern Indian English Literature.* New Delhi: Atlantic Publishers, 2006. Print.

Das, Nigamananda. *The Poetry of Jayanta Mahapatra: Imagery and Vision.* New Delhi: Adhyayan Publishers, 2006. Print.

Das, Kamala. The old Playhouse and other poems. Hyderabad: Orient Longman Ltd., 1986. Print.

Deshpande, Gauri, Ed. *An Anthology of Indo-English Poetry.* New Delhi: Hind Pocket Books, 1974. Print.

Dwivedi, A.N. *Kamala Das And Her Poetry.* Delhi: Doaba House, 1983. Print.

Dweivedi, A.N. *Indo-Anglian Poetry.* Allahabad: Kitab Mahal, 1979. Print.

_____. Ed.*Indian Poetry in English: A Literary History and Anthology.* New Delhi: Arnold Heinemann, 1980. Print.

Dweivedi, S.C. ed. *Perspectives on Nissim Ezekiel*, New Delhi: Kitab Mahal, 1989. Print.

Dodiya, Jaydipsinh. *Critical Essays on Indian Writing in English.* New Delhi: Sarup and Sons, 2006. Print.

Dodiya, Jaydipsinh K.   *Indian English Poetry: Critical Perspectives.* New Delhi: Sarup and Sons, 2009. Print.

Gandhi, Leela.   *Postcolonial Theory: A Critical Introduction.* Delhi: Oxford University Press, 1999. Print.

Gokak, V.K. Ed.   *The Golden Treasury of Indo-Anglian Poetry.* New Delhi: Sahitya Akademi, 1970. Print.

_____.   *Studies in Indo-Anglian Poetry.* Bangalore: Sairatan Agency, 1972. Print.

Iyengar, K.R.Srinivasa.   *Indo-Anglian Literature.* Bombay: International Book House, 1973. Print.

_____.   *Indian Writing in English.* New Delhi: Sterling Publishers, 1984. Print.

_____.   *Two Cheers for the Commonwealth.* Bombay: Asia Publishing House, 1970. Print.

Jain, Jasbir and Veena Singh.   *Contesting Postcolonialism.* Jaipure: Rawal Publications, 2000. Print.

Jussawalla Adil, ed.   *New Writing in English.* Harmondsworth: Penguin Books, 1974. Print.

Karnani, Chetan.   *Nissim Ezekiel.* Delhi: Arnold Heinemann, 1974. Print.

_____.   *Indian Writing in English.* New Delhi: Arnold Associates, 1995. Print.

Khan, M.Q. and Das, Bijay Kumar. Eds.	*Studies in Postcolonial Literature.* New Delhi: Atlantic, 2007. Print.
Kher, Inter Nath. Ed.	*Journal of South Asia Literature.* (Special Number of Ezekiel), Spring-Summer, 1976. Print.
King Bruce.	*Modern Indian Poetry in English.* New Delhi: Oxford University Press, 1987. Print.
_____.	*Three Indian Poets.* Madras: Oxford University Press, 1991. Print.
Kohli, Devindra.	*Virgin Whiteness: The Poetry of Kamala Das.* Calcutta Writers' Workshop, 1968. Print.
_____.	*Kamala Das.* Delhi, Arnold Heimann, 1975. Print.
Kotary, P.C.	*Indo-English Poetry.* Gauhati: Gauhati University Department of Publication, 1969. Print.
Kottiswari, W.S.	*Postmodern Feminist Writers.* New Delhi: Sarup and Sons, 2008. Print.
Kulshrestha, Chairantan.	*Contemporary Indian English Verse: An Evaluation.* New Delhi: Arnold Heinemann, 1980. Print.
Lal. P. Ed.	*Indian Writing in English: A Symposium.* Calcutta, Writers' Workshop, 1961. Print.
Lall, Emmanuel Narendra.	*The Poetry of Encounter.* New Delhi: Sterling Publishers Pvt. Ltd., 1983. Print.

Mahapatra, Kamala Prasad *Nature Culture Metonymy: Quest for Lost Horizons in Jayanta Mahaptra's Poetry*. New Delhi: Adhyayan Publishers, 2013. Print.

Maya, D. *Narrating Colonialism: Postcolonial Images of the British in Indian English Fiction*. New Delhi: Prestige Books, 1997. Print.

Mehrotra, Arvind Krishna. Ed. *The Oxford Indian Anthology of Twelve Indian Poets*. Delhi: Oxford University Press, 1998. Print.

Melwani, Murli Das. *Themes in Indo-Anglian Literature*. Bareilly: Prakash Book Depot, 1997. Print.

Mc Cutchion, David. *Indian Writing English: Critical Essays*. Calcutta, Writers' Workshop, 1969. Print.

Mc Leod, John. *Beginning Postcolonialism*. New Delhi; Viva Books Pvt. Ltd, 2013. Print.

Mohanty, Niranjan, Ed. *Consideration*. Berhampur, Poetry Publication.1985. Print.

Mohan, Ramesh. Ed. *Indian Writing in English*. Madras. Orient Longman, 1978. Print.

Mokshi, Punekar Shanker. P.Lal: *An Appreciation*. Calcutta: Writers' Workshop, 1968. Print.

Mongia, Padmini. Ed. *Contemporary Postcolonial Theory*. New Delhi: Oxford University Press, 1997. Print.

Mukherjee, Meenakshi, Ed. *Consideration*. New Delhi: Allied Publishers, 1971. Print.

Mulloo, Anand.   *Voices of the Indian Diaspora.*
                         Delhi: Motilal Banarsidas, 2007.
                         Print.

Nabar, Vrinda.   *The Endless Female Hungers: A*
                         Study of Kamala Das. New Delhi:
                         Sterling Publishers, 1994. Print.

Naik, M.K. Ed.   *Aspects of Indian Writing in*
                         English. New Delhi: McMillan,
                         1979. Print.

_____.   *Dimensions of Indian English*
                         Literature. New Delhi: Sterling
                         Publishers, 1984. Print.

Naik, M.K., Ed.   *A History of Indian English*
                         Literature. New Delhi: Sahitya
                         Akademi, 1982. Print.

_____.   *Studies in Indian English Literature.*
                         New Delhi: Sterling Publishers,
                         1987. Print.

_____.   *Perspectives on Indian Poetry in*
                         English. New Delhi: Abhinav
                         Publiucations, 1984. Print.

Naik, M.K. et al.   *Critical Essays on Indian Writing*
                         in English. Dharwar: Karnatak
                         University, 1968. Print.

Naday, Pritish.   *Indian Poetry in English Today,*
                         New Delhi: Sterling, 1973. Print.

Narasimhaiah, C.D.   *Indian Literature of the Past Fifty*
                         Years. Mysore: University of
                         Mysore, 1970. Print.

_____. *The Swan and the Eagle*. Simla: Indian Institute of Advanced Study, 1969. Print.

_____. *Essays in Coomonwealth Literature: Heirlom of Heritage*. Delhi: Pencraft International, 1995. Print.

Pandey, S.N. Ed. *Nissim Ezekiel: Dimensions of a Poetic Genius*. New Delhi: Doaba House, 1999. Print.

Paranjape, Makarand P. *Mysticism in Indian English Poetry*. Delhi: B.R. Publication, 1998. Print.

Parker, Michael and Starkey, Roger. Eds. *Post Colonial Literatures*. London: Macmillan Press Ltd, 1995. Print.

Parthasarathy R. Ed. *Ten Twentieth Century Indian Poets*. New Delhi: Oxford University Press, 1977. Print.

Pathak, R.S. Ed. *Creative Forum (Special Issue): Quest for Identity in Indian English Poetry*. V Jan-Dec' 92. Print.

Paul, S.K. *Indian Poetry in English: Roots and Blossoms, Vol-I*.

Amar Nath and Prasad. New Delhi: Sarup and Sons, 2007. Print.

Peeradina, Saleem, Ed. *Contemporary Indian Poetry in English: An Assessment and Selection*. Bombay: McMillan, 1972. Print.

Paniker, K.Ayyappa. Ed. *Indian English Literature since Independence.* New Delhi: The Indian Association for English Studies, 1991. Print.

Perry, John Oliver. *Absent Authority: Issue in Contemporary Indian English Criticism.* New Delhi: Sterling Publishers, 1992. Print.

Prasad, Amar Nath and Rajiv K. Malik. *Indian English Poetry and fiction: Critical Elucidation.* Vol- II. New Delhi: Sarup and Sons, 2007. Print.

Prasad, Amar Nath and S.K Paul. *Feminism in Indian Writing in English.* New Delhi: Sarup and Sons, 2009. Print.

Prasad, Madhusudan. Ed. *The Poetry of Jayanta Mahapatra ; A Critical Study,* New Delhi: Sterling Publishers Pvt. Ltd., 1986. Print.

Radha, K. *Kerala writers in English: Kamala Das.* Madras: Macmillan, 1986. Print.

Rahman, Anisur. *Expressive Form in the Poetry of Kamala Das,* New Delhi, Abhinav Publications, 1981. Print.

_____. *Form and Value in the Poetry of Nissim Ezekiel.* New Delhi, Abhinav Publication, 1981. Print.

Rajan, P.K. Ed. *Changing Tradition in Indian English Literature.* New Delhi: Creative Books, 1995. Print.

Ramaswamy, S.   *Exploration: Essays on Commonwealth Literature.* Bangalore: MCC Publications, 1988. Print.

Rawat, Aniruddh.   *Episteme of Desire: The Poetry of A.K. Ramanujan.* New Delhi: Adhyayan Publishers, 2012. Print.

Reddy, G.A.   *Indian Writing in English and Its' Audience.* Bareilly: Prakash Book Depot, 1978.. Print

Rizvi, S.N.A. Ed.   *Love and Death in Indian Poetry in English.* New Delhi: Doaba House, 1989. Print.

Saha, Subhas.   *Modern Indo-Anglian Love-Poetry.* Calcutta: Workshop, 1971. Print.

_____.   *Insights; Eight Indo-Anglian Poems.* Calcutta; Writers' Workshop, 1972. Print.

Sahoo, Raghunath.   *Tension and Moral Dilemmas in Nissim Ezkiel's Poetry.* New Delhi: Sarup Book Publishers, 2012. Print.

Sarang, Villas. Ed.   *Indian English Poetry since 1950: An Anthology.* Bombay: Disha Books, 1995. Print.

Seshadri, P.   *Anglo-Indian Poetry.* Banaras, Indian Book-shop, 1928. Print.

Shahane, Vasant A. and Sivaram Krishna, M. Eds.   *Indian Poetry in English: A Xritical Assessment.* Madras: McMillan, 1982. Print.

Shaikh, F.A, Vyas, K.B. and Makodiya, V.V. Eds. *New Perspectives on Indian Writing in English.* New Delhi: Sarup Book Publishers, 2009. Print.

Sharma, K.K., Ed. *Indo-English Literature.* Ghaziabad: Vomal Prakashan, 1977. Print.

Sinha, K.K. *Indian Writing in English.* New Delhi: Heritage Publishers, 1979. Print.

Singh, kanwar Dinesh. *Feminism and Post feminism: The Context of Modern Indian Women Poets Writing in English.* New Delhi: Sarup and Sons, 2004. Print.

Singh, Kanwar Dinesh. *New Explorations in Indian English Poetry.* New Delhi: Sarup and Sons, 2004. Print.

Singh, R.A. *Keki N. Daruwalla.* Bareilly: Prakash Book Depot, 1991. Print.

Sinha, Krishna Nandan. *Indian Writing in English.* New Delhi: Heritage Publishers, 1979. Print.

Surendran, K.V. *Indian English Poetry: New Perspectives.* New Delhi Sampand Sons, 2002. Print.

Swain, S.P *Self and Identity in Indian Fiction.* New Delhi: Prestige Books, 2005. Print.

Trivedi Harish and Meenakshi Mukherjee Ed. *Interrogating Postcolonialism: Theory, Text and Context.* Shimla: Indian Institute of Advanced Study, 1996. Print.

Upadhyay, Onkar Nath.	*Perspectives On Indian Diaspora.* New Delhi Sarup Book Publishers, 2014. Print.
Verma, Monika.	*Facing Four Indo-Anglian Poetess.* Calcutta: Writers' Workshop, 1973. Print.
Verghese, C.Paul.	*Essays on India Writing in English.* New Delhi: N.V. Publishers, 1975. Print.
William, Wlsh.	*Reading in Commonwealth Literature.* Oxford Clarendon Press, 1973. Print.
_____.	*Commonwealth Literature.* London: Oxford University Press, 1973. Print.
_____.	*Indian Literature in English.* London: Longman, 1990. Print.
Williams, H.M.	*Indo-Anglian Literature 1800-1970: A Survey.* Madras: Orient Longman, 1970. Print.
Young, Robert J.C.	*Postcolonialism: A very short Introduction.* New York: OUP, 2003. Print.

ARTICLES:

| Acharya, N. Prabhakar. | "Achievement and Failure in Ezekiel' s Poetry", *The Journal of Indian Writing in English.* 14.2, 1986, 73 – 90. Print. |

Aikant, Satish C.   "Dilemma of Nationalism: Siting Post- Colonial Theory", *Journal of Literary Criticism.* 8:2, December 1996: 70 – 80. Print.

Alexander, Meena.   "Exiled by a Dead Script", *The Journal of Indian Writing in English.* 5.2, 1977, 1-4. Print.

Allen, Walter.   "Commonwealth Literature", *New Statesman.* 10, September, 1960, 341. Print.

Amanuddin, Syed.   "Love and Sex in Indo – English Poetry", *Creative Moment III: 1* Spring 1974. Print.

Anand, Mulk Raj.   "The Changeling", *Indian Writing in English,* Ed. Ramesh Mohan, Madras: Orient Longman, 1978, 11- 20. Print.

Anklesaria, Zerin.   "Wit in the Poetry of Nissim Ezekiel", *The Journal of Indian Writing in English.* 14.2, 41- 48. Print.

Anniah Gowda, H.H.   "A Defence of Indain Verse in English", *The Literary Half – Yearly.* 9.2, 1968, 23- 376. Print.

———————.   "Contemporary Creative writers in Indian", *The Literary Half – Yearly.* 10.1, Jan. 1969, 17-39. Print.

———————.   "Perfected Passions: The Love Poetry of Kamala Das and Judith Wright", *The Literary Half- yearly.* 20.1, Jan. 1979, 116 -30. Print.

Anniah Gowda, H.H. "The Use of Images in Contemporary, Indian Verse in English", *WLWE,* 20. 1971, 61-76. Print.

Atma Ram. "An Interview with Kamala Das", *New Quest* No.2, August 1977, 41-42. Print.

Ayyub, Abu S. and Amlan Dutta. "Editorial", *Quest 26.* July – Sept. 1960, 9 -13. Print.

——————————. "Editor's Reply", *Quest 27.* October December 1960, 109-110. Print.

BalKrishnan, Parasu. "Contemporary Indian Writing in English", *Triveni.* 47, 3 October-December 1978, 58-67. Print.

Belliapa, Meena. "Ezekiel's Poet, Lover, Birdwatcher" *The Miscellany.* 46 July – August 1971, 25- 44. Print.

Bernard, J. "The Poet's Audience", *The Journal of Commonwealth Literature.* No.5, 1968, 116-118. Print.

Beston, John B. "An Interview with Nissim Ezekiel", *World Literature Written in English.* 16 No.1. April 1977, 87-94. Print.

Bhabha, Homi. "Indo- Anglian Attitudes", *The Times Literary Supplement.* February 3, 1978, 136. Print.

——————————. "Indo – Anglian Attitudes", *The Times Literary Supplement.* 21 April, 1978, 445. Print.

Birje Patil, J.   "Interior Cadences: The Poetry
                                    of Nissim Ezekiel", *The Literary
                                    Criterion*, Vol. XII, No.2.3, 1976,
                                    198- 212. Print.

Bose, Amalendu.   "Some Poets of the writers'
                                    Workshop, *Critical Essays on
                                    Indian writing in English*. Eds.
                                    M.K. Naik et al, Dharwar:
                                    Karnatak University, 1968, 31-50.
                                    Print.

_____.   "Modern Indian Poetry in
                                    English", *Indian Literature*. 13, 1
                                    March 1970, 51 – 59. Print.

Bose, B   "Indian Poetry in English", *The
                                    Concise Encyclopaedia of English
                                    and American Poets and Poetry*.
                                    Eds. S. Spender and D. Hall.
                                    London: Hutchinson and Co.
                                    1963, 142 – 143. Print.

Chakoo, P.M.   "Ezekiel's Family Poems", *The
                                    Journal of Indian Writing in
                                    English*. 14.2, 24-40. Print.

Chaddah, R.P.   "Women Indo- English Poets",
                                    Commonwealth Quarterly. 1 No.
                                    5, Dec. 1977, 41-52. Print.

Chatterjee, Usasi   "Twenty Five Years of Indo-
                                    English Poetry", *Review of Indian
                                    Poetry in English*. 1947- 72, ed.
                                    Pritish Nandy, *Indian and Foreign
                                    Review*. 1 February, 1973, 8. Print.

Chellappan, K.	"Irony as Understanding and Love in Three Indo- Anglian Poets", *Journal of Literature and Aesthetic.* 2.4, October 1982, 36-40. Print.
Chitre, Dilip	"Poetry in the Enemy's Tongue", *New Quest* 14, March- April 1979, 77-82. Print.
Das, Bijay Kumar	"The Pattern of Thought in Poet, Lover, Bird Watcher', *JIWE.* 7, 2, 1979, 48. Print.
_____.	"Aspects of Modern Indian Poetry in English", *The Indian Journal of English Studies,* Vol. XX, No. 1, 1980, 39-50. Print.
_____.	"Some Indian – English Poets of the Seventies", *Indian Literature.* 25, 3 May- June 1982, 101-109. Print.
_____.	"Indian Poetry in English", Th Illustrated Weekly of India, 27 June 1982, 28 – 29. Print.
_____.	"What's it like to be a Poet? A study of R. Parthasarathy", *Studies in Indian Poetry in English* Ed. O.P. Bhatnagar, Amravati: Rachana Prakashan, 1981, 43-52. Print.
_____.	"Ironic mode in Modern Indo-English Poetry", *Journal of Literature and Aesthetics.* 2.4, 1982, 75-82. Print.

——————. "The Search after Reality: A Study of Nissim Ezekiel's "Hymns in Darkness", *JIWE*. 10. 1, 1982. Print.

——————. "Indo-English Poetry to Recent Years", *Poetry V.* 1983, 32-39. Print.

——————. "Recent Indian Poetry in English", *The Literary Half-yearly.* 25. 1, 1984, 52-58. Print.

Das, Bijay Kumar   Review of "Latter-Day Psalms" by Nissim Ezekiel, *Pratibha India.* 11.4, July-Sept, 1983, 53-54. Print.

——————. "Kamala Das and the Making of Indian English Idioms", *Language Forum.* Vol.XII, 91-98. Print.

——————. 'Nissim Ezekiel and the Making of Indian English Idiom, *IJES.* Vol. XXVI. 1987, 112-122. Print.

——————. "Indian Landscape and Imagery in the poetry ofShiv K.Kumar" *Creative Forum.* 1.1, 1988. Print.

——————. "Indian English Poetry: Before and After Independence", *Triveni,* 56, 3 and 4. Print.

——————. "The Image of the 'Native Land' in the Award Winning Poets", *Chiaroscuro* (Ed.) A.S. Ratnam, Parbhani: Dnyanopasak Prakashan, 1991. Print.

_____. "The 'Self' in Nissim Ezekiel's Poetry", *Creative Forum*, 5, 1992. Print.

_____. "How Memorable is Ezekiel's Poetry ?", *Indian Scholars*. 16:1-2, 1994. Print.

_____. "Nissim Ezekiel and the application of Indian Poetics", *Inner Voice*. 1:3-4, 1996. Print.

_____. "The Poetry of Nissim Ezekiel and the Question of The Reader Response", *Critical Practice*. 4:2, 1977. Print.

_____. "A Modernist Poet or a Post-Modernist?: A Study of Nissim Ezekiel's Poetry", *Mapping Cultural Spaces: Post-Colonial Indian Literature in English*. Ed. Nilufer E. Bharucha and Vrinda Nabar, New Delhi: Vision Books, 1998.

_____. Trends in Post-colonial Poetry", *The Critical Endeavour*, 4, 1998. Print.

De Souza, Eunice. "Kamala Das", *Osmania Journal of English Studies*. 13, 1, 1977, 19-27. Print.

_____. "Introduction" to The Unfinished Man (2nd ed.) Calcutta: Writers' Workshop, 1965. Print.

Deshpande, Gouri,   "Parthasarathy", *Quest 74*. Jan-Feb, 1972. 51-58. Print.

Deswani, Tillotama.   Review of The Exact Name, *The Indian P.E.N.*. 5 XXXII, May 1966, 179-182. Print.

Dutta, Ujjal.   "Problems of Sex, Self and Art in Nissim Ezekiel's Nudes", *Lygunus*. 2, 1, 1980, 50-57. Print.

Dwivedi, A.N.   "Irony as Technique in some new Indo-English Poets", *JLA*. 2, 4, 83-94. Print.

——————.   "Modernity in Ezekiel's Poetry", *JIEE* 14.2, 65-72. Print.

——————.   "Feminine Sensibility at Work: A Comparative Study of Kamala Das and Judith Wright", *The Critical Endeavour*,. 1996. Print.

——————.   "Imagery in Nissim Ezekiel's Later Poetry". *Nissim Ezekiel: Dimensions of A Poetic Genius.* Delhi: Doaba House, 1999: 116-134. Print.

Enright, D.J.   "Modern Indian Writing", *The Miscellancy*. 28. 1968, 61-74. Print.

Ezekiel, Nissim.   "Ideas and Modern Poetry", *Indian Writers in Conference*. (Ed) Nissim Ezekiel, Bombay: All India P.E.N. Centre, 1964, 48-54. Print.

_____. "Two Poets: A.K.Ramanujan and Keki N. Daruwalla", *The Illustrated Weekly of India.* 93, No. 25 (June 18, 1972) 43-45. Print.

_____. "Two Poets: A.K.Ramanujan and Keki N. Daruwalla", *The Illustrated Weekly of India.* 93, No.25 (June 18, 1972) 43, 45. Print.

_____. "A New Arrival in Indo-Anglian Poetry", *Time Weekly.* 1, 29 (1971), On Keki N. Daruwalla's Poetry. Print.

_____. "K.N. Daruwalla", *Quest.* 74s, 1972s, 67-69. Print.

_____. "Kamala Das", *Contemporary Poets.* 2nd ed. James York, St. Martin's Press, 1975, 352. Print.

_____. "How a poem is written", *The Indian Journal of English Studies.* 16, 1975-76, 45-52. Print.

_____. "What is Indian about Indo-English Poetry" ? *Osmania Journal of English Studies.* Vol. XIX, 1983, 49-58.int. Print.

_____. "To Revise or not to Revise", *The Literary Criterion.* 17.3, 1983, 1-9. Print.

German, Micheal. "Nissim Ezekiel – Pilgrimage and Myth", *Critical Essays on Indian Writing in English*. Ed. M.K.Naik et al, Darwan: Karnatak University Press, 1968, 106-121. Print.

Gokak, V.K. "A Question of Variety", *Contemporary Indian English Verse: An Evaluation*. Ed. Chirantan Kulshrestha (New Delhi: Arnold-Heinmann 1980) 41-56. Print.

Gokak, V.K. "The Concept of Indianness with Reference to Indian Writing in English", Ed. Ramesh Mohan, (Madras: Orient Longman, 1973) 21-25. Print.

Harrex, S.C. "Small-Scale Reflections on Indian Engflish Language Poetry", *Journal of Indian Writing in English*. Vol. VIII, 1-2, 1980, 137-166. Print.

Hess, Linda. "Post-Independence Indian Poetry in English", *Quest 49*. April-June, 28-38. Print.

Iradate, Roger. "Indian Poetry in English To-day", *Quest 98*. Nov-Dec, 1975, 72-74. Print.

Iyengar, K.R. Srinivas. "Indian Poetry in English: Yesterday, Today, Tomorrow", *The Literary Criterion*. 18.3, 1983, 10-18. Print.

Jaggi, Satya Dev.   "Indo-English Poetry in the Context of World Standard", *Journal of Indian Writing in English*. 1.1, 1973, 35-38. Print.

Jain, Jasbir.   "Postcoloniality, Literature and Politics". *Contesting Postcolonialism*. Ed. Jasbir Jain and Veena Singh, Jaipur: Rawat Publication, 2000. Print.

Jeffares, A.N.   "Introduction", *Commonwealth Literature*. Ed. John Press, London: Heinmann Education Books, 1965, XI-XVIII. Print.

_____.   "The Study of Commonwealth Writing", *WLWE* News Letter, 15, April 1969, 1 – 15. Print.

_____.   "The contemporary situation in Commonwealth Poetry", *Verse and Voice*, 1965, 17-25. Print.

Jussawalla, Adil.   "The New Poetry", *Readings in Commonwealth Literature*. Ed. William Walsh (Oxford: Claremdonn Press, 1973) 75-90. Print.

Karnani, Chetan.   "The Poetry of Nissim Ezekiel" *Journal of South Asian Literature*. 11, 3-4, spring-summer, 1976, 223-228. Print.

Kher, Inder Nath. "That Message from Another Shore: The Esthetic Vision of Nissim Ezekiel", *Mahfil*. 8.4, (1972) 17-28. Print.

———. "Introduction", *Journal of South Asian Literature: Nissim Ezekiel Issue*. 11, Nos. 3-4 (Spring-Summer, 1976) 3-7. Print.

Kohli, Devindra. "Passionate sincerity in Indian Poetry in English", *Journal of Commonwealth Literature*. 9, 1, (August 1974) 20 – 34. Print.

———. "A new Dynamism or a Dying Phenomenon ?", *Indian and Foreign Review*. 15 February 1971, 16- 18. Print.

———. "Landscape and Poetry", *The Journal of Commonwealth Literature*. 13.3, April 1979, 54-70. Print.

Kohli, Suresh. "Interview with P.Lal", *Indian and Foreign Review*.July 1, 1970, 18 – 19. Print.

———. "Nissim Ezekiel: Pursuit of Perfection", *Indian and Foreign Review*. 1 may 1971, 15-16. Print.

———. "Interview with Nissim Ezekiel", *Mahfil*. 8, 4 (Winter 1972, 7-10). Print.

_____. "Indian Poetry in English", _The Indian Literary Review_. 1, No.7-8, (Nov.-Dec. 1978) 33-40. Print.

Kulshrestha, Chirantan "English verse in India: Some obstinate Questions", _Contemporary Indian English Verse: An Evolution_. New Delhi: Arnold Heinemann, 1980, 9 – 19. Print.

_____. "Half-Baked Thoughts on the Unhoused muse", _The Literary Criterion_. 17, 1, 1982, 67-74. Print.

Kumar, T.Vijay. "Post-colonial or Post-colonial ? Relocating the hypen". _Post-colonialism: Theory, Text and Context_. Harish Trivedi and Meenakshi Mukherjee, Shimla: Indian Institute of Advanced Study, 1996. Print.

Lal, P. "Indian writing in English", _Harvard Educational Review_. 34, 2, 1964, 316-319. Print.

_____. "Indian writing in English", _Indian and Foreign Review_.15 Feb. 1971, 16. Print.

_____. "Nostalgia Indo-Anglia", _Journal of Indian Writing in English_. 3. 1, Jan. 1975, 13-15. Print.

Mahapatra, Jayanta. "The Inaudible Resonance in English Poetry in India", _The Literary Criterion_. 15. I, 1980, 27-36. Print.

_____. "The Decline of Indian English Poetry", *The Journal of Indian writing in English*. 28:1 Jan-2000, 3-6. Print.

Mahashabde, N.C. "Indian Poetry in English", *Quest 50*. July-Sept. 1966, 110. Print.

Mangaiyarkarasi.S "Diasporic Consciousness in the Novels of Bharati Mukherjee", *Contemporary Discourse*. Ed. Sudhir Nikam and Madhavi Nikam. Vol-5.,2. July-2014. Print.

MC Cutchion, David. "Must Indian Poetry in English Always Follow England?". *Critical Essays on Indian writing in English*. Ed., M.K.Naik, et. Al. (Dharwar: Karnatatak University, 1968) 164-180. Print.

Mishra, Soubhagya. "Ezekiel: An Estimation", *Gray Book*. 1. 1, 1970, 18-27. Print.

Mokashi – Pumekar. Shankar, "Keki N. Daruwalla's Poetry", *The Journal of Indian writing in English*. 4. 1, 1976, 24-30. Print.

Nabar, Vrinda. "Keki N. Daruwalla: Poetry and a National Culture", *Osmania Joournal of English Studies*. 13. 1, 1377, 1- 18. Print.

_____. "The Critical Imperative in Indo – English Poetry", *Cygnus*. 2.1, 1980, 33- 39. Print.

Nagrajan, S.   "Nissim Ezekiel", (New York: St. Martin's Press, 1975) 466. Print.

Naik, M.K.   "The Indianness of Indian Poetry in English", *Journal of Indian Writing in English*. 1.2, July 1973, 1-7. Print.

_____.   "Echo and Voice in Indian Poetry in English", *Indian Writing To – day*. 4.1, 1970, 32-41. Print.

_____.   "The Achievement of Indian English Poetry", *The Humanities Review*. 4.1 and 2, Jan- Dec. 1982, 22-29. Print.

Nandy, Pritish.   "Indian Poetry in English: The Dynamic of New Sensibility", *Indian Literature*. 14.1, 1972, 8 – 12. Print.

Narayan, Syamala. A.   "Review of Hymns in Darkness by Nissim Ezekiel", *World Literature Today*. 52.1, Winter, 1978, 177 – 178. Print.

Narayan, Shyamala. A.   "Review of Ten Twentieth Century Indian Poets, ed. R. Parthasarathy, *World Literature Today*. 52.1, Winter 1978, 180. Print.

Nayar, Pramod K.   "Poetry of the Nineties", *Chandrabhaga*. 1/2000, 95 – 119. Print.

Paniker, K. Ayyappa,   "Four Voice and a medium", *Indian Book Chronicle*. 7, 190- 191. Print.

—————————. "The Poetry of Jayanta Mahapatra". *Osmania Journal of English Studies.* 13.1, 1977, 177 – 38. Print.

—————————. "Peacocks Among Partriarch: A Close Look a at Indian Poetry in English", *New Quest.* 2, August 1977, 59 -70. Print.

—————————. 'Beyond irony: The Third Vission of Nissim Ezekiel", *Journal of Literature and Aesthetics.* 2.4, 1982, 105 – 108. Print.

—————————. "Indian Poetry in English and the Indian Aesthetic Traditional", *The Indian Journal of English Studies.* 23, 1983, 137 -151. Print.

Parthasarathy, R. "Whoring After English Gods", *Perspectives Bombay Popular Prakashan.* 1970, 43 – 60. Print.

—————————. "Indian English Verse: The Making of a Tradition, *The Humanist Resview.* 1. 1, July – Sept., 1979, 5 – 8. Print.

—————————. "Foregoining as an Interpretative Device in Nissim Ezekiel's "Night of the Scorpion", *The Literary Criterion.*10.3, 1974, 38 -44. Print.

—————————. "Poet in Search of a Language", *Association of Commonwealth Literature and Language Bullentin.* Mysore, 4th Series, No.2, 1975, 9-11. Print.

_____. "Notes on the Making of a Poem", *Studies in Indian Poetry in English*. ed. O.P. Bhatnagar, Jaipur: Rachana Prakashan, 107 -110. Print.

_____. "Tradition and Freedom", *The Indian Journal of English Studies*. Vol. XXI, 1981 – 82, 47 – 59. Print.

Prasad, Madhu Sudan. "Keki N. Daruwalla: Poet as Critic of Age" *The Literary Half Yearly*. Vol. XXIII, No. 1, 1987, 17 – 38. Print.

Prasad, Mohan V. "A Note on Recent Indo – Anglian Poetry", *The Two – Fold Voice*. Ed. D.V.K. Raghava Charyulu, (Gunur: Navodaya Publishers, 1971) 127- 135. Print.

Rajiva, Stanley F. "Contemporary Indian Writing in English", *Quest*. 60, Jan. March, 1969, 72 – 75. Print.

Raj Kumar. "A New Language for New Indian: A Utopian Dream?" *Punjab University Research Bulletin* (Arts). III, No. 2, October 1972, 267 – 278. Print.

_____. "Doyen of Indo – Anglian Poets", The Tribunel, 10 Feb. 1979.Print.

Rama Krishna, D. "Why more Poets and Poetasters", *The Journal of Indian Writing*. 6.1, Jan. 1978, 58 -70. Print.

RamaKrishna E.V.

"Kamala Das as a Confessional Poet", *The Journal of Indian Writing in English.* 5. 1, 1977, 29 – 34. Print.

—————————————.

"Parthasarathy's Self – world: A Reading of 'Rough Passage' ", *Perspctive on the Poetry of R. Parthasarathy.* Ed., Bijay Kumar Das (Bareilly: Prakash Book Depot, 1983) 52 – 6. Print.

Rao, R. Raj.

"Ezekiel's Bombay Poem: Some Opinions", *Mapping Cultural Spaces: Postcolonial Indian Literature in English.* Ed. Nilufer E Bharucha and Vrinda Nabar, New Delhi. Print.

Rath, Harihar.

"Parthasarathy's Rough Passage': Vision and Attitude", *Perspectives on the Poetry of R. Parthasarathy.* Ed. Bijay Kumar Das (Bareilly: Prakash Book Depot, 1983) 40 – 51. Print.

Rayan, Krishna.

"Contemporary Indian English Poetry and the Gods", *Chandrabhaga.* 1/ 2000, 43 – 52. Print.

Rodrigues, Santan.

"An Interview with Nissim Ezekiel", *Youth Times.* 1 – 14 Feb. 1980. 17. Print.

Saha, Subhas Chandra. "Ezekiel's 'Enterpries' Insight", *The Miscellany*. 40, 1970, 9- 23. Print.

_____. "Kamala Das's The Dance of the Eunuch' Insights", *The Miscellany*. 39, 1970, 63 – 76. Print.

_____. "Search for Indianness in Writing", *Indian and Foreign Review*. 15 March 1976, 8 -9. Print.

Saha, Subhas Chandra. "Parthasarathy's Rough Passage': A Study of its name and Style", *Perspectives on the Poetry of R. Parthasarathy*. Ed. Bijay Kumar Das(Bareilly: Prakash Book Depot, 1983) 71 – 79. Print.

_____. "The Indian Millieu and Ethos in Nissim Ezekiel's Poetry", *The Literary Half- Yearly*. Vol. XXIX, No. 1, 1988, 84- 91. Print.

Sergeant, Howard, Ed. Pergamon Poets 9: Poetry form India (Nissim Ezekiel, A.K. Ramanujan, R. Parthasarathy, Deb Kumar Das), (Oxford: Pergamon Press, 1970). Print.

Shahane, Vasant A. "The Religious – Philosophical strain in Nissim Ezekiel's Poetry", *Journal of South Asian Literature*. 11. 3 and 4, 1976, 253 – 261. Print.

————————. "The return of the Exile: The Poetry of R. Parthasarathy", *Osmania Journal of English Studies*. 13. 1, 1977, 149 – 172. Print.

————————. 'Aesthetics of Irony in Modern Indo – English Poerty ", *Journal of Literature and Aesthetics*, 2. 4, October 1982, 28 – 35. Print.

————————. "Search for Critical perspectives on Indian writing in English", *The Indian Journal of English Studies*. 23. 1983, 126 – 136. Print.

Sharma, I. K. "Mary and Meera: A Study of kamala Das ", *Common – Wealth Quarterly*. 3, 10, March 1979, 36 – 47. Print.

Sharma, K. Godabari. "The Poetry of R. Parthasarathy", *The Indian Journal of English Studies*. 19. 1979, 45- 53. Print.

Simms, Norman, "A Poet of Many Words", *The Poetry of Jayanta Mahapatra: A Critical Study*, Ed. Madhusudan Prasad, New Delhi: Sterling Publishers Pvt.. 1986. Print.

————————. "Rev. of Form and Value in the Poetry of Nissim Ezekiel", Anisur Rahman. *Journal of Indian Writing in English*. 21: 1, 1993. Print.

Singh, Brijraj, "An Admirable Curtain Raiser", *Indian Book Chronicle*. 2., 1977, 241 – 245. Print.

———————. "Four New Voices", *Chandrabhaga*.1. 1979, 68 – 85. Print.

Singh, Satyanarayan. "Ramanujan and Ezekiel", *The Miscllany*. 45. 1971, 47- 56.Print.

———————. "Journey into self: Nissim Ezekiel's Recent Poetry ", *Osmania Journal of English Studies*. 13. 1, 1977. Print.

Siveram Krishna, M. "The Tongue in English chains Indo – English poetry To – day", *Indian Poetry in English: A Critical Assessment,* Ed. V.A Shahane et al., (New Delhi: MacMillan and co., 1980) 1 – 27. Print.

———————. "Curio and Archetype": Modernity in Indo- Anglian poetry", *The Indian P.E.N.* 41. 1, Jan 1975,1- 5. Print.

———————. "The Last Refinement of Speech": The Poetry of R. Parthasarathy", *The Literary Criterion*. 12. 2 and 3, 1976, 151 – 172. Print.

———————. "Contemporary Indian poetry in English: An Appoach", *Opinion Literary Quarterly*. 1. 4, July, 39 – 57. Print.

Sreenivasan, S.	"The self and its Enchanted Circle: A Perspectives on the poetry of Nissim Ezekiel". *Changing Traditions in Indian English Literature*. Ed. P.K.Rajan, New Delhi: Creative Books, 1995. Print.
Srinath, C.N.	"Contemporary Indian Poetry in English", *The Literary Criterion*. 8.2, 55-56. Print.
Srivastava, A.K. And Smita Sinha.	"New Voices: Aimed versions on Recent Indo-Anglian Poetry", *Indian Writing in English*. Ed. K.N.Sinha (New Delhi: Heritage Publishers, 1979) 109-127. Print.
Tambimutta.	"Poetry in India: Its Heritage and New Directions", *Atlantic Monthly*. 192, No.4, 147-148. Print.
Taranath, R., and Meena Belliappa	"Nissim Ezekiel's Poetry", *The Miscellany*. 19, 1966, 47-65. Print.
_____.	"Nissim Ezekiel", *Quest*. 74, 1972, 1 – 5. Print.
Taranath, Rajeev.	"Nissim Ezekiel", *Contemporary Indian Poetry in English*. Ed. Saleem Peeradina, Bombay: Macmillan & Co., 1972, 1-5. Print.

Venkatachari, K.   "Indian Poetry in English Today",
                          Indian P.E.N., 40. 2-3, Feb-
                          March, 1974, 1-6.

_____.   "The Poetry of Nissim Ezekiel",
                          Indian Literature. 15. 1, March
                          1972, 63-75. Print.

Verma, K.D.   "Myth and Imagery in 'The
                          Unfinished Man': A Critical
                          Reading", *Journal of South Asian
                          Literature*. 111. 3-4, Spring-
                          Summer, 1976, 229-230. Print.

Verma, S.K.   "A Linguist's view of English in
                          India", *Indian and Foreign Review*.
                          15 October 1972, 20-21. Print.

Walsh, William.   "The Indian Poets", *The Literary
                          Criterion*. 11. 3, winter 1974, 1-6.
                          Print.

_____.   "Modern writing in English",
                          Indian and Foreign Review. 15
                          October 1972, 17-19. Print.

_____.   "In a Backward Place", *The Times
                          Literary Suppliment*. Feb, 3. 1979,
                          122. Print.

_____.   "Small observations on a Large
                          subject", *Aspects of Indian writing
                          in English*. Ed. M.K.Naik, (Delhi:
                          Macmillan and Co., 1979) 107-
                          119. Print.

Watson, F.   "English Poetry from India", *The
                          Listener*. 28, Sept. 1950, 420-430.
                          Print.

Wells, Henry W. "Poetic Imagination in Ireland and India", *The Literary Half-Yearly.* 9. 2, 1968, 37-48. Print.

Wendt, Allan. "Babu to Sahib: Contemporary Indian Literature", *South Atlantic Quarterly.* 64 Winter 1965, 166-180. Print.

William, H.Moore. "English writing in Free India (1947 – 1967)", *Twentieth Century Literature.* 16 Jan. 1970, 3-15. Print.

Wiseman, Christopher. "The Development of Technique in the Poetry of Nissim Ezekiel", *Journal of South Asia Literature.* 11.2 and 3, 1976, 241-252. Print.

Young, Vernon. "Poetry Chronicle", *The Hudson Review.* 29. 4, Winter 1976-77, 615-630. Print.

Printed in the United States
By Bookmasters